Development Planning and School Improvement for Middle Managers

Marilyn Leask and Ian Terrell

KOGAN
PAGE

First published in 1997

Kogan Page Limited
120 Pentonville Road
London N1 9JN

© Marilyn Leask and Ian Terrell, 1997

British Library Cataloguing in Publication Data

A CIP record for this book is available from the British Library.

ISBN 0 7494 2038 3

Typeset by Northern Phototypesetting Co Ltd, Bolton
Printed and bound in Great Britain by Clays Ltd, Bungay, Suffolk

Contents

Preface

How can schools be improved so that children learn more effectively?

The answer to this question is being sought not only in the UK but also in countries throughout the world. Improving the quality of management is widely cited as one of the keys to school improvement as the international contributions in Chapter 6 make clear. In the UK, the Teacher Training Agency (TTA), a government body responsible for teacher training, identifies the quality of school management at head teacher and middle management levels, as current foci for development.

This book is for middle managers both new to the job and those with some experience. It is designed to support the personal and professional development required for the classroom teacher to make the transition to middle manager.

We consider that middle managers have a pivotal role to play in ensuring that a school improves. In managing the work of a team of classroom teachers in an area (a department or a team), the middle manager is in a key position to influence standards and the implementation of whole-school policies. While the head and the other senior managers have ultimate responsibility for creating the structure and guidelines for the development of the school and its ethos, the middle managers have a central role in ensuring that the policies and procedures that embody that ethos are applied in the classroom in the area for which they are responsible.

In the UK middle managers may receive little training or support when they take on this role. This is in contrast, for example, to practice in Singapore (see Chapter 6). Taking on a middle management post requires not only the acquisition of new skills and knowledge but also psychological readjustment. A good teacher is not automatically a good manager of adults.

The middle manager's role is subject to pressures from those in senior management above and those in the classroom below. Managing 'up' and managing 'down' require the middle manager to act in different ways. The management of adults involves different skills to the skills of the classroom teacher, yet the demonstration of effective classroom skills probably enabled the middle manager to gain promotion in the first place. Middle managers necessarily have a wider role in the school than classroom teachers. They have to think strategically about how their area of work should develop and plan how goals are to be achieved.

We identify four dimensions to the middle manager's role which provide a framework for reflection and analysis about the work of the middle manager. Reflection on individual performance in these dimensions and analysis of the constraints operating provide a basis for understanding how individual performance can be improved in the particular circumstances of the school. The dimensions are:

- the tasks of management;
- how you (as a middle manager) work with people;
- who you are in the context in which you work;
- your values and beliefs about teaching and learning.

These dimensions are recurring themes throughout the book.

If you, as a middle manager, can clearly articulate your philosophy of management as a framework of principles guiding your approach to your work, you may be able to plan change rather than just respond reactively to crises. Crisis management, where management responds to events as they occur rather than undertaking a proactive systematic planning of development, is an approach that damages both adults' and pupils' capacity to work effectively.

Effective management is about getting the best out of people. The ideas in this book are designed to help in the task of articulating your own management philosophy and developing a strategic plan for achieving the goals for improvement for your area of work. Below are some statements that encapsulate particular philosophies of management.

> 'Everyone is a potential winner. Some people are disguised as losers. Don't let their appearance fool you.' (Blanchard and Johnson, 1983, p. 71)

> 'It's no use delegating anything around here, no one else does things properly.' (head of department)

> 'People who feel good about themselves produce good results. (Blanchard and Johnson, 1983, p. 19)

> 'I like to keep people on their toes – they never know which way I'm going to react to them.' (head teacher)

Your beliefs about what motivates people to produce good work will guide your management philosophy. We support the view that *structured critical reflection* is a key tool for middle managers, helping them to check progress towards the goals that they and their staff have for their area of work. At various stages through this book, we suggest that you reflect on the management theories or case studies presented and that you record your response in a *reflective journal*. Using a journal will, over time, either give you a sense of achievement when you look back at what you have achieved, or will provide you with notes to analyse later when you consider how things might have been done better.

We do not take an anti-theory stance as some writers do in this field. We consider such an approach is detrimental to personal growth and development. After all, what are theories? Theories should be based on the analysis of practice or the synthesis of ideas and they can provide an analytical framework (not a recipe or panacea) against which you can assess your practice and experience, and predict future actions. Reflection on theory and practice, may provide a short-cut to improvement as you avoid making mistakes that others have made. In this book we put a number of management theories before you – asking you to reflect on these in the light of your experience, then recording in your reflective journal approaches you wish to try out.

The ideas in this book draw on the contributors' experiences as middle managers, researchers and teachers, working with schools on school improvement issues. We believe that middle managers have a key role in influencing the ethos of the school as well as the professional and personal development of staff. In this book we examine different aspects of the work of the middle manager in order to highlight the areas in which your decisions can enhance the effectiveness of your school.

> 'The focus of a good school is effective learning. This is the reason for its existence and therefore the final criterion against which its management is judged. It is the task of management to create the conditions which enable teachers and pupils to achieve effective learning. Management development is the means of increasing the capacity of school management to undertake this task.'
>
> (Gilchrist and Hall, 1993, p. 7)

We wish you well in your endeavours and we welcome any correspondence with you about the views expressed in this book.

Marilyn Leask, Ian Terrell
1997

Acknowledgements

We thank the many teachers, who have been involved in numerous projects with us, for their cooperation and help in developing, adapting and providing the discussion of the ideas for these materials.

We also thank those members of our families who supported us through the process of writing this book, and Pat Lomax, our editor, for her patience and support.

The Contributors

Mikael Alexandersson PhD, is Lecturer in Educational Research at the University of Gothenburg.

Batia Brauner is studying for an MA in the Department of Education at Anglia Polytechnic University.

Bert P M Creemers is Professor in Education at the State University of Groningen, The Netherlands and Director of GION, the Groningen Institute for Educational Research.

Trond E Hauge is Professor of Education at the Department of Teacher Education and School Development, University of Oslo, Norway.

Dr Doris Henry is an Assistant Professor and coordinator of the K–12 School Administration and Supervision internship in the Department of Leadership at the University of Memphis (Tennessee).

Rolf Lander, PhD, is Assistant Professor in Educational Research at the University of Gothenburg.

Marilyn Leask is a Principal Lecturer in Education at De Montfort University, UK.

Lim Lee Hean is a Senior Education Officer at the Ministry of Education.

Low Guat Tin is Head of the Division of Policy and Management Studies, at the National Institute of Education, Nanyang Technological University.

I T Ofei is Deputy Headteacher at Herman Gmainer International College.

Steve Rowe is General Inspector with responsibility for humanities in an urban local education authority in the UK.

Kath Terrell is Deputy Headteacher at a London Comprehensive School.

Ian Terrell is Senior Lecturer in Educational Management at Anglia Polytechnic University and an education evaluation and improvement consultant.

Paul Tompkins is Deputy Head of an Inner London comprehensive school.

Laurie Wheldon works in the Queensland Department of Education as Senior Policy Officer (Adolescent Education) in the Effective Learning and Teaching Unit.

Gill Venn is Senior Lecturer in Education at Anglia Polytechnic University.

Part I   Foundations

Chapter 1

Middle Management at the Centre of School Improvement

Middle managers play a vital role in school improvement. We use the term 'middle manager' to describe all those teachers working in schools who have some kind of management responsibility for a team of staff, or an aspect of the school's work, below the level of the head teacher and senior management team. The term is only loosely definable and there are many variations in school management structures, both within the UK and across the world. For some, even the head teacher is a manager in a 'middle' position between the school governing body, or local authority and the staff.

Much of the literature on educational management, school improvement and school effectiveness (for example, Hopkins *et al.*, 1994; Fullan, 1991, 1992; Reynolds and Cuttance, 1992) has described the importance of head teachers and senior management in improving the school. There has, however, been a relative neglect of the importance of the role of the middle manager. Our experience, working in schools on a number of school development and improvement projects, leads us to believe that this emphasis needs to be reviewed. We see the middle management role as central to the development and improvement of the school. Much of the literature of school improvement seems to portray schools that are collaborative organisations which encourage 'involvement' of the whole staff. There are few references to middle managers and departments or teams. Yet schools for older students, in particular, tend to be large organisations, having many departments or sub-groupings of staff led by middle managers.

The senior management team and the governors of the school are responsible for the development of the whole school. They develop a strategic plan to ensure that the school is in a sound position for delivering quality education to all pupils both at the present time and for the foreseeable future. While the grand plan works for the whole school and all teachers may be involved in its creation, development and implementation, the departments, subject or year teams are at the core of the large school organisation. Even if whole school development teams are formed from staff working across departmental boundaries, they need eventually to influence the working of the departments if the quality of teaching and learning is to be enhanced.

In this chapter we raise and examine issues of school improvement from a middle management perspective and make a case for middle managers to play a significant role in improving the school.

The case for middle management at the centre of school improvement

A number of factors make it clear that middle managers in large schools are central to school improvement. These include the complexity of the organisation and curriculum, the need for all teams to be fully involved in realising the school vision and in creating the conditions for school improvement.

The size and complexity of large schools

Large primary and secondary schools are complex organisations. A typical UK secondary school may employ 50–70 teaching staff and a further 10–20 support staff of various kinds, including administrative, premises, welfare and classroom support staff. Organisation is often through departments and teams. There will be a range of areas of responsibility within schools and some schools may have several sites. Management responsibilities are, therefore, both devolved and diverse.

The school's immediate clients are on site every day and all day, at least during term time. Other clients, the parents, visit less frequently, and in some cases not at all. School organisations are rooted in the community in which they are based, both influencing and being influenced by it. This frequently means that a number of middle managers are involved in different ways with responding to client groups.

We believe that the effectiveness of school improvement initiatives is limited if the most appropriate unit of analysis, when talking about educational management, is the whole-school. Many practitioners will realise that the school is often a collection of departments and other groupings. The real work of the school, the delivery of the curriculum, is organised and managed through semi-autonomous departments and teams. By tradition, in many schools, departments, if not teams, have operated fairly independently, led by the head of department. In this context, each department could take an independent stance in the approach to its own area of work or subject. Each department could create its own way of working or culture, its own pattern of relationships and so on.

In the UK however, this independence and isolation has been breaking down over the past decade. Increased accountability through the publication of league tables of examination results, greater publicity about what goes on in individual schools and parental choice of schools has led to increased collective responsibility for the performance of the whole school. Hence, it is no longer good enough to be a successful department in an unsuccessful school. A key responsibility of all middle managers is to work with others, including the senior management team, to make the whole school successful.

Creating a whole curriculum for students

Departments and teams are the units mainly responsible for implementing the school curriculum, teaching, learning and assessment policies. Yet the curriculum is not a collection of individual subjects and areas that can be dealt with in isolation. Many links and connections have to be made by teachers and students. The curriculum is a whole experience for students. Middle managers have a central role in ensuring coherence across the curriculum. The nature of this curriculum in the UK is directed by central government.

For example, in the UK, the Education Reform Act (ERA) of 1988 places a statutory responsibility on schools to provide a broad and balanced curriculum which:

- promotes the spiritual, moral, cultural, mental and physical development of pupils at the school and of society; and
- prepares pupils for the opportunities, responsibilities and experiences of adult life. (ERA Section 1(2)(a))

The introduction of the National Curriculum in the UK emphasised the need for ensuring that content was planned as a coherent whole, across different subject areas where there was overlap. There are also cross-curricular themes, dimensions and skills that need to be planned for. The use of information technology (IT) in different subject areas is probably the best example of a cross-curricular theme. The responsibility for ensuring integration of cross-curricular issues into the curriculum falls to middle managers.

Inspection of schools in the UK, under the Office for Standards in Education (OFSTED), focuses on the contribution of departments to:

- the spiritual, moral and cultural development of pupils;
- the development of 'core skills' of speaking and listening, reading and writing and the use of IT.

The National Curriculum guidance documents (NCC 1990) draw attention to cross-curricular elements including:

- Personal and social development;
- Economic and industrial understanding;
- Careers education and guidance;
- Health education;
- Environmental education;
- Education for citizenship.

Much of the responsibility for ensuring the implementation of school policies in these areas, and others, falls on the middle manager, for example, the implementation of the equal opportunities policy, ensuring access to the curriculum for all pupils irrespective of race and gender and meeting the needs of all levels of ability. The Special Educational Needs Code of Practice also places obligations on middle managers (HMSO, 1994; Capel *et al.*, 1995).

The wholeness of the curriculum provides a rationale for middle managers to work together to negotiate the delivery of the curriculum and to achieve the aims of the school.

Whole-school development planning

The notion of whole-school development planning has grown in the UK following the publication of the DES Document, *Planning for School Development* (Hargreaves *et al.*, 1989). School development plans are whole-school documents. The school has identified whole-school priorities, targets for action, tasks and timescales and the people responsible for carrying these tasks at a whole-school level. The plan should identify resources for development and possibly also the staff development activities that will support the development.

Ideally, the development plan for the department reflects the whole-school priorities. While some whole-school priorities may not be particularly relevant to some departments, others may be central. Each different department or team has their own development priorities and particular development needs. Many departments and working groups will feel the need to create their own development plan, which may be partly in response to the whole-school plan. Construction of the plan can simply mirror the cycle for the whole school and Chapter 11 gives detailed advice about departmental plans.

The challenge for the middle manager is to work on a number of fronts in the planning process including:

- ensuring that the development process moves from the identification of needs through planning to implementation and evaluation;

- motivating staff through their involvement and interest in the process;
- developing the skills of staff through staff development activities;
- ensuring development actions take place effectively;
- making an impact upon the quality of teaching and learning.

The importance of the middle manager in the development process is clearly illustrated by the outline of development planning (see Chapter 11). The middle manager ought to be contributing to the process of identifying whole-school needs, at the audit stage. A key role is played by the middle manager, in interpreting and translating the whole-school issues into development within the department. The middle manager is in a good position to be able to link the staff development process with school development so that plans impact upon classroom teaching and learning. Our view is that insufficient attention is paid, in the literature, to the role of middle managers in large schools, in development planning.

Schools as social organisations

Ball (1987), Blase and Anderson (1995) and others have drawn attention to the micro-politics of schools. Ball describes 'baronial' power structures and Blase and Anderson describe the politics of subordination and empower-ment. Clearly, in secondary schools, the heads of departments have tradi-tionally been the power 'barons'. Being aware of the micro-politics of the school is essential for the middle manager. Middle managers have to defend the department's interests, yet those with a whole-school view will try to achieve this without damaging others.

In addition to the exercise of power relationships, the middle manager must consider the interrelationships and group dynamics both within the school and within the department, if efforts for school improvement are to be successful. Cockman *et al.* (1992) describe a number of key 'process issues' to do with group effectiveness, including participation, influence, sensitivity to feelings, dealing with issues and handling conflicts (see Table 1.1).

The process issues in Table 1.1 clearly affect the contribution the depart-ment can make to whole-school improvement. Process issues are part of the culture and ethos of the school that can enhance or inhibit efforts for school improvement. They operate between managers and also within departments. They affect both the motivation and the performance of teachers. Middle managers by their skills at facilitating staff relationships can create a climate for 'process' issues to be worked through.

Developing effective classrooms

Recent work on school improvement has emphasised the need to focus on the teaching and learning in the classroom. This point is made by Hopkins *et al.* (1994) and emphasised in the Improving the Quality of Education for All. Logic suggests that middle managers, often those with responsibilities for areas of the curriculum, are key agents in the development of quality teaching and learning. They are also in a position to create a culture and a set of beliefs and values about classroom life.

Table 1.1   *Process issues related to group effectiveness (from Cockman* et al., *1992)*

Participation
High and low participation.
Treatment of those who are silent.
Who talks to whom? Who leads? Who keeps us on task?

Influence
Who influences and how?
The direction of influence?
Rewards and sanctions?
Assertiveness of individuals?

Sensitivity to feelings of the team
Noticing when people are ignored, interrupted or talked over
Asking each other how they are feeling

Dealing with issues and conflicts as they arise
Recognising concerns or fears.
Creating a climate for saying what you feel.
Handling differences of opinion.

Team atmosphere
Creating an atmosphere of trust.

The culture of teaching has a major influence over the progress and direction of school improvement. Hargreaves has illustrated how the culture of teaching can be either a major obstacle to improvement or a major force for it.

> 'What the teacher thinks, what the teacher believes, what the teacher assumes – all these have powerful implications for the change process, for the ways in which curriculum policy is translated into curriculum practice. Some of these patterns of thinking, belief and assumption are shared among the community of teachers so that they amount to what might be called a broad occupational culture of teaching. This culture of teaching… seriously inhibits practical curriculum change at school and classroom level.'
>
> (Hargreaves, 1989, p. 54)

Clearly, the seed bed for the development of culture, particularly in large organisations, must be the small group, ie the department or team under the leadership of a middle manager. The 'community of teachers', where 'thinking, beliefs and assumptions' are worked through, is to be found within departments and teams in schools.

More recent work by Creemers (1994) goes further. He carries out a study based on a meta-analysis of research, best evidence studies, literature reviews and research reports on effective classroom practice. After constructing a model of best classroom practice, according to the research, he goes on to describe the school conditions that support this practice in the classroom. Creemers' work identifies a number of factors which ensure effective learning in the classroom (Table 1.2). He considers student level factors such as student aptitude, motivation and time spent on task, and he accepts the socio-ethnic variance in these factors. Nevertheless, he minimises this influence and argues for attention to be given to an equally important, but more controllable, factor of teacher and organisational behaviour. He emphasises that what the teacher does in the classroom is important.

He then goes on to describe classroom and school level determinants of effectiveness including quality in policies about classroom instruction and its evaluation, the planning of time for the delivery of the curriculum and the creation of opportunities for learning (Table 1.2). These make a great deal of sense to any practitioner. Following this work, we suggest that the key school managers in leading and developing effective classroom practice are middle managers. It is the middle manager who leads the team and is responsible for the schemes of work for the curriculum area. The middle manager is both the subject expert and pedagogical leader, the manager closest to the classroom teacher, with detailed technical expertise and a remit to manage the people who teach the area for which the manager has responsibility.

Table 1.2 *The factors supporting effective classrooms (adapted from Creemers, 1994)*

Classroom Level

Quality of instruction curriculum
- explicitness and ordering of goals and content
- structure and clarity of content
- advance organisers
- material for evaluation of student outcomes, feedback and corrective instruction

Grouping procedures
- mastery learning
- ability grouping
- cooperative learning
- differentiated material
- material for evaluation, feedback and corrective instruction

Teacher behaviour
- management, and orderly and quiet atmosphere

- homework
- high expectations
- clear goal setting
  - restricted set of goals
  - emphasis on basic skills
  - emphasis on cognitive learning and transfer
- structuring the content
  - ordering of goals and content
  - advance organisers
  - making use of prior knowledge of students
- clarity of presentation
- questioning
- immediate exercise after presentation of new content
- evaluation, feedback and corrective instruction

School Level

Quality (educational)
- rules and agreements about classroom instruction
- evaluation policy and system

Quality (organisational)
- policy on intervision* and supervision of teachers
- professionalisation of teachers who do not live up to standards
- school culture for effectiveness

Time
- time schedule for subjects
- rules and agreements about the use of time
- orderly and quiet atmosphere

Opportunity
- school curriculum plan
- consensus about the mission
- rules and agreements about how to implement the curriculum

---

*Intervision is the mutual supervision of each other's work.

The roles of middle management in the organisation

This book is essentially about the middle management role in a modern large school, meeting the changing and developing needs of society. The quality of middle management is, we argue, a key to successful improvement and development in this environment, but only if their central role is recognised.

Brown and Rutherford (1996) have developed the ideas of Murphy (1992) and created a typology of roles for the middle manager in a 'post industrial school'. These roles include that of leading professional, architect for the organisation, moral educator and servant leader (see Table 1.3).

Table 1.3   *Roles of middle managers (adapted from Brown and Rutherford, 1996)*

Servant Leader
They argue for 'leadership from the centre' based upon 'a web of inter-personal relationships' and 'leadership from professional expertise not line authority'. Leaders operate 'not by controlling teachers but by empowering them'. The task is to build shared purpose and consensus to 'model' and clarify values and work through 'ministering to the needs of departmental staff'.

Organisational Architect
As organisational architect the middle manager should 'focus on change... as change agents', develop 'cooperation, empowerment, community and participation as structuring principles' and create 'adaptive and organic forms of departmental structure' which lead to a greater degree of ownership and a more committed workforce.

Leading Professional
They argue that the middle manager is up to date with curriculum developments, a more than competent teacher who has the capacity to reflect upon their own practice and promote self enquiry.

Moral Educator
Brown and Rutherford see middle managers as moral educators who 'invest much more heavily in activities which have a common purpose and in reflective analysis and active intervention in the classroom'. They are 'motivated by a set of deep personal values and beliefs' and 'view their task more as a mission than a job'. They exercise 'moral authority based upon values of the school' and support 'collaboration... shared decision making... enhancing the feelings of self sufficiency (and) the ethic of care to all'. Above all they operate by 'concentrating on people first, by valuing each member of their department and responding to each person's qualities and needs'.

Social Architect
The middle manager as social architect searches out and implements ways to make schools fit children, rather than vice versa. Addressing the needs of a changing society, the leader is 'sensitive to racial issues and the goals of equal opportunity'.

Being in the sandwich

The middle manager may feel they are in a sandwich between classroom practitioners and senior managers. There are demands for change and improvement from teachers themselves, from outside the school, from governments, local education authorities, parents and the community. There is a pressure to reach higher standards of achievement. Different and higher expectations develop over time, such as ensuring the use of IT and the Internet for learning.

Classroom teachers place a special pressure on middle managers. Some practitioners believe that children are not getting any cleverer or easier to work with. Indeed, some believe that they are getting more difficult, for a variety of reasons, including the influence of the media, distractions of leisure pursuits, a shift in the perceived value of education and so on. Innovative and enthusiastic classroom teachers will have their own solutions to these problems, and perhaps these are not always shared by senior management.

At the centre of the management sandwich is the middle manager, working with the practical difficulties and pressures from below, and the higher aspirations and pressures from above. While the logic, aspirations and value judgements of senior management may be clear, practitioners living with the daily reality of classroom life may have a different view. Handling this tension and creating a strategy for dealing with it is a central task for middle managers.

Middle managers creating the conditions for school improvement

As a middle manager you will need to accept that change is inevitable, systemic and essential. If you have some years' experience in education you will have seen a number of waves of change sweeping through the education system from outside. In the UK these include the introduction of CSE (Certificate of Secondary Education), GCSE (General Certificate of Secondary Education), CEE examinations (Certificate of Extended Education), GNVQ (General National Vocational Qualification), the development of TVEI (Technical and Vocational Education Initiative), the Pastoral Curriculum and Local Management of Schools. The introduction of the National Curriculum and its revisions is a case in point. Some may believe that after such a period of rapid change, a period of stability and consolidation is called for, however, they will be disappointed. There will not be a period of 'no change' because there are too many interest groups attempting to perfect different aspects of the system.

Change is not the same as improvement. Improvement implies that a judgement has been made about values. Therefore, decisions are made about the quality of the existing provision of education and its outcomes, which leads to intentions to improve. The notion of continuously searching for better ways of achieving better results is not new to most teachers, although it has been popularised in much of the literature on change (Peters and Waterman, 1982, Hopkins *et al.*, 1994).

Clearly, the logic of our earlier argument suggests that in large schools the role of middle manager is key to effectively implementing change and ensuring there is continuing improvement. Hopkins defines school improvement as developing the internal capacity of the school to take on external pressures for change and to raise the achievement of all children. Hence, his emphasis is upon not just a single improvement but improvement to the school organisation so that it can continue to change. He outlines six essential conditions found in improving schools. These have been outlined by the Improving the Quality of Education for All Project (Hopkins *et al.*, 1994) as:

- commitment to staff development;
- practical efforts to involve staff, students and the community in school policies and decisions;
- transformational leadership;
- effective coordination strategies;
- proper attention to the potential benefits of enquiry and reflection;
- commitment to collaborative planning activity.

Our argument is that these conditions are developed as much through the leadership and organisation of the department as they are through whole-school management. It is the department to which staff are appointed and belong. It is the head of department who provides the leadership, organisation and resource base for teaching and learning. This idea was put to a group of MA students who were managers in schools and their observations are recorded in Table 1.4. Each one of the six conditions is looked at below and the potential middle management contribution explored.

Staff development

There are difficulties in ensuring that staff development has an impact on the quality of teaching and learning in the classroom. Again, the middle manager is sandwiched between the needs of the school and the needs of the individuals working in the subject area of the school. Departmental middle managers have a key role in developing the skills of staff, particularly in the classroom.

Staff development in the UK has traditionally involved attending courses. More recently there has been the development of school-based projects as a form of in-service training. Less frequently, at least with experienced staff, as opposed to student teachers, coaching and mentoring have been developed.The middle manager has responsibilities to ensure that new staff, particularly those newly qualified, are inducted into the systems and procedures of the school. Clearly, teacher appraisal can be a staff development activity organised from within the department, by the middle manager.

Staff development that really impacts upon the quality of teaching and learning needs to be focused on the team or department and their scheme of work. The leadership and professional expertise of the head of department is then a key to successful staff development. These ideas about staff development are further discussed in Chapter 8.

Table 1.4   *The middle manager's contribution to creating the conditions of school improvement*

Leadership	Coordination
Knowledge	Maintaining relationships
Experience	Organising
Power	Communication
Charisma	Chairing meetings
Vision	Encouraging
Decision making	Supporting
Arbitration	Monitoring
Planning	Linking resources and plans
Taking responsibility	Supporting teamwork
As leading professional,	Supporting collaboration
developing the leadership of others	Giving feedback
Planning	*Involvement*
Creating the scheme of work	Delegating responsibility
Ensuring lesson planning	Sharing decision making
Planning improvement	Collaborating in planning
Planning the development of the team	Collaborating in evaluation
The development of individuals	Ensuring that student views are heard
Evaluation	Linking the department to Senior
Ensuring evaluation feeds into planning	Team
Ensuring the use of evaluation in	
planning the grouping of students	
Ensuring the involvement of staff	
Reflection and enquiry	*Staff development*
Creating a culture of critical reflection	Using evaluation to identify needs
Creating a supportive culture	Using classroom observation
Developing 'evaluation as improvement'	Negotiating targets and goals
Using meeting time for reflection	Providing access to training events
Establishing procedures for evaluation	Supporting the development of skills

*Derived from work produced at the Quality in Middle Management Workshop summer school, 1996

Involvement of staff and the community

As staff are attached to departmental teams or are representatives of the department on whole-school teams, the middle manager can ensure that all staff are involved in school improvement initiatives and that their voices are heard. The middle manager could build collaboration and involvement and delegate key tasks within the department. The success of involvement with whole-school initiatives is dependent upon this leadership.

To achieve genuine involvement, ancillary and support staff such as technicians, classroom support workers and others also need to be recognised. Many of these staff are attached to, or their work focuses on, the subject area. Their involvement is explored further in Chapter 8.

Ensuring the involvement of pupils, parents and the community can be more difficult at a department level. However, it is often at this level that their involvement can have most impact, for example in schemes that develop involvement and support for learning. (This is further explored in Chapter 8.)

Leadership

Current management literature (including Hopkins *et al.*, 1994; Day *et al.*, 1993; Smyth, 1989) emphasises that there should be leadership from within the organisation, rather than solely from the top. Clearly those in middle management positions are central to providing leadership. They have certain advantages: they are experienced and close to classroom teaching and focused upon learning. There are a number of issues that are best dealt with by the middle manager performing a professional leadership role. These include:

- clarifying roles, tasks, duties and responsibilities;
- clarifying accountability, relationships and processes;
- communication and collaborating on building a vision of what might be;
- articulating and emphasising quality criteria and values;
- providing pedagogical leadership.

(Discussion of the leadership role of middle managers can be found in Chapter 7.)

Coordination

The curriculum in large schools is coordinated through middle managers and the teams that they lead. Within these teams the activities of staff are coordinated by the middle manager. Across the school the middle managers have to work in a coordinated way under senior management leadership. (Issues of coordination are dealt with in Chapters 7 and 8.)

Collaborative planning

In emphasising whole-school involvement, the literature on school development planning has neglected planning at departmental level. Interestingly, however, in practice, many large schools, when they first attempted school development plans, organised them by department. This often made the school plan a collection of 30 or so department or team plans. While we agree that the overall school strategic development plan should be a short and concise document, this needs to be supported by detailed department or team plans. Clearly collaboration and agreement can exist at the department or team level and responses can be made to whole-school issues which recognise specific departmental needs. (The structure of departmental planning is discussed further in Chapters 11 and 12.)

Critical enquiry and reflection

Hopkins *et al.* (1994) call for enquiry and reflection as a foundation for improvement. However, we would add that the enquiry and reflection needs to be critical, spurred by a desire to improve, rather than accepting current practice and outcomes. There are many terms associated with enquiry and reflection, including evaluation, appraisal, action research and reflective practice (McNiff, 1988).

The essence of Hopkins's approach to enquiry and reflection is seen in an earlier work. Holly and Hopkins (1988) described three approaches to evaluation. They called these 'evaluation of improvement', 'evaluation for improvement', and 'evaluation as improvement'. 'Evaluation of' occurs after the event to see if the improvement has worked. 'Evaluation for' can occur after and during the process of improving and its purpose is to ensure that the improvement takes place. 'Evaluation as', is about building systems for continuous reflection and enquiry as part of the improvement process and ensuring that the school has increased capacity for future change.

McNiff (1988) describes the reflective process as being a cycle, going through stages:

- identification of the problem;
- imagination of the solutions;
- implementation of the solution;
- evaluation of the solution;
- modification of practice.

Middle managers are in key positions to ensure that enquiry and reflection are supported within the department. Terrell *et al.* (1996) argue that a starting point may be reaching agreement on the problem. Terrell (1996) outlines some of the challenges faced by managers in establishing consensus and collaboration of such enquiries including the need to negotiate clear contracts and agreements, the need to challenge beliefs and values, and the need for a clear middle management role in encouraging reflection and enquiry in the department.

Conclusion

In this chapter we have explained why we consider the middle manager's role to be central to school improvement in large schools. In the rest of this book we discuss how middle managers can continuously improve their effectiveness through enquiry and reflection upon their management approach. We provide examples and activities to undertake as well as provide management ideas and theories that can be used to aid your reflection.

Chapter 2

Competence, Reflection and Improvement

Chapter 1 outlines our argument for a focus on middle management in any attempts to enhance school development and improvement. The argument is based upon the assumption that, while middle managers are highly skilled and experienced practitioners, the effectiveness with which they carry out their pivotal role in school improvement depends upon their ability to continue to learn and to improve.

It is too easy to prescribe a list of expectations of middle managers that only some form of super hero manager could meet. This is not our intention. We assume that most middle managers are appointed to the post because they are good classroom practitioners who have a range of other skills and qualities. While being a good manager is different to being a good classroom practitioner, some qualities may be similar. Classroom teachers have been on the receiving end of management and these experiences will have taught them a range of techniques and approaches to management.

Our view is that effective middle management requires particular skills that can be learnt. We see the development of the skills and knowledge of a middle manager as a dynamic process, taking place continuously over a period of time. The lessons of experiences, in different schools or circumstances, are built upon, applied and evaluated. Our approach is to support the development of middle management skills through raising issues and stimulating reflection on management processes, as well as through providing an introduction to theories of management relevant to the middle manager.

We did not wish to write a book that provided a set of instructions for middle managers. To begin with, the skills of management need to be applied within each specific context in which each manager is working and to the people with whom the manager is working. There is unlikely to be a single set of instructions capable of providing all the answers in every circumstance. Furthermore, each individual brings their own experience to management tasks. However, lists of competences can provide a useful starting point for reflection and analysis about individual strengths and weaknesses. The UK Teacher Training Agency list of competences for middle managers ('Consultation Paper on Standards and a National Professional Qualification for Subject Leaders') was published in November 1996.

This chapter introduces some of the competences middle managers need to reflect upon. We build a case for an individual to undertake structured reflective practice on both teaching and middle management. We then outline the idea of reflecting on four key and interconnected issues, which we call pathways of reflection. This model forms the essential structure to the book.

Management competence

In the UK the vocational training movement has developed lists of competences for all of the key occupational areas. These lists of competences are developed by observing what workers actually do in the occupation. The occupational area of 'management' has been subjected to this analysis and, indeed, this list has been applied to the more specific roles of 'school management' through a project entitled the Management Charter Initiative (MCI).

This has supplied managers with a list of key competences linked to four key roles or functions:

(a)   The management of policy;
(b)   The management of learning;
(c)   The management of people;
(d)   The management of resources.

While such a list provides a useful description of the areas of responsibility of the middle manager in schools, there are a number of criticisms of such a bank of competences.

- The breakdown of competence into small atoms of behaviour creates an illusion of precision. In real management, the sum of all the atoms does not necessarily add up to high levels of competence, since there is little room for variance, for personal difference or for some of the less measurable aspects of management.
- The demonstration of competence in one school should not be assumed to transfer to others. Different schools require different approaches to management and a range of different skills.

- Critical reflection on how competence is defined and what is working in any school context can be undervalued by concentrating upon providing evidence that managers can do the things stated in the prescribed list.
- There can be limited consideration of values and beliefs, yet in schools these are central to teaching and learning and the work of managers, in areas such as equal opportunities, the purpose of assessment or the nature of children's potential.
- The competences are those that managers would be expected to display in the normal course of their work as managers. This is inevitable since they were created as descriptions of what managers do. The model is useful for assessment but not one that illustrates how the competences may be learned.
- Underpinning knowledge or understanding is weakly defined.

The competence model is a useful bank of some criteria for effective middle managers and we would not dispute that the process of providing evidence of competence with an assessor can be a dynamic and reflective process. We have not adopted this approach to management development in this book because we feel that more can be achieved through reflecting and continuously improving management skills.

Indeed, there are other attributes, not listed in the MCI statements, which are important. Some of these are contained in the 'Personal Effectiveness Model', developed by the Department of Employment (Department of Employment, 1993). Its purpose is to allow managers both to monitor and acquire the skills necessary to become effective.

The areas of effectiveness outlined in the model include:

- **Making the most of what is done**
  trying to make things better
  deciding what needs to be done and the order in which to do it
  looking at what had to be done
  looking at what was planned
  and finding if they match

- **Involving other people to get the best results**
  identifying and responding to the needs of other people
  getting on well with other people
  getting people to work together
  getting other people to see you in a positive way

- **Managing yourself to get the best results**
  showing a sense of purpose
  dealing with emotions and pressures which can be within yourself or from others
  being responsible for your own development and learning

- **Using knowledge skills and abilities to make the most of what is done**
  getting information and making sense of it
  identifying ideas and finding ways of using them
  making decisions
  using situations
  deciding on values and working within these.

(Department of Employment 1993)

These statements again provide a useful checklist for self-assessment and development. It is interesting that many of these are examples of the more ephemeral and less measurable qualities of managers, for example 'showing a sense of purpose'.

The reflective practitioner and depth to reflection

The process of experiential learning has been outlined by Kolb (1984).

> 'This perspective on learning is called experiential for two reasons. The first is to tie it clearly to its intellectual origins in the work of Dewey, Lewin, and Piaget. The second reason is to emphasise the central role that experience plays in the learning process. This differentiates experiential learning from rationalists and other cognitive theories of learning that tend to give primary emphasis to acquisition, manipulation, and recall of abstract symbols, and from behavioural learning theories that deny any role for consciousness and subjective experience in the learning process.'

The importance of Kolb's work is that he reminds us that learning from experience is an active process, to be worked upon by the learner, and does not necessarily occur by accident. Kolb reminds us for the need actively to reflect upon and make sense of experience and build understanding through establishing principles, rules and theories. Conflict, in Lewin's terms between concrete experience and abstract concepts, and in Dewey's terms between impulse and reason, needs to be resolved.

Applied to knowledge about management, this suggests that it is always possible for you to develop your ideas about the best approaches to use – to develop your work with different people and in different circumstances and to come to new understandings about what being an effective manager means.

The task of being an effective learner is a difficult one requiring several abilities, as Kolb says, 'Learners, if they are to be effective, need four different kinds of abilities – concrete experience abilities, reflective observation abilities, abstract conceptualisation abilities, and active experimentation abilities'… Learning requires abilities that are polar opposites and the learner as a result, must continually choose which set of learning abilities he or she will bring to bear in any specific learning situation.' (ibid., p. 148)

In the case of writing this book, we propose to offer some abstract conceptualisations of management, in the form of recognised management theories.

These have been selected because our experience shows us that they are the most useful in helping managers come to new understandings. They may also suggest strategies for action. We would wish our concepts to be used as a tool to help to observe and experiment in practice. For this reason we will suggest activities to stimulate reflection.

Critical reflection, according to Bullogh, has 'spawned a myriad of forms, the teacher as researcher, action research and reflective teacher movement' and is 'rarely defined with precision' (Bullogh, 1989). He adds, 'reflectivity is a slippery concept' (p. 15).

Following Powell's (1989) work on reflective practice in nursing, reflection can be on:

1. processes or means;
2. outcomes or ends;
3. moral, ethical and political dimensions;
4. structures and ideologies.

Mezirow (1981) suggests levels of reflectivity. These include the following:

1. Reflectivity – awareness of seeing thinking or acting.
2. Affective reflectivity – awareness of feelings.
3. Discriminant reflectivity – assessment of decision making process, or evaluation of planning or carrying out actions.
4. Judgemental reflectivity – being aware of the value judgements and the subjective nature of these.
5. Conceptual reflectivity – assessment of whether the theoretical concepts used sufficiently explain what is happening.
6. Psychic reflectivity – an evaluation of the adequacy of the evidence used to explain the perceived events.
7. Theoretical reflectivity – awareness that routine or practice taken for granted may not be the complete answer, obvious learning from experience or change in perspective.

The list suggests that much reflection remains superficial, rarely digging deeper in terms of awareness of feelings or exploring value judgements, and almost never changing perspectives and learning from experience.

While the middle manager must reflect upon and develop their own management work, we would expect that the middle manager should build the conditions for their team to reflect upon and develop the process of teaching. The department, being the key organisational element for most staff in the large school, can provide the conditions for enquiry and reflection upon the quality of teaching and learning. Reflection is central to the approach to both evaluation and appraisal outlined in Chapters 8 and 12.

The four pathways for reflection and action

Having justified a reflective approach to learning from experience, our concern in the rest of this book is to analyse key aspects of the middle manager's role which provide pathways for reflection. The aspects are different layers or perspectives to think about in any management activities. They are:

- the tasks of management;
- who you are in the context in which you work;
- ways in which you work with people;
- your philosophy of teaching and learning.

Different aspects can be starting points for critical reflection about the management issues that are faced.

The tasks of management

The middle manager needs to reflect upon tasks of management and the systems and procedures for achieving them. The tasks include:

- planning the programme of lessons;
- ensuring the implementation of the programme and evaluation;
- planning future development;
- holding meetings;
- organising resources;
- monitoring;
- staff deployment;
- administrative tasks;
- appointment of staff;
- planning groups;
- managing assessment of students' work.

Many of the tasks will be common in every school although there may be some differences in how things are done. Thinking about tasks, systems and procedures is important. Without the tasks being done, and without clear systems and procedures, there is little chance of effective work being done in the department. Part IV of this book focuses upon some of the common tasks and procedures, particularly those that make a major impact upon the quality of teaching and learning.

Thinking about the tasks, systems and procedures alone is not sufficient for effective improvement to happen. If it were that simple it would be easy to write a guide book of instructions for tasks to be done and systems and procedures that would fit every school. The problem is that schools are all different places and all people are different to work with. You also need to think about who you are, what you want and where you are going. Lastly, you need to think specifically about teaching and learning, and how your work is impacting upon your central mission of organising effective teaching and learning.

Ways in which you work with people

'Management in schools is all about working with people.' (school senior manager, 1995)

Much of the work of the middle manager is about working with people within the department and across the school. Some of the people may be senior managers, some with more or less experience. Some will be teachers, others non-teaching staff. Working with parents is one further aspect.

Cockman *et al.* (1992, p. 112) outline important 'process' issues concerning the functioning of groups, by which they mean:

- relationships and group dynamics;
- motivation, commitment and involvement;
- management and decision making style.

Many management books fall into the trap of talking about tasks, systems and procedures without giving concern for the people who create and manage them. Further development of these ideas can be found in Chapters 7 and 8.

Who you are in the context you in which you work

Reflecting on one's own strengths and weaknesses is an important part of the process of learning about middle management. Another aspect is reflection on one's own assumptions, beliefs and values about how schools should be, about how people behave. You need to understand the things about your work that make you angry and the things that give you great pleasure. These form a basis of what you expect from people. Understanding these things about yourself helps you to make clear to those you manage what you expect from them.

We all work on our own practical understandings of how people behave and how organisations function. These form implicit theories at the core of our decisions about what to do in any situation. Some of these theories may be derived from academic study, some informally built upon through working in the system. Chapter 4 outlines some issues and activities for identifying the personal qualities, beliefs and values you hold and where they derive from. Chapter 7 provides some insights into your personal leadership style.

Reflection on one's own assumptions and values needs to be balanced with reflection upon the context and organisation that you are working within. The analogy of the sandwich outlined earlier is important. Whatever the middle manager's own values and assumptions, they are expressed in a wider prevailing climate generated by the organisation itself. You may for instance value principles of equal opportunity but your values are not consistently applied across the organisation. At times this may be unproblematic. At other times this may cause conflict between you and the organisation.

There are many ways to conceptualise the organisation. We have already discussed a set of conditions described by Hopkins *et al.* (1994) that underpins school improvement. It should be remembered, however, 'There is no single perspective capable of presenting a total framework for our understanding of educational institutions' (Bush, 1995, p. 142). Our task here is to provide some analytical tools so that you, the middle manager, can conceptualise the kind of organisation you work within, so that you can select appropriate strategies to ensure the improvement you seek. Further development of this idea is to be found in Chapter 5.

The context you work in is influenced by international trends and ideas that cross national boundaries. For this reason we have included some perspectives from a number of different countries. These are to be found in Chapter 6. Here you will find some differences and some similarities as school systems grapple with similar issues. Wherever you are currently, it is helpful to know that the issues are sometimes not just new fads or the invention of some group locally but part of a general movement cutting across national school systems and boundaries.

Teaching and learning

The argument earlier outlined our call for making teaching and learning a central focus of reflection and improvement. Making it a central focus means that you must think through your own beliefs and values about teaching and learning in your curriculum area. Your views must be discussed and negotiated with the people who will put them into practice in their classrooms. You have a clear responsibility for organising the foundations of effective classroom practice including the scheme of work, lesson plans, student assessment, the monitoring systems and the organisation of resources. The final performance of teaching, however, will be left to others in their classroom. Making clear to others what your vision of excellence in teaching and learning in your subject is, starts with being clear yourself. This is looked at in Chapter 9. Then there are some basic foundations to put in place if you are to raise achievement. These are outlined in Chapter 10.

Going forward

The chapter has outlined some of the key issues concerning the effectiveness of middle managers. The argument has been made for individuals to undertake structured critical reflection, focusing on four key themes of:

- the tasks of management;
- who you are in the context in which you work;
- ways in which you work with people;
- teaching and learning.

This section makes some practical suggestions about what you should do so that you can reflect upon and develop quality from a middle management position. We consider four suggestions:

1. keeping a reflective journal;
2. undertaking a collaborative action research project;
3. using a 'quality circle' group;
4. working with a 'critical friend' consultant.

The reflective journal

Some managers have found that keeping a journal of their experiences as a manager over a period of time helps them to make sense of it all and identify strategies for improving their management. The journal may be written or a voice recorded on tape. The most successful use involves going over the journal a number of times to gain new insights. Matching the journal to theoretical models of management, such as ideas about motivation, also leads to new insights. The journal may be used to suggest the collection of more information about situations, for example, by asking staff of their perceptions.

Collaborative action research

The systematic collection of information about management processes so that strategies for improvement can be formed, implemented and evaluated can be termed 'action research'. The model is often regarded as a cycle of collecting data, analysing it, planning and implementing strategies and evaluating the outcomes. The research need only be small scale and need not be quantitative. Working collaboratively enhances the perspectives brought to bear upon the situation and helps to ensure agreement among the participants about effective strategies. Some examples, drawn from recent middle management enquiries from MA students, include enquiries into:

- approaches to school development planning;
- changing attitudes to student self-assessment;
- developing and implementing an approach to monitoring;
- developing a consistent teacher assessment policy within a faculty.

More information about action research can be obtained from Hopkins, (1993) *A Teacher's Guide to Classroom Research* and McNiff (1988) *Action Research: Principles and Practice*.

The critical friend consultant

You may be able to reflect in depth with a critical friend consultant. The critical friend may be another manager or someone with the skills to help you reflect and come to your own conclusions about what to do to improve your management approach. The style of facilitating your reflection is important. Those who frequently prescribe their own solutions to your problems may not prove to be helpful. Those who listen carefully and ask questions that help you think through your work might be more useful to you. You might want someone to challenge your interpretations or highlight some of your inconsistencies, such as in what you say and appear to do. Alternatively, you might need someone just to listen to your feelings about being a manager. With luck, you will find someone to use all these strategies at the appropriate times.

More information about approaches to such consultancy can be found in Cockman *et al.* (1992) *Client Centred Consulting*.

Management quality circle

Anyone who organises in-service training for teachers will be familiar with the comment that the training was all right but just finding time to talk to other professionals about the job was the really rewarding part of the activities. The management quality circle is a group convened to talk about management issues. It works best where there is a set structure so that dates, times and venues are known and there is an agenda of items that can be discussed. Issues can arise from participants in turn or be drawn from management literature such as that on motivation, appraisal, monitoring staff and so on. The group can be chaired as in a meeting or activities can take place such as brainstorming ideas, or working in pairs of co-consultants.

Conclusion

This chapter has introduced the notion of developing your skills as a manager through reflection. Several practical suggestions for structuring reflection have been made. If you are a middle manager or are aspiring to be one, you might find it helpful to start a reflective journal now, identifying the issues this chapter has raised and strategies for resolving them.

Chapter 3

The Wider Contribution to the Teaching Profession

Chapters 1 and 2 have focused on the middle manager's role within the school organisation. However, middle managers have a role to play as leading professionals, not just within the school but also in the wider educational community. For example, they are responsible for teaching approaches, for professional development of staff and, in many cases, the training of student teachers in their care. In these roles, middle managers are playing an active part in the wider professional community beyond the school – a part which involves them in the development of professional knowledge and practice in education.

In this chapter, as an introduction to wider professional debates in which, we suggest, middle managers have a responsibility to take part, we raise issues about the development of professional knowledge and practice and the education of student teachers.

The process of developing professional knowledge

As leading professionals, middle managers are expected to be up to date with developments in their area of expertise and, where they participate fully in professional associations, they will be forming and disseminating new practice. But how does knowledge about teaching and learning develop? What are the influences on change?

Sir Isaac Newton is said to have acknowledged the work of his predecessors with the statement 'If I have seen further than others, it is because I have stood on the shoulders of giants'. This idea – that each generation builds on the work of the preceding generation – can be applied to the process of building knowledge in any sphere of life. Each generation probably has the opportunity to push forward the barriers of understanding a little further – building on the thinking and experience of the generation before.

For teachers in the UK state education system, changes in the shared body of professional knowledge and practice are influenced principally by ideas emanating from any of six sources:

- professional organisations;
- local education authorities;
- the Department for Education and Employment (the voice of government);
- higher education institutions (HEIs);
- the media;
- processes within the individual school.

To what extent are you aware of current thinking and developments coming from each of these sources? New ideas which contribute to professional knowledge are, for example, developed through practice and/or research (eg collaborative action research groups working within the school and HEIs) and disseminated through professional networks, conferences, in service education and various types of publication. The Collaborative Action Research Network (CARN) is an example of such a network; professional associations provide other networks. Collaborative professional work taking place in such networks provides ongoing development of professional knowledge within the profession.

Politicians and policy makers at the national level clearly influence the development of professional knowledge, for example through speeches, legislation and through fiscal control.

Activity 3.1 Your wider involvement

Consider in what ways you are involved in the wider educational community. How would you like to extend this commitment? What do you have to do to achieve this? Record your plans in your reflective journal.

At the national level in the UK in recent years, there seems to have been a constant struggle among different political groups for the power to influence policy. There has been rapid change as Secretaries of State for Education have come, introduced major changes and gone, without seeing through these changes. Ball (1994, p. 30) acknowledges these tensions in his examination of how 'traditionalists' wrested power from 'modernizers' and 'progressive vocationalists' in the 1980s.

> 'the losers in the policy making arena (in the eighties) were a coalition of educational "modernizers": a loosely constituted group made up of "new progressive" educators, especially from the science and mathematics education communities, and "progressive vocationalists" representing the educational concerns of many of the UK's largest multinational companies.' (ibid., p. 30)

In the UK a whole raft of legislation was passed which was designed to change the education system radically. This legislation related to the curriculum, the management of schools, competition between schools, local education authority involvement with schools and so on (Goddard and Leask, 1992, provides details). Similar changes are being implemented in other countries too, for example New Zealand, Australia and The Netherlands. The rash of changes has produced casualties and contradictions in the system.

Of course, the education system cannot be static; much as teachers, parents and pupils may wish it otherwise. The speed with which society is changing, and with which technology is changing ways of living and working, means that the knowledge, skills and attitudes of yesterday's curriculum may not be appropriate today. This presents challenges for society and for schools and teachers as they try to adjust. The middle manager is the person at the forefront of the implementation of such changes in knowledge, skills and attitude in the teaching practised in their department. An understanding of the need for ongoing change and of ways to help staff and pupils adapt to change must then be desirable attributes for middle managers.

There is pressure in England and Wales for distancing the school education system from direct political control, for the 'professionalisation' of teaching. Those arguing for the formation of a self-governing body for teachers (eg The Education Council for England and Wales, 1993) are to the fore in this debate. However, experience from the Australian system shows that such governing bodies are still subject to political interference when they depend on government money for their operation.

Professionalism and teaching

The notion of teaching as a profession is a contested assumption. There are, for example, a number of publications in which the notion of professionalism in teaching is debated (Hoyle and John, 1995; Langford, 1978; Calderhead, 1988).

Various criteria are used in the attempt to differentiate between the working practices of 'professionals' and those of 'non-professionals'. One national group which claims to represents the professions in the UK is the UK Inter-Professional Group (UKIPG). The UKIPG lists 18 professions as member organisations and these members include the major professional groups such as the British Medical Association, Royal College of Nursing, Library Association and the General Council of the Bar. However, teaching is not included. Whether the criteria used to define a profession by the UKIPG are appropriate criteria is a debate outside the scope of this book. The fact that teachers are not included in the membership of a body claiming to represent the professions, indicates that work in the education sector does not fit criteria which do apply to other recognised professions.

Activity 3.2 Teaching – profession or trade?

What is your view of teaching? Do you view teaching as purely skills-based, ie as a trade or as a profession, ie requiring the exercising of professional judgement beyond that required in the exercising of skills which can be directly taught? Consider how those with whom you work view teaching. How do their views influence the way they carry out their work?

An examination of the *'Principles of a Profession'* as defined by the UKIPG, and quoted below, reveals that a major difference between teaching and the professions which are members of the UKIPG is that there is no independent governing body for teachers in England and Wales. The existence of an independent governing body for a profession features significantly in these 'Principles':

'The UKIPG believes that the following principles can be identified as those which characterise a profession, and the obligations its members owe to the public.

1. A profession must be controlled by a governing body.
2. The governing body must set adequate standards of education as a condition of entry or achievement of professional status.
3. The governing body must set ethical rules and professional standards which are to be observed by its members.
4. The rules and standards enforced by the governing body must be designed for the benefit of the public, and not for the private advantage of the members.
5. The governing body must take disciplinary action if the rules and standards it lays down are not observed or a member is guilty of bad professional work.
6. Some types of work should be preserved to the profession by statute, not because it is for the advantage of the members, but because for the protection of the public, it should be carried out only by persons with the requisite training, standards and disciplines.

7. The governing body must satisfy itself that there is fair and open competition in the practice of the profession.
8. The members of the profession must be independent in thought and outlook.
9. In its particular field of learning the profession must give leadership to the public it serves.'

(UK Inter-Professional Group, 1995, p. 9)

In some countries or states, for example, Scotland in the UK, Queensland in Australia, British Columbia in Canada, such a governing body for teaching does exist. So although teaching may come close to satisfying the UKIPG criteria for recognition as a profession in some countries, this is not the case in England and Wales, where Hoyle and John (1995) describe teaching as having the status of a 'pseudo-profession'. Teaching, Hoyle and John argue, has only some features in common with recognised professions.

Currently changes in the curriculum can be dictated by government and such freedom may be constrained by a professional governing body. So there may be financial and political issues hindering the formal recognition of teaching as a profession in England and Wales. For example, a professional governing body with responsibility for the quality of training would carry the responsibility for setting standards. Short cuts to training would then be controlled in a way which has possibly not happened in England and Wales before. The qualifications of the teaching force could be scrutinised more easily as, in common with other professional bodies, a register would be produced which would be open to public scrutiny. Currently teachers may hold a variety of professional qualifications or, indeed, in some cases, teachers may have no qualifications in education. Exposure to public scrutiny of such variations in qualifications may create pressure for change.

These debates about professionalism, change and control over the curriculum are just some of the debates in which you, as a middle manager and an 'extended professional' (ie with an active interest in education as a whole, not just the work in your own classroom), may wish to become involved. Another current issue in the UK is the appropriate way to train teachers.

Models of teaching

Few assumptions can be made about the professional knowledge held by teachers or indeed about the training they have undergone. In the UK, some in teaching positions may have had no formal training, while others may have been trained and worked in only one school. Some will have had one year's training in education after a degree course, others will have spent four years undertaking an education degree. In England, where the accepted models of teacher training are more varied than in a number of other countries, some student teachers are trained entirely in schools without an input from higher education. Italy is only now developing formal training for secondary teachers. In The Netherlands and Australia the one-year route to teaching is much less common than in the UK.

The values and beliefs individuals hold about teaching as a profession influence their views about the form of education that is appropriate for teachers. As a middle manager you may also have responsibility for student teachers and you may be expected to have a considered viewpoint about what is appropriate in this role.

There are different views about how and what student teachers are to be taught. Three contrasting models are identified by Furlong and Maynard:

> 'New Right thinkers such as O'Hear (1988) talk of the importance of "learning through the emulation of an experienced practitioner" – a form of unreflective apprenticeship. Such an idea follows logically from the conception of teaching as an almost mystical process, dependent primarily on personality and "natural" skill – not susceptible to systematic analysis… In sharp contrast those advocating a competency model advocate a more systematic, skills-based approach to learning to teach… others, insist that teaching is a complex intellectual and moral activity.' (Furlong and Maynard, 1995, pp. 178–9)

We believe that there is a body of professional knowledge to be acquired which goes beyond the basic classroom management skills identified in Furlong and Maynard's first and second models. The third model, 'that teaching is a complex intellectual and moral activity', is closer to the model of teaching espoused in this text. Capel *et al.* (1995, 1996), argue that three facets of professionalism, the teacher's professional knowledge, their professional judgement as well as their professional skills, have to be developed beyond initial training through reflection on experience and further education. The case is made that these aspects of a teacher's professional life need to be under continual development, and that evaluation and planning skills provide professional tools for such ongoing development. Simons (1984), Sparkes, (1991), McNiff (1993) and Schratz and Walker (1995) are among many supporters of the reflective practitioner approach to teacher development.

Students on initial training courses are, naturally, particularly concerned with developing curriculum and lesson planning skills together with class management skills. Deep learning about pedagogy – the science of teaching – may be more appropriately provided for teachers who have acquired the basic skills. There is nothing new in this idea. The James Report in 1972 in the UK recommended sabbatical terms for teachers for refreshment and professional development and, up to the mid-1980s, teachers could apply to their local education authority for sabbaticals although these were restricted in number. Sabbatical terms are available to teachers from, for example, Australia where the notion of 'long service leave' has been established for decades. Clearly, initial teacher education can only provide part of a teacher's education. What happens next depends to a considerable extent on the management philosophy of the middle manager with whom individual teachers work. Teacher–researcher projects can provide a useful avenue for professional refreshment and reflection. Chapter 12 discusses these in the context of departmental evaluation.

Conclusion

Extending your horizons beyond the world of the school to the education system may give you a perspective on change which may allow you to accept and understand the changes demanded of schools – even if you do not agree with them. Playing a full role in the debates accompanying such changes is a role that middle managers who have a commitment to the teaching profession, will want to take on.

Part II   Who You are in the Context in which You Work

Chapter 4

Values, Beliefs, Vision: Where do You Stand?

How you perform and how others see you depends on the environment in which you work and the criteria others use to judge you. Behaviour considered normal in one context may be interpreted as unacceptable in another. Similarly, beliefs and values about how and what to teach vary. Differences of beliefs and values about management, and about learning and teaching, can render middle managers ineffective if they find themselves in an environment where their values and beliefs are not viewed sympathetically.

So, before you can effectively contribute to school improvement and the development of your department, we suggest you consider how your beliefs, values and working practices fit in with those of other staff in the department and the school. If you are new to leadership of a department, you will need to consider how your new role changes your relationship with colleagues.

Throughout this book, you will be given opportunities to assess your strengths and weaknesses against various descriptors of the tasks of middle management. In this chapter we focus in particular on three of the four dimensions of the middle management role which we identified in Chapter 2.

- *How you are in the context in which you work.* How does your individuality have an impact on the context in which you are now working?
- *Your philosophy of teaching and learning.* How this was formed and how well you can tolerate differences.
- *How you work with people.* Your personal characteristics which help or hinder the forming of effective working relationships.

Your capacity to manage these different dimensions of the role will affect your ability to turn your vision for your area of work into reality.

To what extent do you know yourself? In this chapter you are encouraged to reflect on your own values and beliefs about teaching and learning, and about working with people, in order to understand better your strengths and weaknesses as a leader of a department or team. The chapter starts with a discussion about your values and beliefs and how your vision for your department or team stems from these. Interpersonal skills and qualities form the focus of the last section, together with an analysis of how power is exercised in organisations.

Your values and beliefs about management

Your personality and your prior experience influence your expectations of your line managers and your expectations of those for whom you are now a line manager. What motivates you to do good work? What values do others hold which motivate them to work well? Do you share the beliefs and values which underpin the ethos of your school? What level of fit is there between your beliefs and practices about how schools, teaching and learning are best managed, and those beliefs and practices of the teachers whom you manage? If the fit is not close, then conflict may be inevitable unless you are able to accept and work with these differences, developing good working relationships with staff who have different priorities, beliefs and practices.

Chapters 7 and 8 introduce a range of strategies related to the management of people and leadership from which you can analyse your own approach to leadership and management. How do you view staff potential? We quoted Blanchard and Johnson's (1983, p. 71) optimistic view in the Introduction: 'Everyone is a potential winner. Some people are disguised as losers. Don't let their appearances fool you'.

You may find some of the staff with whom you have to work difficult but there is no point in wishing they were different – part of your role is to help all staff grow and develop. How you deal with difficult staff depends on circumstances and in dealing with these problems you can expect help and support from senior management. However, protecting the pupils' rights to high quality education must be to the fore when you are involved in decisions about staff performance.

Your values and beliefs about teaching and learning

We argue that it is both relevant and useful for teachers to become overtly aware of their personal values and beliefs about teaching and learning. Undergoing a process of personal reflection on your own conceptual framework of teaching and learning, and its potential origins, is an essential starting point if you are to move towards sharing your perceptions across the department. It is also important that these views are shared and understood between members of the department. In Chapter 9, we argue that the process of sharing these views is an important element in developing a professional dialogue about teaching and learning within the department or team.

We each have a unique set of values that have been and continue to be constructed from a variety of sources. Many of these values, if not all, impact in some way on our teaching. They inform our behaviour and guide us in developing professional relationships with colleagues, pupils and parents. They helped shape our view of teaching when matched or mismatched with ideas expounded during our initial training about models of learning and teaching styles. They play a part in determining our view of acceptable classroom behaviour and our expectations of pupils and colleagues. Whitaker (1993, p. 48) links values with *experience, personality* and *will* – identifying these as factors determining 'our uniqueness as individuals'. He describes this combination as the interpersonal landscape, in that these four factors impact on our thinking and in our communication with others. He cites childhood, school, work and society as the influencing experience factors, and attitudes, beliefs, assumptions and prejudices as the values that emerge partly as a result of our experiences.

Defining our beliefs about teaching can be complex and difficult. Exploring the sources of these beliefs can also be daunting. One useful 'way in' might be to consider the various role models of teaching that we have experienced, both as a child and as a practising teacher. On the next page is an example of one teacher's experience.

In 1996 these issues were explored by Gill Venn with groups of mainly mature BEd secondary student teachers at the end of their course and with groups of experienced Israeli teachers and head teachers. She discovered that early childhood influences were seen as key by the individuals in terms of their teaching practices in the classroom. Using a 'timeline' approach the students were encouraged to brainstorm, then mark on to the timeline, key events and key people who influenced their thinking in terms of teaching and learning.

Various events were detailed, many of which expose painful memories of being humiliated or publicly sanctioned by teachers when young. Others charted key teachers whose approach had made a real impact on their young lives and who, in adulthood, had become something of a role model. Wragg and Wood (1994) discuss the way in which student teachers initially often simply teach in the way they were taught themselves at school. The BEd secondary students felt very strongly that, despite several important influences from their university course and from their periods of school experience, essentially their attitudes towards teaching and learning had not greatly altered from when they started the course. The experienced Israeli

Norman: A philosophy of teaching

My views on the quality of teaching originate with my own experience at a boys' grammar school. The general teaching philosophy was to motivate pupils to try harder by always focusing on the mistakes they made. So no matter how well you did the teacher would always find something wrong with it. If you were doing fairly well then this approach could prove motivating. I was always determined not to let them get me down and their negative comments stimulated me to work harder. However, this approach had the opposite effect upon my brother. He found the work a bit more difficult and all the negative comments eventually made him feel that he was a failure and he gave up. The teachers were quite happy to label him as a failure. He left the grammar school with no examination passes. He was not a rebel and I feel the system failed him rather than vice versa. This helped me formulate my fundamental philosophy of teaching: the teacher should always develop a positive relationship with each pupil, any criticism should be constructive and every pupil should be treated as an individual with the teacher responding to individual needs. This still remains the cornerstone of my criteria for evaluating the quality of teaching.

colleagues also expressed a real sense of these early experiences having a profound impact on their teaching approaches. Undertaking such an activity with colleagues, working within the department, might encourage initial discussions of how thoughts, beliefs and values about teaching and learning have been influenced by such early personal experiences.

Every teacher has a unique personal construction of what is meant by 'teaching'. This unique conceptual framework has been formed and shaped by the individual's combination of experience, beliefs and values and their resulting attitudes. How the individual has interpreted these experiences and her or his exposure to beliefs and values may, in part, be influenced by their personality.

This conceptual framework of teaching may influence the individual's response to suggestions for innovation, change or improvement. If the suggestion for change complements the framework, the individual might accept the possibilities for inclusion into their own practice more readily than if the suggestion confronts or challenges their assumptions or framework.

There are clearly a number of potential elements which combine together to create a personal sum of values and beliefs about teaching and learning – an individual conceptual construction of teaching and learning. Table 4.1 presents nine such potential elements.

Activity 4.1 Your personal values and beliefs about teaching and learning

Work through each element in Table 4.1 and consider which construction fits best for you. How might you best describe your view of the role of the teacher? You might feel that the role of the teacher is to deliver knowledge and the National Curriculum. Or you might believe that the role of the teacher is to facilitate the pupil's learning through a variety of means. Whichever descriptor fits best would be your personal construct of that element. Use the table below to 'map out' your beliefs and values under these headings. The descriptors are suggestions. If none fit for a particular element, create your own.

Table 4.1   *Your personal values and beliefs about teaching and learning*

Element	Potential construction
Role of the teacher	as educator?
	as deliverer?
	as facilitator?
	as carer?
	as mentor?
Role of schools	in relation to society?
	in relation to the individual?
	cultural bearers?
Notion of child(hood)	empty vessels?
	inherently good/inherently evil?
	small 'people' with differing needs?
	expectation of learners?

| Models of learning | transmission of knowledge? |
| | constructivist? |

Model of motivation	theory X and Y (see Chapter 8)
	through fear?
	through enjoyment?
	influence of self-esteem/motivation?

| Curriculum models | notion of entitlement, breadth and balance? |
| | differing values for different subjects – ie subject worth |

Grouping of learners	setted?
	streamed?
	by age?
	mixed ability?
	by interest?

| Role of parents/wider community | active involvement or hindrance? |
| | potential partners or interference? |

Intrinsic worth of education	empowering?
	controlling?
	school based or lifelong?

How we arrive at the sum of our framework will depend on the experiences, attitudes and values to which we have been exposed.

Personal skills, knowledge and qualities

Accepting what you cannot change and keeping your vision to the fore while dealing with the realities and constraints of the environment in which you work are two characteristics worth developing. Idealism tempered with pragmatism is an approach which is likely to allow you to keep your sense of humour, lessen your frustration and allow you eventually to reach your long-term goals. Recognise when a problem cannot be solved by you and pass it on. To reach this point, you will have developed quite a lot of self-knowledge: knowledge of how to defuse situations by allowing those involved space to reconsider rather than forcing them into a corner; knowledge of how to be assertive rather than aggressive.

Activity 4.2 Assessing your personal qualities

Compile a list of the qualities and skills you believe an effective middle manager should possess. Table 4.2 provides some suggestions but you will need to add your own ideas. Once your list is complete, assess yourself in terms of each quality. Give yourself a score out of 5. On which areas do you need to work? How can you develop in those areas? Record your goals for development in your reflective journal.

Table 4.2   *Your personal qualities*

	score out of 5
Administrative skills	
Willingness to share power	
Counselling skills	
Ability to deal with conflict constructively	
Sense of humour	
Sensitivity	
Ability to give and receive criticism	
Sense of fairness	
Awareness of curriculum developments	
Understanding of the role of the department within the school	

Managing power

We have already discussed the fact that as a middle manager you will possess more power than the class teacher. In any interpersonal interactions, power relationships will be operating even at a subconscious level. It may help you in developing working relationships with other staff to think about the power relationships operating within the department and the whole school organisation. As a middle manager, on what basis do you expect staff to let you have power to make decisions?

Fritchie and Thorne (1988) write about the need to understand power in organisations:

'An understanding of organisational politics is important for a number of reasons:

1. It is a crucial aspect of getting things done in the organisation – you need to know who will help or hinder you, and why.

2. Your career progress depends to some extent on your "track record" which in turn depends on being able to get things done in the organisation, so… back to Item 1 above!

3. Your career progress also may depend on knowing who the powerful people are in the organisation as far as your promotion is concerned, and what will influence them to support your cause.

4. Organisations have cultures – preferred ways of doing things, ways of treating people, valued ideas or beliefs, acceptable way of thinking. The people who determine what the culture will be like are the people who have the most power in the organisation. If you want to ensure that the culture reflects *your* values and interests, it is important to gain and exercise organisational power.'

They identify four bases for power in organisations:

- formal authority
- expertise
- resource control
- personal skills.

You may wish to reflect, for a moment, on which of these give you power in your context. However, other factors can influence your ability to use power appropriately, for example, the micro-politics within the organisation.

Micro-politics

Your use of power is affected by the micro-politics operating in the organisation and the importance of considering this was stressed in Chapter 1. The micro-politics within the educational system influence the implementation of any change and hence cannot be ignored when you as a middle manager consider introducing innovation. The informal culture operating in institutions and the passive resistance of staff to change can effectively block initiatives. Ball (1987) and Davies (1994) in particular warn of the impact of micro-politics on the implementation of innovations.

Bullying and harassment

Unfortunately, some middle and senior managers use their power to bully staff.

'The NASUWT claimed at its recent annual conference that 10000 teachers were victims of bullying by colleagues and that it was becoming the biggest cause of stress related illness in the profession. A survey by the union indicates that most bullies are headteachers in their forties, although deputies and department heads were also among the main offenders.' (Whitehead, 1996, p. 6).

Whitehead goes on to identifying the characteristics of bullying:

> 'Bullying among adults usually involves a kind of psychological warfare by someone in a position of authority against a subordinate involving such tactics as constant criticism, public humiliation, undermining of the victim's confidence and setting unreasonable performance targets. Bullies also resort to shouting at the victim in front of colleagues or pupils, arbitrary removal of responsibilities, threats, intimidating use of discipline or isolation.' (ibid.)

We have also come across the giving of bad confidential references in order to prevent good staff obtaining other posts. This is an insidious form of bullying which may only come to light by accident. One member of staff we know of in this situation found out in interview. His strategy for avoiding this in the future was to ask the head for a testimonial (ie an open written reference) and to give the deputy head as the confidential referee. Others report inconsistent behaviour on the part of the manager, such as denigration of work, lack of back-up or setting conditions for failure.

Activity 4.3 Bullying and Harassment

What circumstances do you consider give rise to bullying and harassing behaviour? If you have experienced bullying tactics yourself, reflect on your feelings at the time and the ways in which you dealt with the situation.

As a middle manager you may need to support staff who are experiencing such treatment from others in the school or you may find that you experience this yourself. To work with people effectively you need to be able to resolve such situations. Your union is an obvious source of advice on these matters.

Developing your vision for the department

The following examples (pages 43–6), present the visions of a group of middle managers for their own departments or areas of the school. They show a number of ambitions and desires and clearly at their roots is a fundamental set of values held by each individual. The need for motivated staff and pupils, the drive for good working environments and the link between academic and pastoral work are examples.

There is also a strong emphasis upon the working with people element of management. Managers, quite naturally, want other staff to have a set of positive attitudes and to respond in positive ways, ie colleagues should share experiences, pupils are treated like adults (by staff) and so on. This emphasises that managers need to work with and through others.

There are some interesting anomalies, contradictions and questions that arise from the vision statements. For example, what is behind the statement about perceived 'economic viability' (Dipak, page 44). What is the concern about 'homework' being expressed (Frank, page 46). How does one equate talking about being 'part of the school and not out on a limb' with the reference to the rest of the school as 'they' (Dave, page 45), in terms of 'they will understand, they will appreciate'?

Vision statements reveal a lot about our concerns, beliefs and values. A critical friend may be particularly helpful in helping you unlock the vision you hold as a middle manager.

The middle managers providing these vision statements were also asked what difficulties they faced in implementing the vision, that is they were asked to reflect upon the difficulties they might predict. These views are presented in Table 4.3. Again the list suggests a high degree of concern for what other people might do or not do to hinder the development of the vision in practice. This suggests that building the vision together with other people should be an imperative. Getting others to be as enthusiastic as you are about it and letting them contribute to the developing vision is a central task if you are to be successful.

Chris: Vision for year seven

- The transition to secondary school is not traumatic
- There is academic progression from primary school for all levels of ability
- Children are stimulated and socialised by extra-curricular activities
- Children feel safe and secure
- Children are familiar and comfortable with the culture and demands of secondary school
- Children look forward to returning to school in year 8.

Anita: Vision of the maths department

- Pupils to love mathematics
- Pupils discuss maths at every opportunity
- Attainment is raised
- Colleagues share their classroom experiences
- Colleagues in other areas are using maths ideas as starting points for their own work
- Colleagues are willing to share ideas and experiences with other departments
- A culture of success is established.

Dipak: A vision for the school

The kind of school I would like to teach in would value pupils as individuals who can be encouraged to excel in academic and non-academic areas. Pupils are secure in the knowledge that their future is valued and that the staff take an active interest in this. There is an open door policy and relaxed and respectful parent–teacher relationships. There is a healthy balance between academic and non-academic areas. Strong pastoral support is built into every department and not perceived as a separate issue. Pupils are encouraged to follow their own interests and goals, regardless of what is perceived to be 'economically viable'.

Jen: IT across the school – looking to the future

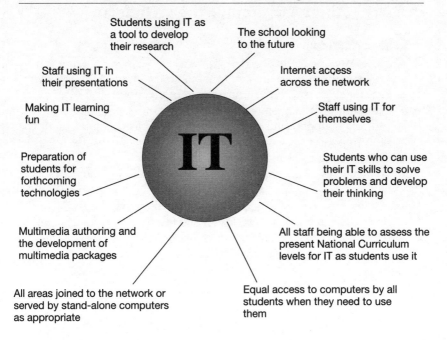

Students using IT as a tool to develop their research

The school looking to the future

Staff using IT in their presentations

Internet access across the network

Making IT learning fun

Staff using IT for themselves

Preparation of students for forthcoming technologies

Students who can use their IT skills to solve problems and develop their thinking

Multimedia authoring and the development of multimedia packages

All staff being able to assess the present National Curriculum levels for IT as students use it

All areas joined to the network or served by stand-alone computers as appropriate

Equal access to computers by all students when they need to use them

---

Dave: A vision for the drama department

Staff and pupils create an enjoyable, positive atmosphere to work in. The department within the school is a positive, busy, creative area as a functioning part of the whole school, not in isolation. The main body of the school will understand and appreciate the contribution of drama to the overall vision of the school.

Ajita: A vision for the sixth form

- The best VI form
- Pupils want to be there
- Pupils motivated, committed to work and study
- Good results, social life, being ahead of the times
- Wonderful working environment
- Staff offer support and guidance to improve the knowledge and skills of pupils
- Staff treat pupils as maturing adults
- Students become empowered to enquire, they should enjoy learning, have respect for other people's views and opinions
- Staff engage in learning themselves, understand the problems others have when learning. They have respect for the pupils they teach, are self-critical but listen to the views of others. They are prepared to change to improve the learning opportunities of others.

Frank: A vision for lessons

Pupils and teachers arrive for the lessons with an enthusiastic sense of purpose, knowing that they are going to learn something (about the subject, the world, about themselves and each other). They will feel physically and emotionally safe but challenged. They will enjoy being in an attractive and evolving physical environment and be sad to leave at the end of the lesson. They will feel proud of what they have learnt and want to learn more. They will be eager to rush home and complete their homework which they know will enrich them.

Activity 4.4 Articulating your vision

In your reflective journal write your own vision statement for your department or area. Consider how you could work with others in the department on a vision statement. Are the values you express likely to be shared? What are the problem areas? Will you need to accept differences of values and direction or are there ways of working together to develop shared values?

Table 4.3 lists some of the difficulties in putting your vision in place. These were identified by a group of experienced middle managers.

Table 4.3 *Difficulties of implementing the vision*

- Getting consistency across all staff (see Chapter 16).
- The minority destroys the work of the majority.
- Not having control.
- Finances controlled by SMT (see Chapter 15).
- Dependence on others to succeed.
- Pressure of time and concern for standards (see Chapter 13).
- Lack of professionalism.
- Utopia being a long way from reality.

Activity 4.5 Analysing problems in implementing the vision

In your reflective journal note the issues to be resolved in the quest for shared commitment to a vision for the whole department or team with whom you work. Spend some time reflecting on the various solutions to the problems identified in Table 4.3 and develop an action plan setting out what has to be achieved to move forward. This activity is designed to encourage strategic thinking about change and it leads on to the development of your personal strategic plan in Chapter 11.

Some staff may never accept this approach to planning and working and it might be that you decide that the investment of time and energy required to change their views is not justified – focusing your energies on the areas where change is more likely may be the most effective strategy to adopt in the context in which you find yourself. Turning the vision into action is the focus of Chapter 11.

Conclusion

Because your effectiveness is determined to a large extent by the context in which you work, a considerable part of this book is devoted to developing your understanding of how your values and beliefs about teaching, learning and management fit with this environment. Your ability to understand yourself and the micro-politics of the organisation, and to work effectively within these boundaries, is crucial to success in your career. Staff in your department will hold differing values and beliefs about teaching, schooling, education and learning. Discovering the values and beliefs they hold is explored more fully in Chapter 9. The extent to which you are able to work with these differences will to some extent determine your success in building an effective department in which both pupils and teachers are achieving high standards.

Chapter 5

The Nature of Organisations

Earlier chapters of this book have introduced the notion of reflection on the practice of middle management as a key to improving management performance and developing the skills of management. In the previous chapter you are invited to identify your beliefs and values, and your personal qualities and skills. Another aspect influencing the effectiveness of your work as a middle manager is the nature of the organisation in which you work. Effective management is dependent both upon you fitting into the organisation and you having a positive effect upon it. As was outlined in Chapter 3, what may be effective management in one school may be inappropriate, ineffective or even disruptive in another.

People who are not managers in different schools have different traditions and ways of working. They expect different things from those who are managers. Indeed, their concept of management itself is different. 'The way in which things are done' is a loose definition of the culture of the school. Managers need to think carefully about the kind of organisation in which they are working, so that they can adapt their approach to take account of what the school expects. This is not to say that you might not wish to work in a different way, in time, but you should do so after careful consideration.

This chapter describes several different theoretical models of school management. The models exist as different perspectives. Do not expect that your school fits exactly one of the models. It is more likely that management practice in your school has some of the attributes of several of the models. You are asked to consider which model fits most closely the management behaviour in the school. You may also wish to consider which model describes your own approach to management and what this leads you to expect from staff.

The context for middle management in your school

A good starting point for looking at the school management context is to ask yourself which metaphor sums up for you what working in your school as a middle manager is like. A recent group of managers came up with the following suggestions:

- a boxing ring
- a garden
- a funfair
- a railway station
- a production line
- a telephone exchange
- a social club
- a sponge.

These images suggest different working conditions and different expectations of the middle managers. The boxing ring describes, perhaps, the constant battle and confrontations and of having to fight your corner. The garden is quiet and peaceful but perhaps needs careful tending to make sure that it blooms. The telephone exchange is the constant relaying of snippets of information across different channels and to different sets of people. The sponge contains many different pockets of activity involving many different people. Each of the images demands a different approach to management.

Activity 5.1 Dimensions of management

Table 5.1 is a selected list of dimensions and associated aspects of management. Which of these are the best descriptions of the place in which you work? Which are you most comfortable with? Which reflect your beliefs and values about management? Identify the key qualities that describe your organisation and the expectations placed upon you. Record your comments in your reflective journal.

Table 5.1 *Selected dimensions and associated aspects of management*

Decision making	Rational	Non-Rational	Irrational
Involvement of staff			
Consensual	Normative	Moral	Conflictual
Calculative	Limited	Individual	Problematic
Dependent			
Individual roles			
Specialist	Specified	Autonomous	Negotiated
Self-interest	Generalist	Ambiguous	Fixed
Dynamic	Flexible	Wide ranging	
Degree of centralisation			
Centralised	Devolved	Variable	Unclear
Management functions			
Control	Command	Monitor	Resource
Report	Facilitate	Coordinate	Disseminate
Negotiate	Lead	Bargain	Spokesperson
Entrepreneur	Liaise	Uncertain	Dictate

More formal models of management have been outlined by Bush (1992). The basis of Bush's classification is that there are four main elements that distinguish management theories. These are differences about:

- goals;
- the meaning and validity of organisational structures;
- the relationship between the school and its external environment;
- the most appropriate leadership strategies.

The models that Bush proposes include:

- *Formal Models* which can be structural, systems based, bureaucratic, rational or hierarchical. They are goal oriented and goals are often determined by the head and others. Support from staff is not a problem dealt with by these models. Staff belong to structures within the organisation and have specific roles. Interaction with the external environment only occurs at the most senior levels in the main. Leadership is from the top where policy decisions are designed by a rational process.
- *Collegial Models* are based upon sharing power and decision making. They assume that there is a common set of goals and values. The models are felt to be particularly suited to large organisations, staffed by professionals. There are clear and representative structures to make collegial decisions.

Consensus is all important. Leaders are responsive to the professionals within the school.

- *Political Models* emphasise power and decision making as a bargaining process. The goals of the departments and other subunits may be diverse. The structure of the school is determined by the power over decision making. Decision making bodies are the battlegrounds of the 'power barons'. Leaders have their own values, interests and policies.

- *Subjective Models* are based upon the notion of the individual. Each individual has a different set of goals and plays a part in creating a structure. Clearly, some, particularly the head, are likely to have more influence than others. There is little attention paid to the external environment .

- *Ambiguity Models* stress the uncertainty and unpredictability of the organisation. Goals are vague. Structures are loose and subject to change. Decisions are made through committees and working parties. Schools are sensitive to the needs of the external environment. Leadership is problematic because of the ambiguous nature of goals, power, experience and the nature of success.

- *Cultural Models* of management emphasise the identification of a culture through the expression of goals. The structure is the physical manifestation of the culture and the environment is probably the key creative force. The leadership develops and maintains the culture.

The ethos and culture of schools

The model of management in operation indicates the values and beliefs about management, and about teaching and learning, held by those leading the school. In Chapter 4 the point was made that if you are to work effectively in the role of middle manager, you need to be aware in which ways your values and beliefs fit with the ethos and culture of the school and in which ways they differ. This understanding of the context in which you work will determine which of the ideas in the rest of this book can be effectively applied by you in your position as middle manager. Torrington and Weightman (1993, p. 45) discuss the difference between these two concepts.

'The concepts of ethos and organisational culture are very similar but there is a slight difference. Organisational culture is the characteristic spirit and belief of an organisation, demonstrated, for example, in the norms and values that are generally held about how people should treat each other, the nature of working relationships that should be developed and attitudes to change. These norms are deep, taken for granted assumptions that are not always expressed, and are often known without being understood.

The history and traditions of a school tell one something of a school's culture because the cultural norms develop over a relatively long period, with layers and layers of practice, both modifying and consolidating the norms and providing the framework of ritual convention in which people feel secure, once they have internalised its elements.

The ethos of a school is a more self conscious expression of specific types of objective in relation to behaviour and values. This can be in various forms such as a formal statement by the headteacher, and in such comments as "we don't do things that way here".'

If the ethos of the school is such that your values and beliefs are at variance with those that are dominant then changes you wish to introduce may run counter to those which staff are likely to accept. Torrington and Weightman (1989, p. 40) discuss the balance between effectiveness, control and autonomy of decision making within the school. The way the balance between these two aspects is managed is, they suggest, crucial: 'A balance between a tight central mission of a school coupled with a loose decentralised autonomy of how to put that into practice seems to make for effectiveness.' The generally held beliefs and values about development and change to be found in your school will, of course have a major effect upon your impact as a middle manager at the centre of stimulating improvement. Hopkins *et al.* (1994) refer to four types of school in relation to attitudes to change. These are as follows.

- *The stuck school:* Here, staff are not much interested in change. Things are said to have been tried before and failed. Factors external to the school such as the type of children and their parents are identified as the major ones influencing the condition the school finds itself in. There is a strong feeling of powerlessness. Externally imposed change, such as changes in curriculum, are regarded as tasks which have to be undertaken, even though it is felt it will not make things better.
- *The wandering school:* Here, there are many different innovations that are started. Some do not get fully implemented or disseminated across the whole school. Groups or individuals are enthusiastically following their own development agendas without any coherent plan or focus. The underpinning assumptions and goals of all the different innovations are not agreed. Staff are fragmented and become exhausted with innovation.
- *The promenading school:* Here, change is felt to be unnecessary because the school has a history of impressive achievements which have, in the past, made the school a successful one in the eyes of staff, students and parents. Staff have often been at the school for a long time. Success is assumed to be something that is guaranteed if the school keeps working in the same way. Changes imposed from outside, such as by exam boards, are regarded with suspicion and some regret.
- *The moving school:* Here, there is a healthy blend of change and stability. There is an acceptance of change and a desire for continuous improvement. The direction of the school is discussed and planned by all the staff. The staff, in development terms, are clear about where they are and where

they are going, yet there is a calmness about the way they accept externally driven changes.

Understanding the school and department

What is the nature of the organisation that you work in and the department that you manage?

Activity 5.2 The context in which you work

Table 5.2 provides a checklist which will enable you to make an assessment of the kind of organisation that you work in. For each of the statements, circle 4 if you strongly agree with it, 3 if you agree, 2 if you disagree and 1 if you strongly disagree.

Consider which of the five descriptions, A, B, C, D or E, you agree most strongly with. Invent a name for this type of organisation. Some names that you might use are:

- bureaucratic
- collaborative
- individual
- ambiguous.

In your reflective journal, note your thoughts about how you might need to work in and adapt to such an organisation. In which sort of organisation would you prefer to work? What works and what does not work in your organisation? How does this make you feel? How could the problems you experience be solved?

Table 5.2 *Evaluation of the management context*

A

1. Issues are thought through and decisions made on the best evidence.	1	2	3	4
2. There are rules, policies and systems in place to get things done.	1	2	3	4
3. It is made clear to everyone what they have to do.	1	2	3	4
4. There are experts in different fields who are called upon to give specialist knowledge, when required.	1	2	3	4
5. There are effective channels of communication and decision making.	1	2	3	4

B

1. The issues are discussed and courses of action agreed.	1	2	3	4
2. Everyone can more or less get on with their own work, without interference.	1	2	3	4
3. People work together where their work crosses boundaries.	1	2	3	4
4. Managers coordinate and facilitate discussion.	1	2	3	4

C

1. People stick to their own work and areas of the school.	1	2	3	4
2. People have their own interests, projects or agendas.	1	2	3	4
3. Sometimes the interests of different groups clash.	1	2	3	4
4. Some people have a great deal of influence.	1	2	3	4
5. Things need to be bargained for.	1	2	3	4

D

1. People get on with their own work.	1	2	3	4
2. Each person has their own goal and aspirations.	1	2	3	4
3. You are able to do your own thing.	1	2	3	4
	1	2	3	4

E

1. There is no clarity about who makes the decisions and how.	1	2	3	4
2. It is not clear who is responsible for any area.	1	2	3	4
3. Tasks can be undertaken by many different people.	1	2	3	4

Conclusion

This chapter has outlined some of the theoretical models of management and school cultures. You have been invited to analyse the organisation in which you work and to think about the norms of behaviour and the expectations of others. From this starting point you are able to devise strategies for managing.

Chapter 6

International Perspectives

Contributions in this chapter are drawn from eight countries and they illustrate a variety of ways in which school systems operate, as well as differing expectations of the middle manager. While the tasks of middle managers may be seen to be similar around the world, for example managing a team, focusing on the quality of teaching and learning, and developing policies for the area of responsibility, the support given to the middle manager varies.

The extent of the training offered to middle managers in the Singaporean system may come as a surprise, as may the focus on teaching and learning espoused by the Queensland (Australia) Education Department. The experimentation described in Norway will strike a chord with readers in different countries – constant change is not a feature peculiar to the education systems of any one country.

A number of the contributions take up the concern that we are equipping pupils for a future which is likely to provide a more rapidly changing environment than has been experienced before.

These different perspectives on management in education are included to extend the ideas discussed in this section of the book about how you are moulded by the context in which you work. The one lesson to be drawn from all contributions is that change is endemic and that there are various solutions to any one problem.

Australia: Middle Management in the Queensland Education System

Laurie Wheldon, Queensland Department of Education

Overview

The purpose of this contribution is to raise issues of significance in middle management in Australian government schools and to identify trends or features of the Australian system, their implications for teachers and their implications for middle managers.

Brief context and description of Queensland schools (compulsory schooling)

Primary schools cater for ages 4 (pre-school) to 12 (year 7) and junior secondary schools for ages 13 to 15 (years 7 to 10) offer traditional academic education. The non-compulsory senior secondary schooling for ages 16 and 17 (years 11 and 12) offers general academic and vocational education. All public schools are administered and staffed as a whole at state level with regional offices providing local administrative support.

Assessment of students is criterion-based, conducted at individual school level. The public examination system was abolished in the early 1970s. State curriculum documents are provided to be interpreted according to local community, teacher and student needs. A system exists for moderating individual school results across the state to ensure comparability of standards. School-based subjects are also offered to students. These are not moderated externally. Junior and senior secondary schools have been largely organised in a traditional way with one teacher responsible for one group of students for each subject/key learning area. Over the past decade moves have been made to encourage teacher teaming and to minimise the number of teachers faced by students in any one year. Mixed ability grouping is the main principle for student organisation – a full non-streaming model is applied. From year 9 onwards student's own interests and abilities are the major criteria for organising classes.

Middle managers in junior and senior secondary schools usually take two forms – heads of department (HODs) and year level coordinators. HODs usually manage a content area across the five years of secondary schooling except in the case of very large schools with more than one HOD per content area. In this case roles are often shared as junior school and senior school HOD. During the 1980s there was an increasing awareness of the importance of how learning occurs and the effect of the teaching process on student motivation and teacher satisfaction. A number of teacher professional development programmes were introduced to encourage teachers to reflect on and share successful teaching practices regardless of the subject area being taught. This spawned a focus on identifying the learning and teaching principles under-pinning effective practice (see Appendix). In 1991 a restructuring of the Queensland Department of Education provided an opportunity to highlight the importance of these by establishing in its Studies Directorate a unit specif-ically dedicated to effective learning and teaching (Effective Learning and Teaching Unit) and separate from the traditional academic subjects (Key Learning Areas).

Initially these principles provided a language to describe classroom prac-tice, however it gradually became obvious that they apply to all learners and learning situations including teachers, middle managers, senior managers and parents. Hence a programme was introduced to assist managers to reflect on the effectiveness of their work groups using the same language.

Factors affecting Australian education at present

Previous articles have highlighted many of the factors which affect Aus-tralian education at present:

- an emphasis on collaborative action, power of the group (synergy) and responsibility/accountability of individual to group and group to indivi-dual;
- increased involvement of the range of partners in education;
- shared leadership and empowerment of individuals regardless of official role;
- site-based management;
- a movement away from traditional subject-based curriculum towards greater integration of content areas;
- a focus on common competencies which cross traditional content areas for example, problem solving, interpersonal skills, learning how to learn);
- student needs-driven curriculum rather than subject-driven curriculum.

However, one most important factor that has seeded educational change in this country has not yet been raised here: any school or classroom practice needs to be grounded in appropriate long-term future-oriented learning out-comes for our students.

While this may sound obvious (or trite), a focus by teachers and schools on learning outcomes that are relevant and meaningful for students is, in fact, often neglected. This is not necessarily a deliberate choice. It is most often caused by the constant immersion of teachers in the day-to-day business of the classroom with insufficient time and opportunity to reflect on the longer term view of the appropriateness of the direction being taken. Curriculum is often planned on past experiences as though driving a car looking in the rear-view mirror. What educators need to be taking as well is a futures approach – driving with the headlights on constantly searching in front of ourselves for the most appropriate route. We also need to take a much wider view which includes past, present and future – perhaps a helicopter ride to reflect on both where we have been and where we hope to go.

We are living in a period of unprecedented change. Today's students need to be well prepared to cope with rapid changes in technology and in society's structures. Students have to be flexible, able to handle increased information and prepared to move between occupations during their working life. They need to feel confident working alone as well as in teams, to recognise the importance of continuing to learn and empowered to take control of their own learning.

Schools have to reflect these changing needs or face the prospect of becoming irrelevant to the students' own experience. Crucial in tackling this challenge is the way teachers teach and learners learn, and the way schools are organised. If we need to encourage students to be self-directed, lifelong learners we must encourage and support our teachers to be lifelong learners as well. Teachers (and indeed all school personnel) need to model continuous learning, to take the initiative to find answers, to continue to grow, change and take a proactive stance in creating a positive future.

What are the implications for middle management in secondary schools?

We need to keep abreast of the big picture in education and globally – the helicopter ride:

- modelling ongoing learning;
- building a safe environment for teachers, underpinned by trust, mutual respect and integrity;
- valuing and using individual talents and differences, openness and sharing;
- working collaboratively and in teams;
- involving teachers in planning and discussion;
- sharing power with others;
- playing a change agency role, bringing about changes in the hearts and minds of staff by helping them understand the reason for school reform.

How are these being addressed in Australia (especially Queensland)?

The traditional role of the head of department comprised subject expertise, development and administration of work programmes and assessment requirements, and supervising a collection of individuals who teach that subject area.

Middle managers are encouraged to take a proactive strategic role in curriculum and assessment, to ensure that the curriculum is as up to date and relevant as possible. Being critically reflective, conducting action research and building partnerships among key groups in education are actively promoted. One vital partnership being explored is that between the traditional subject departments with a view to boundaries being broken down, looking for links and integration occurring to maximise time spent with students and minimise re-teaching and excess overlap.

Understanding the process of learning and teaching and making it explicit is a vital facet of the role of the middle manager in Queensland classrooms. Several programmes have been introduced since the early 1980s to assist teachers and middle managers. As a result of the earlier work the state government education authority has developed and is in the process of implementing a policy on effective learning and teaching. Middle managers encourage staff to use the principles as a language to discuss classroom practice.

From line management to team management

Line management was formerly the norm; teachers worked largely in isolation, and swapping ideas and resources was uncommon. With the change in emphasis from independence (the teacher as expert model) to interdependence (teachers are learners too), a major cultural adjustment has been asked of teachers regardless of depth of experience. Middle managers need to find ways to operate that provide opportunities for teachers to work interdependently, to establish a culture that allows and values initiative, that accepts individuality and difference in the context of responsibility to the team.

Planning and teaching in teams is actively encouraged. Timetables are increasingly being organised to maximise this. Schools are gradually moving to days structured with fewer, longer lessons. In an increasing number of places, teams of teachers work with one cohort of students to maximise the positive effect of the deeper relationship that results. Such teams share responsibility for the development of the curriculum and assessment used for that cohort.

Actual leadership is shared across all team members. Middle managers act as facilitators of this process, monitoring and supporting the group as required.

In some Australian schools the middle management role is shared and is not attached to one person for life. For example, in Alice Springs (Northern Territory) one high school has abolished the official role completely and the leadership is shared across teaching teams. In one Queensland non-government school, a greater than normal number of floating middle management roles has been created so that the responsibility can be shared across a greater number of teachers. Teachers move in and out of the role as appropriate.

From administrivia to professional development

One increasing role of the middle manager lies in professional development of staff. Many opportunities exist for a culture of ongoing learning and shared leadership to be established. In Australian schools, they include:

- using team meetings as professional sharing times (eg discussing a partic-ular journal article; problem-solving together; brainstorming a range of strategies);
- running seminars (regular meeting times, after school or away from school) for staff on particular issues identified by the group;
- providing time for critical reflection individually and in groups;
- using peer coaching (by staff) as a means to highlight the expertise of exist-ing staff to others.

Departments in Secondary Schools in The Netherlands

Bert P M Creemers, Groningen Institute for Educational Research

In some countries such as the USA, secondary schools have been organised in departments since the 1930s. In The Netherlands, departments did not become essential components of the organisation of secondary schools until the 1960s. Their increasing importance was partly caused by the increase of scale of individual schools and by processes of educational innovation in which departments played an important role (Witziers and van Vilsteren, 1990). Nevertheless, until recently educational research paid little or no atten-tion to departments and the role of the middle management. Maybe this lack of attention was caused by the idea that schools are organisations where indi-vidual teachers and principals as educational leaders play the most impor-tant role. Moreover, most educational research studies in The Netherlands concentrated on the primary school level, where departments hardly exist. Since 1990 the attention for research and theory-oriented studies in the field of departments has grown, especially concerning the relationship of depart-ments and educational effectiveness.

Departments within the school organisation

Within any organisation, coordination is an important activity that regards the processes in the organisation as well as the relationship between the different activities and the aims and goals of the organisation. Departments can play an important role in the coordination of activities for a specific school subject. Generally speaking, the decisions that have to be taken with respect to subject areas are delegated to departments. The primary task of departments is to take care of and to be responsible for education in a specific subject content. In this respect departments contribute to the quality of education, by coordinating teaching and instruction with respect to their subject area. Furthermore, departments can contribute to the quality of education, for example by the development of a policy for in-service training, the guidance of new teachers, the division of tasks, the allocation of classes to teachers and so on (Witziers, 1993).

The main task of departments is to contribute to educational quality. Departments can develop a specific curriculum or activity plan for their subject area. They can achieve agreement, for example, about the way in which the curriculum should be offered to the students, the textbooks that should be used, the way specific chapters should be taught and so on. By doing so, they plan and evaluate the instruction provided by the individual teachers at the classroom level. Moreover, departments can also contribute to the quality of education at the school level by providing support and by contributing to a school policy. As such, departments are seen as staff organisations which contribute to a school policy based on their own expertise and experiences. As a staff organisation they can give their opinion and they can advise with respect to exam policies, grade repetition and school climate and discipline.

The place or position of departments in school organisations can be different. In a study about departments (Marx, 1975), three kinds of organisations are discerned: the segmented organisation, the line-staff organisation and the collegial organisation. In the segmented school organisation there is hardly any coordination. Neither educational leadership nor policy making and cooperation between teachers can be found. Teachers are totally isolated. They act as autonomous individuals who make decisions about teaching and instruction without collaboration and deliberation with their colleagues. Even when there are departments in this kind of school organisation, they are only departments by name. When meetings are organised, teachers do not discuss the educational policy of their department.

In the segmented school organisation the position and the influence of the heads and deputy heads is minimal too. That is the difference between the segmented organisation and the line-staff organisation. In the latter organisation, the influence of the directorate of the school is important. The school directorate influences what happens at the classroom level but also at the departmental level. In fact, the principal likes to impose school policy on the department and the individual teachers. The position of departments is somewhat stronger, but the department is mainly an instrument to influence individual teachers. The teachers have direct relationships with their principal and for the major part they are still autonomous in their decisions about how and what to teach (within the boundaries set by the principal or the deputy principal). In the collegial organisation, the principal is more process oriented, creating the conditions for teacher cooperation at the departmental level. Departments are strong units which formulate their own educational policies and contribute to school policies and to activities of individual teachers in classrooms.

These three models make it possible to analyse the school organisation and the functioning of departments and individual teachers within the school organisation. However, the models are highly theoretical. They may merely be ideals which exist to some extent in educational practice. In the 1990s, several research projects addressed the departments and their contributions to educational quality (Hylkema, 1990; Witziers, 1992, 1993, 1996; Friebel, 1994). A very important objective of departments is the development of an educational policy for their specific subject areas, a policy on what and how to teach. Dutch departments in secondary schools discuss the goals of education in their subject area, the use of the method, the content of education and especially the way testing and evaluation take place, for example the use of common tests (usually six per school year).

Both Hylkema and Witziers conclude that teachers have some freedom, especially in pedagogical and instructional matters, but this freedom is rather relative. Their second conclusion is that the ability to develop and maintain a policy is reasonably developed within departments, with an exception for the evaluation of education. Evaluation requires a combination of reflection on educational practice and scientific knowledge with respect to education, but also a willingness of teachers to discuss their own functioning and teaching as well, as the functioning and teaching of their colleagues. Hylkema mentions that departmental deliberation depends on the size of the department and usually is only formal. Teachers do not often talk about didactical matters. They mainly discuss the textbooks, the choice of a new textbook and subjects that are addressed in lessons (Hylkema, 1990). Witziers (1992) draws somewhat more positive conclusions based on his data. Teachers in his study find it easy to discuss all kinds of matters with respect to education, but they are less positive about mutual control and evaluation. Still, they also mention that when colleagues do not stick to the rules and the agreements of the department, they can be asked for an explanation.

Recently Witziers (1996) reanalysed the data of his study, which pertain to 376 teachers and 103 departments dispersed over 97 schools. A cluster analysis yielded three clusters. Departments in the first cluster show only a small amount of educational deliberation and educational policy. Teachers can make their own decisions about instruction. Coordination by the principal is weak. The second cluster shows the opposite characteristics and the third cluster takes an intermediate position. In this third cluster, coordination by the management is quite weak but there are a lot of deliberations within departments and the department has a strong influence on decisions about education. These cluster analyses confirm more or less the theoretical models mentioned before (Marx, 1975). In the segmented organisation, there is a weak influence of educational leadership on departments. The line-staff organisation shows more influence of the departments and a strong leadership by the principal and the deputy head. The collegial organisation shows a strong position of the departments (Witziers, 1996).

In a study about curriculum planning and educational effectiveness, Friebel (1994) found that formal deliberation about education and instruction takes place at the department level, more in departments for Dutch language than in departments for mathematics. He found evidence for the conclusion by Hylkema that deliberation in departments occurs more frequent in relatively small schools. Large schools are more formal about organisational matters, while smaller schools are more formal about the contents of education.

The position and role of the head of department

From an organisational point of view, the heads of departments are the leaders of the departments. Most of the time, however, they do not have formal power to direct the processes in their departments, nor the education and instruction given by the teachers who are members of their departments. Heads of departments have a dual role. They are in charge of leadership but they are also colleagues of the department members. This situation can easily cause loyalty conflicts. On top of that, heads of departments are rarely selected on the basis of their competencies, their leadership capacities and their subject matter knowledge. They are mainly selected on the basis of their teaching experience. In general, the way the tasks are carried out depends on their own ideas and opinions. In most schools, the school management does not give any direction at all in this respect (Hylkema, 1990).

Smets (1986) found that heads of departments can fulfill their roles in different ways. They can act as messenger boys, representatives or team leaders. As a messenger boy, the head of the department distributes information, organises common tests and so on. As a representative, he takes care of the position of the department in the relationship with the management of the school. As a team leader, he is responsible for the educational functioning of the organisation and he plays an important role in motivating the teachers. Hylkema and Witziers found that heads of departments do not often act as team leaders. The influence of the heads on education and instruction as it is executed by the department members is minimal. Moreover, the head of the department is not the person teachers will easily address to discuss problems they experience in education. Witziers's research, however, shows that the head of the department can have an important influence on the climate of cooperation in the department. By activities like motivating colleagues for deliberation and by making an agenda for meetings, the head of the department can stimulate cooperation between teachers.

Departments and educational effectiveness

The concept of educational effectiveness overarches school effectiveness and instructional effectiveness. Research has shown that educational effectiveness, defined as added value in the learning results of students, is predominantly explained by factors at the classroom level. The classroom is the place where students are supposed to learn in order to achieve their objectives. Instruction provided by teachers using textbooks, grouping procedures and other kinds of materials is directed to initiate, maintain, facilitate and structure the learning processes of students. Other levels in the school system like departments and the school management can provide conditions for teaching and learning at the classroom level. In this respect, departments can contribute to the quality of education and the effectiveness of education at the classroom level (Creemers, 1994). Departments can especially contribute to the stability, consistency, coherence, constancy and control of educational effectiveness. This can be achieved by maintaining effectiveness of one grade level to another grade level and between teachers of the same department, and by formulating arrangements and agreements between department members with regard to educational matters in their subject area.

This theoretical notion about the contribution of departments to the effectiveness of education is empirically supported by Witziers's research. Departments can play an important role by formulating an explicit educational policy, by means of clear explicit formulations of the goals of education, the priorities within the goals, the relationships between the different grade levels and by formulating an evaluation policy with respect to student results. According to Witziers this means that cooperation, deliberation and democratic decision making are not sufficient for educational effectiveness. They can be important but there has to be a relation between these characteristics of the functioning of departments and the curriculum, the organisation and the instruction. Witziers's position is supported by the study of Friebel, mentioned earlier. He found that effective schools differ from ineffective schools with respect to the planning of education in several aspects:

- the attention for the planning of education;
- the attention for contents and the tasks that have to be fulfilled by students;
- high expectations of the head of the department;
- shared decisions, shared mission about the responsibility of the school for training and instruction in cognitive abilities;
- motivation by the head of the department of the members of the department.

Based on the further development of more autonomous schools Friebel expects that the need for strengthening educational management will increase and become manifest in stimulating more frequent curricular consultations at the level of the department, and between the school management and the department.

Conclusions

In Dutch educational research, the department was a neglected area for a long time. Departments are now more the centre of attention for several reasons, such as the organisational development of schools (especially the development of large school communities with different levels of secondary education) and the attention for educational effectiveness. Departments can play an important role by providing and creating the conditions for effectiveness which is ultimately achieved at the classroom level. In particular, departments can provide conditions for effective teaching and learning. In this respect, departments can contribute – even more than the school level – to educational effectiveness of their specific subject areas, the contents, the methods and the instruction. In that way they can contribute to coherence, consistency, constancy and control, and thus increase the stability of effectiveness. Although Dutch research so far does not provide strong evidence for the importance of the role of the heads of departments, theoretically speaking this role is very important in motivating teachers and stimulating cooperation between teachers and participation of the department members. In this respect more attention should be given to the role of heads of departments in the professional organisation. Maybe more than principals they are able to act as educational leaders among equals. That enforces their position and their tasks in educational matters in specific subject areas.

Middle Management – An Opportunity for School Improvement? A Norwegian Perspective

Trond Eiliv Hauge, University of Oslo, Norway

Middle management plays a crucial role in improving schools, but seems to be a neglected area of concern in the national policy guidelines for school development and leadership training in Norway. In this section the Norwegian situation will be illuminated through an analytical approach to the understanding of middle management in Norwegian secondary schools. The topic is discussed by referring to actual management models, experiences and evaluations in the field and national school leadership philosophy. Middle management functions in different ways in different schools, fulfils different purposes and puts a different pressure on the school organisation concerning improvement. Organisational features, leadership roles nurtured by central and local policy makers, as well as the expectations and traditions of teaching and learning in school, which are held by the teachers, are forces behind this difference. Middle management also imposes a set of dilemmas running a school, which sometimes are counterproductive and other times 'facilitating' to school improvement. These problems will be addressed below.

The context of middle management in secondary schools

Roughly described, secondary education in Norway is divided into two types of schools. The first are lower secondary schools for students aged 13–15 years. These students belong to the nine year comprehensive school, called the basic school (will be ten from 1997). Primary education is organised for students aged 7(6)–12 years. This basic school is administrated by local authorities at the municipality level. Upper secondary schools for students aged 16–18 years are separate from the basic school and offer vocational and academic education. These are administered by authorities at county level.

Lower secondary education is compulsory for all children while upper secondary education is optional. The total number of subjects offered in lower secondary is about 15, while upper secondary offers a total number of 350. The subject teacher holds a strong position in upper secondary schools and the students are to a great extent organised according to their individual subject choices, especially in the second and third year. In lower secondary schools students are put in classes in which they stay for three years, except for a small portion of time allocated to optional subjects. Teachers are assigned to classes according their subject qualifications, but the classes are usually organised through modules. All basic schools, both at primary and lower secondary level, are obliged to practise mixed ability grouping as the main principle for student organisation and teaching. It is a full non streaming model. At upper secondary level, from year 2 and onwards the students' own interests and abilities are the major criteria in organising classes and groups of teaching.

Concerning the opportunities for middle management, the organisational structure in upper secondary schools provide a more complex situation regarding teacher collaboration, compared to lower secondary schools. The main differences may be described in this way: in upper secondary schools students have to go to their subject teacher, while teachers in lower secondary are assigned to students in their classes. As a consequence upper secondary teachers in general meet a larger number of students in different classes and at different grade levels. This organisation and the heavy subject tradition forces teachers in upper secondary schools into a subject-oriented collaboration model crossing classes and grade levels, often named as the department model. Planned collaboration outside this model, eg between teachers teaching in the same class, seems more difficult to implement because of the complex time schedule. Heads of departments may be looked upon as the middle managers in upper secondary schools.

Lower secondary schools are normally populated by fewer students than in upper secondary schools. Teachers are also expected to take on teaching on a broader subject scale than colleagues in upper secondary. These provide important conditions for widespread class team or grade level models for teacher collaboration in lower secondary schools. Team leaders may function as middle managers in these schools.

The culture of school leadership

The concept of middle management varies according to organisation factors, leadership approaches and the tasks involved. The question we may ask heads of departments and team leaders in Norwegian secondary schools is whether or not they are functioning as middle managers and to what extent they look upon themselves as leaders in their school organisation. As an overall assessment it is fair to say that a variety of middle management functions are taken care of in many schools, but it is also true that the consciousness regarding middle management as part of school leadership understanding as a whole varies widely among teachers and principals. This ambiguity may be looked upon from at least two different perspectives.

The middle management concept at local school level is not and has never been a visible part in the national guidelines for practising school leadership in Norwegian schools. Leadership is first of all brought forward and implemented by the principal. This is clearly stated in White Papers on school governing (St. meld. 37 (1990–91)), and confirmed in the guidelines of a recent national training programme for principals (KUF, 1996). Looking back at leadership policies in the 1970s and 1980s we can see that there is now more pressure on the principal in the 1990s to be accountable for both managerial, staff related and educational tasks in school. The expectations of the principal being a visible leader in the school community and being responsible for implementing national and local education policies at local school level has increased. Extensive national curriculum reforms from 1994 and onwards (St. meld. 29 (1994–95)) and the proposal for the new joint education act for primary and secondary education 1997 (NOU, 1995:18) are strengthening this school leadership profile. We may add that the concept of middle management is a neglected topic in the above mentioned reforms and programmes.

Most primary and secondary schools, above a minimum size of students, have one or two vice principals or assistant managers. They are responsible

for specific sub-domains in the organisation, eg time scheduling, special education, substitute teachers or student welfare in school. Advisory teachers
may also be part of leadership teams in school. Usually these assistant leaders are not looked upon as middle managers in school. They belong to the top
administration of the school, and play their roles according to tasks defined
in the bureaucratic school model. However, in primary and lower secondary
schools this traditional leadership model has been questioned and challenged during the 1970s and 1980s, as a consequence of a strong movement
towards democratization of decision making processes in school and the
development of teacher professionalism. As curriculum reforms in the middle of the 1980s strongly recommended the use of teacher cooperation and
school development planning as tools in the implementation process (Mønsterplanen, 1987), principals and local school authorities have been searching
for alternative models governing their schools. Organic and horizontal leadership models have been developed in many schools, in which the concept of
middle management is an integrated one. However, with this background it
is an anachronism that the education reforms in the 1990s, intentional or not,
put such a strong weight on rational and vertical leadership models.

Our analysis so far points to the fact that the culture of leadership in Norwegian schools is moving tensionally between a vertical and horizontal leadership model. It is fair to say that middle management as a tool for school
improvement first of all has evolved in primary and lower secondary
schools.

Organising middle management in secondary schools

Middle management may operate under quite different organisational conditions and is modelled in different ways. A main question for us here is
whether or not the model functions as an ordinary management tool or a
vehicle for school improvement. The answer is more or less depending on the
principal's vision for her or his school, organisational traditions, decision
making structures, collaborative cultures in school and the teachers' preparedness and willingness to participate in school management and development work. I believe, that middle management at its best fits leadership
styles and schools grounded on an organic organisation philosophy (cf.
Burns and Stalker, 1966). Criteria I use for this assessment are whether or not
middle managers function as communicating links between the principal,
the school board and the teachers, as support agents for the teachers in their
daily work and as stimulating forces to the improvement of teaching and
classroom practice.

According to a Norwegian group of empirical studies in primary and
lower secondary schools (Hauge, 1982, 1990, 1991; Hauge and Engeland,
1994; Hauge *et al.*, 1995), the differences between schools regarding middle

management functioning may be described as a difference between management and control of the teachers on the one side and development and support to the teachers on the other side. The different middle management features observed also mirror different school cultures. The conclusion that may be drawn in a reanalysis of these studies is that middle management means different things in an organic and a mechanistic/hierarchical school culture.

What are the middle management models used in lower and upper secondary schools? Three teacher team models may be described as the main basis for the solutions in lower secondary schools:

- *A grade level team model:* Teachers working with the same students at same grade level are organised in one team. One of the teachers is appointed as a team leader. The size of the team depends on the number of parallel classes and which subject teachers' groups are included. This model makes a total of three team leaders, each for each grade level.
- *A class organised team model:* Teachers are allocated a maximum number of teaching hours grouped in one or two classes at the same grade level in order to reduce the number of teachers for those classes. In some subjects teachers may function as assistant teachers. The number of team leaders may vary according to the number of classes at each grade level.
- *A block organised team model:* The school is organised in vertical blocks of students, ie students in 7th, 8th and 9th grade are grouped together in blocks. Teachers are allocated with a maximum number of teaching hours in one block. The number of blocks, usually three to four, defines the number of team leaders.

Middle management at school level arises when team leaders are organised in a leadership group along with the principal and other assistant managers in school.

In upper secondary schools none of these three team models is used. As already stated the department model is a dominating one. However, the department label is not a uniform concept. It covers different collaborative solutions, for example:

- Teachers who belong to a block of subjects, a subject domain or an educational course group are organised in one department. This unit operates as a sub-organisation in the school governed by an assistant principal or a head leader. Organised teacher cooperation inside the department takes on different solutions depending on culture and traditions in the block or school.
- Subject teachers in the school are organised in different departments. Teachers teaching the same subject in different classes at different grade levels are included in this unit. The model may be classified as a vertical collaborative model. Each subject department is assigned a head leader.

The upper secondary education reform of 1994 seems so far to be a force for change in enhancing cooperative behaviour between upper secondary teachers, especially at the first grade level, due to the reorganisation of the basic courses, the reducing of the subjects offered the students and the introduction of obligatory project work for all students. Teacher team solutions, as described for lower secondary schools, do appear, but, the consequences for middle management traditions are unforeseen at the moment.

The question of school improvement

Elaborate leadership models, middle management and well-organised teacher collaboration cannot guarantee school improvement. Recent literature on school effectiveness and development tells a rather complicated story. There is no straightforward link between principalship, middle management, teacher collaboration and improvement in teaching and learning in school. School effectiveness studies have over time emphasised the importance of the principal's leadership of the school as a key factor to effectiveness (Reynolds *et al.*, 1994; Teddlie and Stringfield, 1993; Mortimore, 1993). The studies do not address, however, either the effects of middle management or different teacher collaboration models.

Hallinger and Hausman (1994) describe the ambiguity of the principal's role in restructured schools, and emphasise the tensions arising when restructuring initiatives change decision making structures and processes in school. Middle management provides a pressure for shared decision making, which in turn highlights the micro-political processes in school. Murphy and Louis (1994) describe this changing leadership position through the idea of 'leading from the centre', which means to lead from changing positions in the organisation, based on shared decision making with various groups of teachers and other stake holders. The importance of this shared leadership style is also confirmed in an intensive follow-up study of improvement processes in secondary schools done by Louis and Miles (1990). They conclude that principals must give up some of their singular 'authority' within the school if they wish to have real influence over the innovation process. Principals need to promote genuine leadership roles by others in school (ibid.). The question of what school improvement is all about arises when analysing these studies. If the improvement of teaching and learning is the central issue, then it still remains to see what are the effects of restructured leadership.

Hargreaves (1994a) makes a distinction between contrived collegiality and collaborative cultures in school, the former indicating among other things that teachers' collaborative working relationships are administratively regulated, fixed in time and space, implementation oriented and compulsory. The latter tend to be voluntary, spontaneous, development oriented and pervasive across time and space (ibid.). The important implications derived from

Hargreaves's studies are that teacher collaboration means different things under different contextual and cultural conditions, besides the phenomenon that contrived collegiality may be counteractive to school improvement by overruling teachers' professional autonomy. This warning against an excessive pressure towards collaboration seems not to be an argument for any structuring of teacher collaboration at all. According to studies of Stoll and Fink (1996), Hargreaves (1995) and Lieberman (1994) the need for a collaborative structure in school is well documented as a prerequisite for professional discourse and school improvement. In building a professional community, there must be opportunities and time for disciplined enquiry. However, the question of what role the middle managers have to play in this context remains unanswered in the research literature, apart from evidence stating that the maintenance of a professional community depends on empowered teachers being in charge of leadership functions, formal as well as informal (Lieberman, 1994; Goldring and Rallis, 1993).

Reading studies of school effectiveness and school improvement focusing on the impacts of school culture is sometimes bewildering, because of the diversified use of the school culture concept. However, the evidence is strong for saying that school cultures have a significant impact on dimensions of teaching and learning. Concerning middle management, the question is how this structure interacts and influences school culture and improvement efforts. To answer this question there is a need to make a distinction between different types of cultures that reflect features of the specific school organisation. The typology of the mechanistic and the organic school organisation (cf. Burns and Stalker, 1966) may be a useful one when vertical and horizontal leadership structures are analysed. A study of Norwegian lower secondary schools shows that team leaders and middle managers play quite different roles in school development work in mechanistic and organic oriented school cultures (Hauge, 1982). This assessment may also be turned the other way by saying that these cultures are conditioning different preparedness by leaders and teachers to utilise innovative efforts in improving their school, according to another Norwegian study of eight primary and lower secondary schools located in four different school districts (Hauge and Engeland, 1994; Hauge 1995). D H Hargreaves (1995), in his typological description of different school cultures, also points to this phenomenon, when analysing the mechanistic–hierarchical development structure in school. Putting these experiences into the discussion of different collaborative cultures' impact on school improvement, the question of middle managers' innovative roles becomes a complicated one.

Middle management experiences

Experiences with the use of middle managers in primary and lower secondary schools in a municipality south of Oslo (Hauge, 1990) may illuminate the dilemmas described above. Seven schools participated in a restructuring programme in 1989–90. The schools made use of a grade level teacher team model as a basis for middle management. Three primary schools let each of their middle managers manage two grade levels. The middle managers were all members of the school's planning committee, together with the principal and vice principal. The goals of the programme were threefold.

The middle management structure should contribute to:

- a decentralisation of leadership functions. Decision making should be moved down to those who are in charge of implementation;
- a shared decision making with the teachers concerning school development planning;
- a better utilising of teachers' knowledge and school resources in an attempt to improve the learning environment and the teaching in school.

The implementation of the programme produced three main lessons, which are based on an analysis of programme documents, principal interviews and teacher questionnaires.

Shared decision making

The teachers were in general positive about the middle management structure in the decision making system of the school. They felt it was easier to be heard concerning their daily needs and the information flow was better. In some of the schools teachers criticised the system because of a feeling of over-administration and bureaucratisation of their work.

School development and curriculum work

The schools reported positive effects on educational discourses among the staff. Middle management gave support to joint curriculum work in the schools, but the discourses about school development planning first of all concerned issues for the school as a whole and less the planning and teaching at classroom level. Too often educational questions got a low priority in team discussions because of the need to handle ordinary management questions. However, the middle managers were seen to make positive contributions to the educational discussions in the teacher teams.

Collaboration and leadership

The middle management system seemed to have a positive effect on staff cooperation in general and planned collaborative behaviour in school. However, tensions arose due to redefined leadership roles between teachers and the ordinary management group in school. The defining of responsibility concerning management work, educational tasks and staff relations caused discussion and some insecurity in the schools. The question arose as to who really benefited from the restructuring. Some of the teachers felt that the middle managers too often became the principal's assistants instead of being support agents for the teachers. Principals were in general positive about the structure and the widened opportunity to discuss management and development work with their teachers.

Experiences in this district based programme push to the surface the tensions and dilemmas of shared leadership and micro-policy in schools. It should be noted that the local school authorities did not develop an extensive middle management structure after the programme period. The schools went back to the traditional management structure, but chose to continue, more or less, with team representations on the school planning committee. There are many explanations for this backtracking. Referring to the changing school leadership philosophy in Norway in the 1990s, principals in charge and principals who are accountable for school outcomes seems to be preferred. Shared leadership is blurring this idea. The evolving trend towards the self-managing school also put a pressure on a leadership model built on a distinct authority structure. Part of this problem is the conflict between a traditional political and bureaucratic control of schools, and a trust in the collegial and professional school community (Murphy and Louis, 1994; Hargreaves, 1994b).

Lessons from development programmes

Principals, team leaders and teachers need time to reflect on their practice, to share experiences and plan cooperatively. Improvement does not just happen but is a product of a professional discourse and leadership in school. The struggle between regulated technical managerial work and open-ended professional discourse is at the heart of the school improvement problems. Norwegian principals are struggling daily to get these tasks balanced (Møller, 1995; Anker and Hauge, 1993). How do we get around or break through this dilemma? How is it possible to nurture a shared culture of leadership in school, in which teacher leadership is a natural part of the school development processes?

Some experiences and findings pulled out of the leadership training and school based evaluations programmes, in which the Department of Teacher Education and School Development has been a partner in recent years, may give an opportunity to reflect on these leadership problems. The programmes have been running since 1992 in close cooperation with regional and local education authorities. One of the programmes comprised all upper secondary schools in Oslo – about 30 schools. Four other programmes were run for groups of 10 to 15 basic schools separately in different municipalities. One programme involved eight basic schools in four different municipalities collaborating on a pilot project for dissemination of school-based evaluation knowledge. All programmes were organised for a period of about two years. They were action oriented, ie each school had to define a development project, make an appropriate project organisation and allocate resources for implementing their local governed project work. These local processes were brought together through joint courses, in which theory and the sharing of experiences and planning were highlighted. The schools' organising committee which attended these courses was in charge of the local development work. With the exception of the Oslo programme, the school's representatives were composed of the principal and teachers who held leading positions in their school, either as team leaders and/or as members of the school planning committee. In the upper secondary programme in Oslo the representations were made up of vice principals and ordinary teachers who were interested in this area. Part of the programme experiences are described in Hauge and Engeland (1994), Hauge *et al.*, (1995) and in project reports produced by local authorities.

Some of the main lessons concerning leadership and improvement in school, drawn out through a reanalysis of programme experiences, are described in the following paragraphs. Evaluations of the above mentioned pilot project on middle management (Hauge, 1990) are also utilised in the reanalysis. Since the programmes described all have been trying to improve the professional discourse in the schools, the concept of the organic organisation is laid down as a main principle behind the recommendations.

1. The process of restructuring decision making in school

Shared leadership implies a restructuring of the traditional bureaucratic decision making structure in school. A school planning committee comprised of teacher team leaders may be a process helper in redefining decision making structures and building confidence between team leaders and principal.

2. Qualifying for teacher leadership

Shared leadership presupposes qualifying leadership arenas for the teachers. Teachers must be given the opportunities to share leadership both at class or grade level and at school level. Experiential learning through teacher team collaboration is a valuable way of nurturing leadership competences. Qualifying for teacher leadership has to build on tasks important for teachers' instructional work in classrooms. An important aspect of shared leadership in school is to give priority to teaching and learning in the whole school planning processes.

3. Middle managers and legitimacy

Being in a position of middle management presupposes trust and confidence among teachers, but also legitimacy given by the organisation and the principal. In inviting teachers into middle management positions they must be given real responsibilities, which in turn have to be clarified with the teachers, the principal, the school board or other stake holders in school. Middle managers need a double legitimacy; one which is grown out of the professional teacher culture and the other linked to the professional management culture of the school.

4. Middle management and school improvement

Middle management is no recipe for school improvement itself. In enhancing the professional community teachers do not need any further authorities or control functions governing their work. These functions are usually well taken care of inside traditional structures. However, by using middle management as a complementary or additional leadership competence in the organisation the improvement processes may be facilitated. Middle managers may play a crucial role in making school planning and evaluation processes meaningful for teachers. In changing school based curriculum work from a technical piece of work to a professional activity in school these managers also are taking care of important functions. Middle managers may contribute in giving status to and being facilitative to teacher collaboration based on collegial values.

5. School improvement and 'leading from the centre'

School based development planning and evaluation as continuous processes are contradictory to the lonesome 'leader from the top'. These functions are at the heart of school improvement work, but need to be nourished by the principal through appropriate management and shared decision making. 'Leading from the centre' seems to be a necessary condition for improvement in the main activity domain in school; teaching and learning in the classrooms.

6. Organisational features of secondary schools

The complex structure of secondary schools in Norway, especially upper secondary schools, has to be taken seriously when moving them into reform and improvement processes. The lessons from development programmes for primary and lower secondary schools concerning middle management tell that the system is functioning at its best when teacher teams and middle managers are organised in clearly set out units of work. The structure in upper secondary schools makes it more difficult to organise such working units, but the problem may be addressed by semi-structural solutions inside the departments.

Final comments

Our review of middle management in Norwegian secondary schools reveals no secrets. It rather confirms the experiences found internationally. We may conclude that middle management provides a constructive way of changing the leadership structure in school in trying to enhance improvement processes. However, middle management may do more harm than good when being introduced in strong bureaucratic cultures or as part of a contrived teacher collaborative structure. Teachers may look upon the system only as another managerial control mechanism to their work. Middle management will be at its best when the school culture is open for shared decision making, and the leadership in the professional community is at the focus of change. Concerning the national policy on school leadership dominating at the moment, the idea of middle management, based on shared collegial leadership, is moving in the opposite direction.

Singapore – Heads of Department and School Improvement

Low Guat Tin and Lim Lee Hean, National Institute of Education, Nanyang Technological University

In the Singapore education system, middle managers or heads of department (HODs) are recognised as a significant source in ensuring that quality education reaches out to the pupils. The National Institute of Education (NIE), offers a one-year full-time departmental headship training course. All heads of department in Singapore's primary and secondary schools attend the one-year programme on full pay leave of absence from their schools. Upon graduation, participants are awarded the Further Professional Diploma in Education. This section focuses on the key aspects of the headship as well as ancillary features which are pertinent to the Singapore context. It highlights salient features that pertain directly to the HODs' role of improving quality education for pupils.

One of the numerous tasks of the HOD in Singapore is to finalise the departmental annual self-appraisal, and proceed with charting departmental direction and building ownership of the overall plan for the following year. HODs, together with teachers in their department, plan a comprehensive teaching programme. The schemes of work for each subject, ie what is to be taught in each term of each academic level are worked out for each of the four school terms. These schemes of work are subjected to modification, depending on the needs of pupils, but they have to be in line with the core syllabus which prepares pupils for the Cambridge General Certificate of Education.

Throughout the year, the HODs play an important role in ensuring at least the basics of teaching are delivered and learning takes place. This entails effective programme monitoring, programme evaluation and staff supervision. Besides informal observation, formal classroom observations and checking of assignments to ascertain staff performance and pupils' needs are the norm in Singapore. Beyond administrative requirements, the constructive feedback given to staff after each lesson observation also serves to develop them professionally. Specific areas of weakness and areas of strengths are identified. Ways to improve their areas of weakness are then discussed and teachers are often monitored throughout the year, either formally through classroom observation or informally through discussion in the staffroom. Principals often hold HODs accountable for the performance of the teachers in their department. Thus HODs ensure that teachers in their departments prepare their lessons and assess students' performance regularly. Implementation of quality checks of this nature has great impact on the actual classroom conduct and consolidation of pupil learning. However, we would like to add that classroom supervision by HODs is still a sensitive issue with some teachers, albeit a minority, and requires tact in implementation, as the probable resultant permeation of distrust can affect support and generate negative groundswell.

In Singapore, the HODs are officially required to teach two-thirds of a teacher's normal workload. In this way they are in a better position to empathise with colleagues with regard to pedagogical issues. Inevitably, teachers also look up to them as role models in teaching, hence HODs are aware that they have to develop and adapt effective teaching strategies in their subject area. Often the exemplary conduct set by the HODs in classroom delivery and management helps to promote learning in school. It is necessary that HODs are aware of their role as instructional leaders. Their credibility in counselling, coaching and motivating staff to engage in effective management of pupil learning only holds good when their teachers see that they are successful in the classroom.

The HODs in Singapore are required to attend zonal (the island is divided into five zones) or national subject meetings, where specialist inspectors of the subject area keep them abreast of national education policies, current trends and issues, and specific curriculum requirements. Sharing sessions and presentations by selected HODs are invariably incorporated into such official meetings. After such meetings HODs are expected to disseminate the necessary information and share the professional input with their staff back in school. The onus is also on the HODs to ensure implementation of the curriculum in their respective schools. The core concern in schools today is the interest and motivation of the pupils, that they be given the opportunities to maximise their potential in the process of acquiring the necessary knowledge, skills and attitude in subject learning.

Effective implementation of the departmental programme recognises the appropriate utilisation of human and physical resources and coordination of activities. HODs in Singapore are constantly reminded not to overwhelm staff with tedious meetings, unnecessary paperwork, task abdication or inefficient material production, for these tasks sap energy and drain motivation. A concerned HOD is mindful that the limited staff time and energy must be channelled towards meaningful pupil-centred work. This encompasses staff doing the right things like preparing lessons, effective delivery, identifying pupils' entry behaviour and needs, providing adequate and appropriate pupil homework, proper marking of pupils' assignments to ensure basic consolidation and feedback, tracking and evaluation of pupils' progress, transmitting expectations of quality work, conducting supplementary lessons for pupils with special needs, proper utilising of available teaching aids to facilitate pupil learning, guiding and reviewing pupils' projects for enrichment purposes, establishing teacher–pupil rapport within and beyond curriculum time to enhance learning, as well as staff training and development via courses, workshops and seminars. In-house professional sharing of a repertoire of teaching strategies and resources that prove to be effective in the school can have an immense impact. The emphasis is on pupils learning to learn and teachers creating the necessary conditions to enhance the learning. The HODs' role is to facilitate classroom learning and to ensure that teachers have the resources to carry out their work. Under the mentorship of capable HODs who demonstrate and inspire dedication to the profession, teachers can accomplish much as reflective practitioners and the pupils benefit as a whole.

Usually regarded as subject experts, the HODs act as feedforward, concurrent and feedback advisers to the principal on all matters in their domain. This covers a broad spectrum, ranging from departmental vision in conjunction with school mission, staff deployment and appraisal, to the nitty-gritty aspects like allocation of subject resources and teacher–pupil ratio in specific settings like computer laboratories.

In building quality school education, HODs in Singapore are called upon to conceptualise beyond the myopic departmental level towards a helicopter view of school concerns. Acute awareness and accurate assessment of the political and situational constraints of the school enhance the setting of realistic targets after identifying, analysing and prioritising needs. However, attributing school deficiency or improvement solely to the influence of the HODs would be a distortion of reality. In Singapore, the facts of practice lead inexorably to one conclusion: the synergy of a school team in nurturing a learning climate propels a school to greater heights. Within their span of control, the middle managerial level of HODs serves as a vital motivating link that fosters quality practice at grassroots level.

Middle Management and Quality Development: A Swedish Perspective

Mikael Alexandersson and Rolf Lander, University of Gothenburg, Sweden

Middle management in Sweden was introduced by the state in 1980–1, together with the working unit, in which different teachers of the same pupils in comprehensive schools should plan, coordinate and evaluate the teaching of basic competences and remedial teaching. This work involved meetings chaired by one of the teachers, appointed as 'study leader' for one year or more at a time.

The implementation of the working unit and study leader was slow, especially at the lower secondary level (grade 7–9 of the comprehensive school) where they competed with the subject departments and head-teachers (Ekholm, 1987). However, it still looked like the middle manager was to become a characteristic feature of Swedish schools. In the 1990s, however, management philosophy focused strongly on the head teacher as a result of changes in policy makers' conception of decentralisation. The result was that many municipalities downgraded the importance of study leaders' importance. Municipal interest to a large extent was concerned with how to make head teachers loyal representatives of municipal power.

Is there still a need for middle management? Can they make a contribution to quality development within schools? Is middle management approved of by the teachers? Let us start with the last question.

Survey data from 1991 show that teachers only rarely used the working unit as an arena of serious and regular discussions about school improvement and in-service training (Lander and Odhagen, 1992). But data also show that the study leader had gained some trust as someone who could give direct and stimulating support in improvement work. Nearly 70 per cent of primary teachers and more than half of secondary teachers said that they had at least one such study leader nearby; 90 and 75 per cent respectively felt that this was a legitimate role for study leaders. So the situation for the middle management didn't seem that bad, even if teacher cooperation could be better.

What contributions can middle management make to quality development? When working units function well they are often designed to ensure well-planned and organised pupil care and remedial teaching. The situation of every pupil is then regularly scanned. When problems arise remedial plans are put up and evaluated. Class superintendents and study leaders take special responsibilities for this, but it is felt vital that all teachers of the working unit also participate (Lander, 1996).

We, however, feel it is necessary to broaden our views on middle management and not restrict it to study leaders. Other positions and roles may have similar functions. These case studies also show that staff for pupil care (school

nurses and social advisers called curators) can also have informal management positions, eg when remedial plans are set up and evaluated. Those
newly educated as special needs teachers can build a potential middle management role as they are supposed to have a leading role in the planning and
evaluating of remedial teaching. We have seen cases where these teachers also
work as mentors to colleagues who need to change their teaching repertoire.

Schools often set up temporary or short and fixed term developmental projects, led by a 'middle manager'. In a study of two upper secondary schools,
teachers working as project leaders more often than their colleagues showed
preference for what Fullan (1991) calls 'critical interaction' and their life experiences indicated that this had evolved by changing social experiences over a
long time. These teachers often play leading roles in developmental projects
and thereby influence the social ecology by strengthening the school's meso
system, ie relations connecting the micro systems of departments, etc. This
was a vital factor behind developmental success at these two schools compared to three others that were also studied. The study illuminated the project leaders' importance in creating a feeling of competency among their
fellow teachers. Test items measured feelings of competency by questions
about how well they understood project ideas, how well they managed tasks,
and how effective and confident they felt about their new repertoire. Compared to formal school leaders and to colleagues within the project groups,
the project leaders had by far the most important influence on teachers' feelings of competency. This feeling correlated with some self-reported changes
of teachers' working habits (Hägglund and Lander, 1991).

Middle management roles, thus, can make a big difference in school
improvement and quality development. We think that permanent and tem-
porary/project middle management should not compete. But permanent
middle managers run the risk of being consumed as an administrative support function to the head teacher (Kallòs, 1985; Nestor, 1991). This is less
likely with temporary middle management contracted for two to five years
on different improvement projects, and then primarily used for pedagogical
leadership and working with hands-on-consulting among teachers.

We also believe that such a middle management can make another problem
easier. The official decentralisation policy demands evaluation at every level
of the school system. A questionnaire indicates, however, that about 70 per
cent of Swedish teachers would like to deny the head teacher the responsibility for evaluating within the schools, a task given to them by law. They
would prefer teachers to control the evaluation. Swedish teachers are not used
to the same supervision and evaluation from head teachers or department
heads that, for example, American teachers seem to be (Siskin, 1991).

There is, however, an imbalance in the use of evaluation as a local governing mechanism. At present both schools and municipalities are very interested in measuring the opinions of stake-holders about schools. Some define
such opinions as a quality measure, other see them mainly as a pressure upon

schools to open up their work for insight and influence. Some pioneers also try quality assurance. The problem with the concept of evaluation underlying these efforts is that they are predominantly based on learning as feedback, and not as cognitive learning from challenges to development (cf. van der Knaap, 1995). While feedback is a way to preserve and refine quality, it is not enough for quality development.

What is also at stake here is the monopoly of teachers in knowing what teaching really is about. At worst opinion polls and similar methods will empty the concept of quality. What teachers could fear is that the new tools of evaluation are taken over by administrators, who are not professional enough to design evaluation with validity for teacher work and pupil learning and development. Administrators have been partly set aside during the decentralisation period, and a technical issue like evaluation may give them a chance to recover lost territory backed up by consultants selling rather easy solutions (Granström and Lander, 1995).

We feel schools need evaluation, made by the authorities and the head teachers, which does not hesitate to exert legitimate control over teacher work and pupil results. But schools also need evaluation controlled by the teachers that also fulfils important professional needs for them. This brings us to the popular ideas of 'learning to learn' by reflected evaluation and the 'learning organisation'. Below we briefly evaluate these ideas in order to point to a future development of evaluation as school improvement (Holly and Hopkins, 1988) and a possible way for teachers to balance the evaluation situation with a more professional view.

Learning to learn means being able consciously to reflect upon one's own experiences and then reconsider one's actions. Teaching is the central mean for teachers' learning, but the focus is on pupils' learning. The teaching process and pupil success or failure is foremost noticed in the more traditional evaluation. How the pupil conceptualises and understands different content and how the pupil chooses his own methods of dealing with the contents is the main issue for reflective evaluation (Alexandersson, 1984). The learning is for the teacher both his or her own field of knowledge, 'to be able to teach others to learn', and also a process for continually developing his or her own professional knowledge.

In reflected evaluation the rule is that every situation of teaching and learning is unique: the knowledge obtained is situated. Reflected evaluation begins by making one's own preunderstanding for teaching and learning obvious. Experience and preunderstanding complete one another in a continuous circle. The greater experience, the broader is preunderstanding, thus making subtle differences perceptible. Consequently, a reflected evaluation should be regarded as any analysing process in which, through doubts, one is moving to and from different perspectives and conceivable methods of explanation. According to Schön (1990), the excellent practitioner is distinguished just by the fact that he or she can convert practical problems so that various solutions become apparent. However, this makes demands on the ability to describe, interpret, analyse and talk about one's own experiences.

This kind of learning needs a dialogue with colleagues and pupils. Learning is thus also a social process (Kolb, 1984). Through exploring the presumptions regarding teaching, ambiguities and inconsistencies in the individual, thinking can be analysed and discussed. Openness, respect and mutual confidence are required. For the management this is a question of creating 'knowledge-seeking alliances' among teachers, rather than dividing up teachers according to organising and administrative principles. When teachers are reflecting together, several aspects of teaching practice will be mentioned at the same time. Collective understanding often can be used in a more constructive way than the individual one. If the teachers together develop their ability to reformulate practical problems, their own knowledge of teaching and of the pupils' learning can be deepened: from a seeking for short-sighted and practical solutions to a more conscious analysis in a field of conflicting demands. For instance, they define questions about teaching and learning, they reformulate their intentions and through increased awareness they change their teaching.

Reflected evaluation has close relation to the discussion about 'the learning organisation', in which the personnel are involved in a perpetual learning process – the learning consisting of daily experiences. To transform experiences from daily situations, by learning processes, into knowledge, some organisation is needed, that encourages a continuous learning before control, before demands upon responsibility and accountability. The task for middle management will, therefore, be to focus the local processes of knowledge. That will be made possible by arranging meetings – times and places – so that teachers can meet and draw up questions about their own practice. The purpose is to initiate such activities (ie pro-activities) which support a teacher's own sense of responsibility and which contribute to increase self-reliance, giving teachers the opportunity to learn from their own practice.

Of course people responsible for reflected evaluation will have to be trained. We are engaged in developing such training and using networking among teachers in order to facilitate learning. But if this is a trustworthy description of what reflected evaluation could aim at, we would guess that no group other than a teacher-dominated middle management can achieve it.

Quality education in the United States

Doris A Henry, EdD, The University of Memphis Department of Leadership

Quality education is a term employed with increasing frequency by many school systems internationally. The literature pertaining to quality education in the US is scant. Although this term is not frequently used in the US, it is the crux of the reform efforts to improve education for all young people. Therefore, quality will be addressed in the context of restructuring and the implications for the middle managers/principals. In addition, a specific restructuring effort and the lessons from this will be given.

Background

The Effective Schools Research in the late 1970s was one of the first to identify the indicators for effective schools that was research based. The various subsequent national reports, beginning with 'A Nation at Risk' (National Commission on Excellence in Education, 1983), further clarified the expectations of American schools. Replete in the reports and studies was the critical leadership role of the principal. The emphasis on the principal as the change agent was a switch from the predominant past view of a manager.

External forces to which schools also had to respond were equalisation of funding within the states, the requirement to provide information reported to parents, marketisation of information to create competition among high schools and a continuous thrust to provide equity within diverse populations of students. Given all these forces, the quality of education is dependent upon the leader of the school, the principal and his or her ability to lead.

Glasser (1992) stated, 'The purpose of a Quality School will be to educate children according to the following definition of education: Education is the process through which we discover that learning adds quality to our lives' (p.186). Improvement of instruction, staff development, student learning and curriculum are the integral components in a quality school. These are developed through caring relationships among all the stakeholders.

Some of the concerns critics have of this approach have been whether schools can be held accountable and can consistently have equity and excellence. These concepts appear to be conflicting. Major restructuring efforts have occurred in two waves.

The purpose of the first wave about a decade ago was to increase the quality and effectiveness of public policy mandates and inducements. Little change occurred as a result of these mandates and inducements (Sergiovanni *et al.*, 1992). A significant part of the second wave has been to increase capacity-building and changes that strive to transform schools through democratic approaches to learning and teaching, leadership and the identification of outcome performance goals (Sergiovanni *et al.*, 1992). One of the primary tools for change during the second wave has been site-based decision making (SBDM).

No initiative impacts on all schools – currently no national curriculum or standards exist. There are, however, several nationally recognised initiatives that have been successful. One initiative that is part of Goals 2000 predicted to have a large impact is the New American Schools (NAS). NAS began in 1991 as a joint venture between business and education. NAS invited educators to submit designs that would serve as models for improving schools, 11 of which were selected and 9 piloted in schools over the full 3 years of development. In 1995, school districts and states were invited to apply to NAS to be a 'jurisdiction' which is either several schools in a district or a state that would implement one or more of the designs over a five-year period. Criteria for selection were set. In March 1995, ten jurisdictions were selected: Cincinnati (Ohio), Dade County (Florida), the State of Kentucky, Los Angeles and San Diego (California), the State of Maryland, Philadelphia and Pittsburgh (Pennsylvania), the State of Washington Alliance (Seattle and partner school districts), and Memphis (Tennessee). (For more details see Stringfield *et al.*, 1996.) Memphis City Schools (MCS), the fifteenth largest public school district in the US with 106,000 students, selected six of the NAS designs (Audrey Cohen College System of Education, ATLAS Communities, Co-NECT, Expeditionary Learning Outward Bound, Modern Red Schoolhouse, and Roots and Wings), and two additional nationally recognised models, Accelerated Schools and Paideia. SBDM teams selected from the eight designs. The uniqueness of this approach is that each school selects the design that best meets the needs of the students and community. This is a recognition that there is no one best way to restructure.

Prior to the 8 dramatically different designs being implemented in 34 schools, there had been several changes instituted in the school district. There was a system-wide school restructuring initiated in 1992; curriculum, instruction and outcomes assessments were developed; introduction of school-based decision making through 'leadership councils', school improvement plans written as part of a strategic plan; strengthened support by business and community groups; and a close collaborative relationship developed between MCS and the University of Memphis (Ross *et al.*, 1996b).

Factors that impact school improvement

The factors for improvement identified in the initial evaluation of the MCS initiative are similar to other initiatives in the US. One factor found that permeates improving schools was a strong, positive relationship between the school and the community. Also, communication with the public is no longer an option, but a necessity. Public perceptions are important to the continued improvement of schools. The heart of the NAS initiative in MCS aimed at the revitalisation of schools/teachers with the new school organisations and teaching strategies. Superintendent Dr N Gerry House encouraged and supported the schools.

Principals and teachers were given professional development to function better as teams; to participate in the decision making process; to enable teachers to be leaders; to strengthen communications; and better to utilise resources.

Implications for principals

Some of the lessons gleaned from the MCS initiative focus on the level of implementation, working with people, community involvement, teacher evaluation, change processes, funding, and the changing roles of the principal, teachers, students and parents (Ross *et al.*, 1996a). Strong leadership and communications were found to be a foundation to the success of the restructuring.

The level of implementation or the extent to which the school moved from the introduction to institutionalisation of an initiative is dependent upon the match between the model, the student need and leadership of the principal in involving teachers, parents, community leaders and students in the effort. The more aligned the goals are, the more likely the programme will be implemented and quality will improve.

One design, the Accelerated Schools, provides one year of 'taking stock' and planning for the next year. Teachers are given time during the instructional day to meet as a team. Also, professional development selection was based on the goals outlined in the School Improvement Plan (SIP). The SIP is developed by a team of faculty, staff, parents and community leaders, and is a product of their strategic planning. It is reviewed yearly for progress and revisions. Schools may elect to have an accrediting agency, one external to the district and state systems, to review the school to determine if the school meets the standards of the agency and the SIP. The results of the review are given to the school for dissemination.

Because the restructuring models are based on teams, working with people is fundamental to successfully improving student achievement. School teams who have similar goals and values tend to progress faster to full implementation. Involving the community is a major challenge for principals. It can be accomplished if they involve the community in ways to ensure different perspectives are heard. This requires seeking out parents and welcoming them into the process by providing information and training, continuous communication and establishing a place where risks are encouraged. For example, if the community has several ethnic groups, then meeting with the groups, preferably in their respective communities, is important. This builds greater trust and understanding. Hearing dissenting voices helps to better understand the level of acceptance and potential problem areas.

It is important to maintain a continuous dialogue about the change process and its challenges, frustrations and joys. Reflecting on the changes keeps the focus of the team on the goals.

Existing teacher evaluation systems frequently do not match the demands of the changes. Teachers are expected to instruct differently, but are evaluated by criteria that may no longer be appropriate. Designing a teacher evaluation that reflects the goals of the changes was one of the suggestions that teachers gave.

A major element in the success of the change efforts is the support that NAS gives to schools via supplemental funding. Without such additional funding, it would be difficult for school districts to provide the extent of professional development, outreach and resources with this undertaking. A highly trained support person for each of the models, as well as a trained facilitator at each school, are examples of the increased funding.

Last, the roles of principals, teachers, parents and students will continue to change. Principals must move from being the person in the office to a people and community-oriented person. Interpersonal relations skills are essential to lead a school and its community. Communication, especially with the advent of technology, is imperative. Informing communities should be a central responsibility of the principal. This is especially true because approximately 75 per cent of the people in the school community have no direct connection to schools but are asked to provide financial support for schools.

Conclusions

American schools have struggled with restructuring to improve the quality of teaching and learning. The role of the principal can change, but only with support, trust, knowledge and enthusiasm. Responsibility for educating the young people in a community is no longer dependent on one person, but the entire community. There are five points that may be helpful to principals. They are:

- assess the needs of the students and their community and identify models that fit best;
- be facilitators who will develop ownership and trust;
- communicate continuously and effectively with all stake holders;
- practice effective interpersonal relations skills that address individuals, facilitate groups and communicate with adult learners;
- promote professional development that supports all stake holders as their roles change.

* The author would like to thank Mike Milstein, Professor of Educational Leadership at the University of New Mexico, for his suggestions on an earlier draft.

Middle Management in Two Ghanaian Schools

I T Ofei

There are many different types of school in Ghana. Some aspects of the educational system reflect the strong influence and impact of the British Colonial administration, including the examination system. Other aspects are much influenced by the position of Ghana as a developing West African country, including the importance of charity schools. Two such schools are SOS-Hermann Gmeiner International College, a school established by SOS-Kinderdorf International, and Achimoto School.

SOS-Kinderdorf International is a charitable organisation which looks after orphaned and destitute children all over the world. It operates in 125 countries where it builds villages consisting of a cluster of family houses, in which 8 to 10 children are looked after by a 'mother'. SOS-Hermann Gmeiner International College was established in 1990 to provide education for the most gifted children from all the countries of Africa who do not have access to such provision. The college is focused on providing high standards of education in preparation for entrance to university, while also aiming to develop a strong sense of international understanding and a sensitivity to world cultures and languages, as well as an appreciation of Africa's role in the world. It is a boarding school which offers the International General Certificate of Secondary Education and the International Baccalaureate. Currently it has 200 students from 13 countries and 30 teachers.

Achimoto School was established by the British Colonial administration in the 1930s to train Africans to become administrators after independence. It is a boarding school with 2,000 students and 120 teachers, offering the new Ghanaian National Curriculum for senior secondary schools. Previously the school administered the West African Examination Council 'O' and 'A' level examination.

In both schools, heads of department play a pivotal role in the teaching and learning process. They are the front line managers of the whole school system. They are directly in touch with the teaching staff and students, and are aware of their needs through day-to-day experience. Their jobs require them to be responsive to these needs, and continually to improve teaching and learning to enhance student achievement. Middle managers in Ghana lead and manage their departments and serve as conduits for information flowing between teachers in their departments and senior management, thereby ensuring teacher input in school policy formulation. They serve as channels for policy dissemination.

The role of head of department includes monitoring and evaluation of teaching and learning as well as feeding this information into the process of school policy formation. Heads of department are responsible for ensuring that teaching and learning are effectively planned and that resources are available for the effective delivery of the curriculum. The department is a useful forum for critical assessment of the effectiveness of teaching in the subject. At this level there is mutual understanding of the problems faced in the specific subject area. Discussion can be frank and different points of view aired without judgemental or punitive interference from 'outsiders'.

Occasionally, middle managers can be involved in observing actual teaching rather than depend upon teachers' written evaluations. Unfortunately, there is no scheduled time on the timetable for this.

There is a major role for heads of department in terms of staff development. This should be encouraged not least through creating an atmosphere which enhances collegial problem solving and support. Teachers should be empowered to use their creative energies and talents to bring about innovation, and continuously to improve the knowledge base of the department and of the school.

The head of department can act as activator, initiating ideas to stimulate activities in the subject and strategies to assist students with particular problems. Through keeping abreast of developments in the subject area the head of department can create a stimulating academic environment for students and teachers.

The department is the unit in which teachers work as a team and it provides both support at both the personal and professional levels. The head of department is required to have a high degree of skill and to be firm, fair and objective, to act as mentor and counsellor and use his or her qualifications and experience in the support of staff. A high degree of interpersonal skill is required.

Perspective on Middle Management in Israeli Secondary Schools

Batia Brauner

> 'Mother: (calling upstairs in the morning) It's time to get up for school.
> Chris: I am not going to school!
> Mother: Why not?
> Chris: Because everybody at the school hates me – the teachers, the kids, the janitor – they all hate me!
> Mother: You have to go. You're the principal.'
>
> (Fullan, 1991, p. 144)

Fullan (1991) reports Martin and Willower's (1981) and Peterson's (1981) observations of principals who found that:

> 'Principals' full workdays were sporadic, and characterised simultaneously by brevity, variety and fragmentation and observed that secondary school principals perform an average of 149 tasks a day, with constant interruptions.

> Over 59 per cent of their observed activities were interrupted. Most (84 per cent) of the activities were brief (1–4 minutes). Principals "demonstrated" a tendency to engage themselves in almost all current and pressing situations.'
>
> (Fullan, 1991)

It was observed that they invested little or no time in effective thinking. Instruction-related activities took up only 17 per cent of their time. Sarason (1982, Ch. 9) observes that most of the principal's time is spent on administrative, housekeeping matters and maintaining order. Many principals expect or feel that they are expected to keep everyone happy by running an orderly school, and this becomes the major criterion of the principal's ability to manage – no news is good news, as long as everything is relatively quiet.

A very similar picture emerges from the study of 137 principals in Toronto (Edu-con, 1984). They all reported they felt overloaded. 90 per cent reported an increase over the previous five years in the demands made on their time and responsibilities, including new programme demands and new directives. In the same study, principals were also asked about their perception of effectiveness: 71 per cent reported a decrease in principal effectiveness and 84 per cent reported a decrease in the authority of the principal; 76 per cent reported a decrease in trust in leadership of the principal. The question 'Do you think the principal himself can effectively fulfil all the responsibilities assigned to him/her?' was answered 'No' by 91 per cent.

The frustration and discouragement felt by principals in attempting to cover all the bases is well described by a response from interviews conducted by Duke (1988) with principals who were considering quitting:

> 'The principalship is the kind of job where you're expected to be all things to all people. Early on, if you are successful, you have gotten feedback that you are able to be all things to all people. And then you feel an obligation to continue to do that which in your own mind you are not capable of doing. And that causes some guilt.' (p. 309)

In interviewing principals about why they considered quitting, he found that sources of dissatisfaction included policy and administration, lack of achievement, sacrifices in personal life, lack of growth opportunities, lack of recognition, relations with subordinates and lack of support from superiors.

In studies carried out in Israel these findings are confirmed, the overwhelming emphasis of the principals' daily work is oriented towards:

1. maintenance;
2. student disciplinary control;
3. keeping outside influence under control;
4. keeping staff conflicts at bay; and
5. keeping the school supplied with adequate materials.

Why is this so? Where does this conservative tendency in the principalship have its roots?

Michael Fullan quotes Sarason (1982), claiming that being a classroom teacher by itself is not very good preparation for being an effective principal. The situation is even worse if a teacher's experience is limited to one or two schools. Sarason's conclusion is that the narrowness of preparation and the demands for maintaining or restoring stability encourage principals to play it safe and try not to delegate tasks.

In Israel, principals seem to be overloaded even more, not only because comprehensive schools are very big (1,000–5,000 pupils), but also because of conservative, centralistic tendencies caused by the military tradition and its credo that 'There is only one commander in each battle, all the rest being mere soldiers'. Very often the position of principal is held by veteran military men who have retired from the army and, as a compensation, were given a principalship.

If schools were rational organisations, and not highly resistant to change, the function of vice principals would be perceived in a completely different way. This report will therefore focus on the vice principal's function only, for heads of departments are not even associated with management tasks. 'Coordinator' is the best definition at the moment. Heads of departments are perceived as professionals, competent in their fields, having no say about school policy or staff employment. Heads of departments' financial compensation is almost none – they get a small percentage added to their total income, and the structure of their salary, unlike principals and vice principals, is identical to that of teachers.

There has been a growing need for task delegation, empowering staff and middle management development, yet the field has seen very little change. There has been a growing awareness that the middle management in its broad sense should become a source of school improvement and change. Despite all this, even the function of vice principal still lacks a clear definition and is highly controversial.

A well-known Israeli journal dealing with school principals' problems, called *FORUM*, published a survey describing discussions and interviews with different vice principals from various high schools. Most of the schools mentioned are in Tel Aviv or are located centrally, where one might expect less conservative approaches and new trends to arrive sooner. (Peripheral areas in the north and south of Israel tend to follow a more traditional approach.) The title of the survey was 'Vice principal – function or fiction'. The survey deals with the following questions:

1. Is it a meaningful function, is it well defined, challenging?
2. Is it a good starting point leading to principalship?
3. At the present moment, what does this function consist of?

The survey tries to show how vice principals cope with difficulties, to what extent they get moral and financial compensation, what frustrates them and who is interested in the present state of affairs. Frustration, disappointment and lack of satisfaction characterised all the participants. The only difference was found to be their individual ways of self-compensation and search for meaning in things that seemed to be meaningless.

Vice principalship is perceived both by vice principals and teachers as a purely technical task, lacking independence, a task which even 'silences' initiative. The function consists mainly of boring daily routine and banal activities, such as taking care of class equipment, timetable organisation, simple regulations and sometimes extra-curricular activities.

Vice principals' routines don't contain 'meaningful' managerial acts, such as:

1. staff employment;
2. financial decisions;
3. equipment acquisition;
4. the right to sign instead of the principal;
5. being partners in philosophical disputes;
6. the right to 'punish' or 'reward' students, without asking for the principal's approval;
7. involvement in staff disciplinary procedures.

One of the participants, who started the job with great enthusiasm, because as he said 'education was important to him', gradually saw himself as a servant, of pupils and teachers. The everyday routine was not the only frustration vice principals encountered. Another frustrating thing is working with the principal: 'I want to insert my style, my suggestions, and it is impossible. I want certain things to happen and they don't, to be listened to, to become "acceptable". To become just a little bit dominant takes so much of my energy'. Vice principals complained about not being able to represent the school as far as the external agencies are concerned (ministry of education, municipality, parents), and hence not being able to participate in discussions with these external agencies.

Those who where ambitious, complained about lack of formal training. Being a principal means being professional, and fulfilling both pedagogical and administrative functions. Being vice principal means doing some of this as well and they found it was impossible without training. They realised that formal training would be extremely difficult since, unlike in other fields, where the vice manager or other deputy functions are already defined, in school, the principal deïnes the function and redefines it at will.

Vice principals described the price that the principals usually pay, in that they are approached, consulted and bothered constantly, having no time to 'manage'. Teachers can't always teach well and they are left with no answers, since there is no time to answer everybody. Nobody sees how inefficient this system is, because teachers, principals and vice principals are not familiar with other organisations.

Some of the vice principals confessed that their dream was to be promoted to become a principal. Unfortunately, they felt that the inside experience they have is not considered an advantage when competing for principal positions. They realised promotion is usually based on public opinion, and being vice principals they are anonymous. Everyday hard routine doesn't supply opportunities for public relations and connections.

An interesting case is that of a senior, well-known veteran teacher, who was a vice principal for 25 years. This summer he had a chance of fulfilling his dream – to become principal – and still he failed. When asked whether he was sorry to have invested so many years in the project of his life, he said he had liked every minute of it, he liked his present task and didn't care about honours. Looking for new meaning in his old task he decided to concentrate on weaker pupils in technological classes. He could even console himself by saying that in a way he was fortunate to not get the job:

> 'I will stay young, for I am constantly in the company of students. It is my life. I try to connect between the pupils and the organisation. This reinvented interest is a compensation for the lack of real authority and for dealing mainly with:
>
> 1. maintenance – order
> 2. discipline
> 3. equipment.'

Conclusion

Reading this survey one realises that a reorganisation is needed to bring a redefinition of middle management functions; to limit principals' centralistic position. So far, no real investment has been made in Israel to train middle managers, in general, and vice principals in particular.

People do not want to take responsibility if they are not paid well. Vice principals are paid badly; the structure of their salary depends mostly on the principal's decision and sometimes on local agreement. Thus, schools have to look constantly for new volunteers (very often women), for whom such a situation would be convenient. If, by chance, a vice principal is ambitious, has a vision, aspires to excellence and becomes dominant, the principal is considered a failure and the management system in his school pathological.

In big comprehensive high schools, there is enough work for both the principal and the vice principal. Once better care is taken of:

1. job definition;
2. selection of people;
3. training;
4. reward system;
5. dialogue about the career prospect.

Principals have to understand that career development is not the exclusive property of senior management, but should be shared by middle management and teachers. There will be a new opportunity for middle management to stand in the middle of educational change and school development.

One day perhaps we shall be able to rewrite the anecdote about Chris, and his mother's concluding sentence will be: 'You must to go to school. You are vice principal.'

Part III   Working with People

Chapter 7

Leadership from the Middle

Middle managers are leaders of departments or groups in secondary schools and they provide leadership from within the school. The following definition describes the leadership role:

> 'Leadership is a force that creates the capacity among a group of people to do something that is different or better. This could be reflected in a more creative outcome, or a higher level of performance. In essence, leadership is an agency of change, and could entail inspiring others to do more than they would otherwise have done, or were doing.'
>
> (McKenna, 1991, p. 355)

While the terms of leadership and management are sometimes used interchangeably, we see management as being more concerned with the maintenance of routine activities and tasks, of organising, planning, scheduling and communicating information. These are important aspects of middle management which are dealt with in Chapters 11 to 17. As McKenna outlines above, leadership concerns that capacity to influence a group of individuals to achieve specific goals.

Middle managers can be a positive force for change and improvement within the department, and if they are they are indeed leaders of their department, rather than merely managers of it, they can contribute to improving the school. Middle managers, as leaders, have a vision of where they would like their department to be, based upon a series of values and assumptions about their work and the context in which they are working. Much school improvement must come from the work of individual departments working on their own internal processes and agendas for improvement.

Middle managers are also leaders of the school, and this is particularly true of those who work in schools that have moved towards a 'flatter' management structure by removing layers of senior managers, for example by not appointing the second or third deputy, or by removing senior teacher posts. In curriculum and management committees, middle managers can take up a wider management responsibility beyond their own department and across the whole school. Here, middle managers may become leaders inspiring creativity and higher levels of achievement.

This chapter is about developing appropriate leadership. The word 'appropriate' is used because any leader needs to develop an approach which both recognises and acts upon the unique circumstances within the school. The leader needs to work within the constraints of the context and conditions of the time. Yet the leader also needs to work towards improving those circumstances and conditions. It is not possible to describe a style of leadership which will fit all circumstances or to give the details of what to do as a leader, because so much is dependent upon the context.

Leaders, therefore, need to analyse their own strengths and weaknesses in the ways in which they work with people and those of the group in which they find themselves working. They should not forget their focus upon the quality of teaching and learning, yet they must think about how the tasks of management are impacting upon their leadership: ie the way they are in the context in which they work. These are the four themes of this book and are again central to this chapter.

This chapter identifies a number of dimensions of leadership as a middle manager. You are invited to evaluate your own approach to leadership and develop a leadership style to meet the needs of your school.

Defining leadership and management

'For many the word leadership implies that one person is the dictator: he makes all the decisions and does all the work of leadership. That is wrong. In groups of more than two or three there are too many functions required for any one person to do it all himself [sic]. The good leader evokes or draws forth leadership from the group. He works as a senior partner with other members to achieve the task, build the team and meet individual needs.'

(Adair, 1988)

In the early writings on leadership, there was a quest to describe categories of leadership styles, as though successful leaders had a particular set of characteristics that were drawn upon in every situation. Usually descriptions of leadership revolved around the concepts of democracy and consultation. Hence, typologies using terms such as autocratic, paternal, consultative, *laissez-faire* and democratic were typical in the work of Lippet and White (1968), Tannenbaum and Schmidt (1967), and Likert (1973).

More recent studies of leadership take the view that style of leadership is dependent upon a number of factors associated with:

The Leaders
The leader's values and beliefs
Confidence in the staff involved
Personality and style
The leader's need for control
The degree of stress

The Staff
Their perceived competence in achieving the task
Their motivation
Their need for direction, or support
Their tolerance of ambiguity

The Task
The nature and complexity of the task
The time scale
The importance of the outcome

The Organisation
The power position of the leader and the group
The culture of the organisation.

It follows, thus, that what you do as a leader is largely a matter of choosing to work appropriately, depending upon the circumstances and the context you are working in, hence the need for a great deal of reflection on the context and circumstances.

Activity 7.1 The characteristics of leaders

Identify the characteristics of leaders whom you have enjoyed working for and whom you believe got the best out of you. Now think about the characteristics of those whom you have not enjoyed working for and who didn't get the best from you. Record your thoughts in your reflective journal.

Over 70 teachers from Israel and the UK were asked about the characteristics of the leaders who motivated them and got the best result, the leaders they would 'die' for, and the characteristics of the worst, those that make you cry because they are so poor. Their responses are shown in Table 7.1.

Table 7.1 *Leadership characteristics*

Characteristics of leaders who your would die for	Characteristics of leaders who make you cry
Celebrates the achievements of others	Vague
Makes others feel valued	Talks as if they know everything
Cares for people	Sloppy
Charismatic	Sets targets too difficult to achieve
Inspirational	Tunnel vision
Works with you	Creates an impression of listening
Has a vision that can be shared	Forgets detail
Clear direction	Talks about their own achievements
Respect staff for their knowledge	Changes mind
Articulate	Critises frequently
Has strong moral values	Looks at faults
Clearly defined boundaries	Talks but does not listen
Good memory for detail	Does not do the work themselves
Creative	Delegates but takes credit
Listens to ideas	Does not know the people they work with
Trusts	Never follows up
Is positive	Forgets things that have happened
Is enthusiastic	Changes direction
Values people	Manipulative
Will admit lack of knowledge	Lacks commitment
Can do the job	Dictatorial
Welcomes constructive criticism	Rare to praise – quick to blame
Praises and thanks	Two faced
Empathetic	Lazy
Pays attention to detail	Not honest
Works as hard as you do	Frightened by others
Visible	Divisive
Builds self-esteem	
Earns respect	
Respects others	
Supports the development of others	
Supports the participation of others	
Approachable	
Strength of character	
Honest	
Will take advice	
Dependable	
Ethical	
Empowering	

Activity 7.2 Yourself as leader

Consider your performance in relation to the qualities outlined in Table 7.1. How do others see you in relation to these qualities? What goals for improving your leadership would you set yourself? Record your thoughts in your reflective journal.

Accountability, authority and power

As a middle manager you need to be clear in your own mind about your own position in terms of accountability, authority and responsibility. You may be held to account for the work of your department or team by a number of people from within and outside the school. You may need to hold others to account for their work. You may be seen by senior managers and by the staff whom you lead as an authority in your particular field of expertise. Clarifying the authority that you have will be a helpful foundation to your leadership. You need to know the power you have, particularly if you wish to influence people or get them to change what they are doing.

The professional freedom of teachers has been a tradition and cornerstone of teaching, in the UK, at least until recently. Teachers have been able to close the classroom door and take responsibility for the teaching and learning. With increasing 'accountability' of both teachers and middle managers it has become necessary to rethink this freedom. In the UK, stimulated by OFSTED inspections, there has been an increased emphasis upon managers monitoring and evaluating the work of the department, and of course the teachers within it.

Middle managers are being held to account by a variety of people. Immediately, we can consider being accountable to the senior management and the governors to the school. There is an accountability to the pupils and parents. In local authority schools, middle managers may be accountable to the local adviser or inspector. There is also a professional accountability to one's colleagues and the profession as a whole. Here, there is a management duty to ensure the highest standards of professional behaviour in all aspects of the work.

While middle managers need to think through to whom they are accountable, they also need to think about the issue of holding others to account. This is particularly problematic for new heads of department, those with relatively little experience and those who may have teachers in more senior positions working within the department.

Your professional authority is based upon your knowledge and expertise, particularly in your subject area, in the teaching and learning process, and in your management knowledge and experience. You are the leader responsible for a department or area of the school. You have your own specialist technical expertise, language and technology which can set you apart from others. Yet, you are also working under the authority of others, including the senior management team and governors of the school.

French and Raven (1958) distinguish five different types of power:

- *Reward power:* where the leader can use tangible or symbolic rewards which have value;
- *Coercive power:* where the leader is willing to use tangible or symbolic penalties that are disliked, including the withdrawal of status or privileges;
- *Referent power:* where the leader through charisma provides a role model which is lived up to;
- *Legitimate power:* where the leader is seen to have the right to direct;
- Expert power: *where superior knowledge and expertise which is relevant to the task are seen as key characteristics of the leader.*

The categories are useful ones for the middle manager to think about in terms of the use of power and the powers at your disposal.

Activity 7.3 The power strategies that you use

Consider the ways in which you try to get people to do things. What powers do you think you are using? What powers do your colleagues think you are using? What symbolic rewards do you use and when? How far do your colleagues see you as having a right to direct? How do you feel about exercising your power?
Record your thoughts in your reflective journal.

In the main, you may feel that you are relatively powerless and that people follow your leadership because they like you and see you as having the expertise to do the job well. The appropriate use of coercive power requires clarification. The term 'coercion' is pejorative. Yet, it is not clear under which conditions the use of coercive power is justified, morally, ethically or professionally. At one extreme endangering the physical well-being of pupils by neglect requires some form of coercive action by those in authority. So, too, it may be argued, persistent poor performance as a teacher which endangers pupils' intellectual well-being and life chances requires some form of intervention including coercion.

Activity 7.4 The use of coercion

Can you think of examples where you are, or might be, coercive, that is you use tangible or symbolic rewards and punishments to get people to behave in a certain way? What are the reactions of staff to different rewards and punishments? Under what circumstances are you prepared to be coercive?

Record your thoughts in your reflective journal.

Yukl (1981) has built upon the French and Raven Model, by looking at the outcomes of the use of power in terms of staff commitment, compliance and resistance. Reward power, Yukl argues, is likely to lead to staff being committed, only while the reward lasts, there is some compliance but resistance will grow if there is a hint of manipulation. Etzioni (1975) regards this as calculative involvement. Coercion leads to low levels of commitment and high levels of resistance. The use of legitimate, referent and expert power is likely to develop commitment and reduce resistance, particularly where requests are legitimate, persuasively argued and goals are shared. Etzioni regards this as 'moral involvement'.

These works are useful reminders that whatever leadership strategies we use, there is likely to be a number of different possible responses from the individuals in the group that we lead. Table 7.2 outlines a number of so called 'power gambits' and possible 'responses'.

Table 7.2   *The power–response equation*

Power gambits	Responses	
pay	**Commitment, compliance and**	
resources	**resistance**	
facilities		
equipment		
acknowledgement	immediate	reluctant
attention	conditional	unconditional
abuse	commanded	chosen
shouting loud	calculative	emotional
privileges	self-interest	pupil interest

control	begrudging	willing
freedom	enduring	short-lived
charisma	dependent	unconditional
personality	resistant	supportive
warmth	compliant	committed
skill	disinterest	enthusiasm
role model		
having the right to act	Commitment:	
knowledge	to the reward	to goals
experience		to the group
position		shared goals
strength of case		shared values
values and vision	to the leader	to the task

Activity 7.5 The consequences of power strategies

Reflect on times that you have been really committed to something. How did this feel? What created your commitment? Have there been times when you were resistant? What influenced your resistance? Consider what has really motivated or demotivated you in the past?. What really motivates your staff?

Record your thoughts in your reflective journal.

The use of power in your leadership is influenced by and influences the response of the members of your team. It would be difficult to imagine a department that operates on rewards and punishments alone, a kind of 'What's in it for me?' mentality would pertain. The basis of much leadership must be professional and moral involvement which is committed, active and energetic about the values and vision of departmental and school improvement.

Vision and transformational leadership

Considerable interest has been shown in the notion of 'transformational' leadership. McKenna describes this as the type of leadership that needs to be developed in periods of change. He quotes Bass (1990), who lists three characteristics:

- charisma;
- intellectual stimulation; and
- consideration of the emotional needs of each employee.

Leaders who 'transform' are good at establishing and communicating values and beliefs. They communicate aims and direction and have a strong sense of vision. These form the basis of setting long-term goals, which are reduced down to specific and individual short-term goals. 'A vital part of the process is the ability to project the mind forward into the future and to visualise what intended results will look like' (Whitaker, 1993, p. 114).

Middle managers have their own vision of their department's development and they also have a key role in developing and implementing the vision of the head teacher, conveying the head's vision to the staff, involving them in developing the vision, and converting it into everyday practice. Part of the middle manager's contribution is through the specific vision that they have of their own departmental area.

The purpose of the vision may be to:

- serve as an energising and mobilising focus;
- convey values;
- provide security of direction in a confusion of activities;
- provide a baseline for handling external pressure and initiatives;
- be a symbol of disappointment at existing provision and commitment to improvement;
- provide a baseline for being held to account.

Fullan, quoting Miles suggests that vision involves two dimensions:

> 'The first is shareable, and shared vision of what the school could look like; it provides direction and driving power for change, and criteria for steering and choosing... The second type is a shared vision of the change process... what will be the general plan or strategy for getting there.'
>
> (Fullan, 1991, p. 50)

Fullan goes on to emphasise the need for the vision to be shared by all. This emphasis is simplistic. There may be several reasons why the vision is not and cannot be fully shared. The vision may involve the removal of posts, consideration of factors as yet unknown to the participants or perhaps part of the vision is not yet fully worked out. Fullan outlines the process of developing a shared vision, yet the starting point may be the leader. Clearly, although large elements of the vision needs to be revealed, tactically and practically it may be inappropriate to share the whole vision.

At a simple level the middle manager, as leader, needs to have a vision of how things could be in the department. Knowing your vision for the department is an essential area of self-knowledge as a middle management leader.

The vision you need to focus upon is how you want the department to be. Chapter 11 develops these ideas further.

Leadership of learning

A key area of transformational leadership for middle managers working in schools is the establishment of the values and beliefs about learning and teaching within their own department and beyond, for the whole school. This is where leadership within schools differs from the leadership described in other organisations. The transformational leader as middle manager needs to be clear about and make clear to others:

- the principles and values that are the foundation of the teaching and learning process;
- the place and purpose of the subject in the curriculum.

These issues are taken up in more detail in the chapters on learning (see Chapters 9 and 10).

Dimensions and tensions of leadership

The literature on leadership is littered with theoretical models alleging that leadership can be broken down into dimensions. The dimensions commonly discussed include:

Consideration – Initiating Structure (Fleishman and Harris, 1972)
Concern for People – Concern for Production (Blake and Mouton, 1985)
Relationship – Task (Hersey and Blanchard, 1982)
Assertiveness and Cooperation (Thomas, 1976)

While such models are deliberately focused upon important characteristics of leadership, they are also simplifications of reality. Nevertheless, they provide useful tools for reflecting upon and analysing your own leadership, and the situations in which you find yourself working.

Another aspect of the middle management sandwich concept is that the dimensions operate at the same time as a kind of layered sandwich (see Figure 7.1). The discerning, reflecting middle manager will pick the model which most applies to them and reflect upon how this model helps to bring light to their situation and to suggest strategies for improvement. The concepts are developed further below.

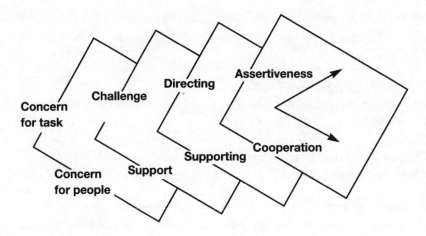

Figure 7.1 The dimensions and tensions of leadership

Concern for task: concern for people

One model that has been outlined by a number of authors, although they often use different terminology, is a model that contains a 'task' and a 'person' component (Following the work of Blake and Mouton, 1985). Leaders may display characteristics that orientate them towards either low or high concern for task. At the same time they can score on a dimension for concern for people (see Figure 7.1). The implications of the model are that a manager showing too much concern for task and too little concern for people may be seen to be ineffective. Similarly, too much concern for people and the task will not get done. Theoretically, there is some optimum level.

The model has some flaws. We may have doubts that 'concern for task' is not related to 'concern for people'. Often they will be the same thing. Talking about targets and achievements can be task orientated but can be undertaken in a way that builds the self-esteem and confidence of the staff concerned. It could be argued that the balance of any individual leader may vary with circumstances.

Nevertheless, particularly considering the features of effective managers outlined above, the model is useful as an albeit rough and ready diagnostic tool for reflection. You may reflect upon how far you feel that you concern yourself as a leader with tasks and people.

In the 'people' dimension you may consider how much you:

1. give the impression that you are happy to be in the school;
2. show an interest in staff as people;
3. are available to discuss personal issues of concern;
4. acknowledge and understand the personal circumstances of staff;

5. express appreciation of the efforts and talents of staff;
6. recognise the demands of the personal circumstances of staff;
7. demonstrate consideration for personal feelings on an informal basis;
8. make time to listen to staff as individuals;
9. boost staff morale and self-esteem;
10. are sympathetic to staff feelings;
11. provide constructive feedback;
12. treat differences of opinion as positive occurrences;
13. encourage collaboration and involvement;
14. listen to staff concerns.

A major aspect of concern for people is concern for the development of their skills and experiences. Some leaders are good at developing the skills and qualities of others around them. A group of more than 30 teachers in a workshop activity produced the following list of characteristics of leaders who were effective at developing people:

- good communicators and good listeners;
- have vision, transfer desire into action and make policies work;
- have understanding and knowledge;
- energetic;
- well organised, work on priorities;
- take risks, prepared to make a mistake and take responsibility for it;
- accept criticism;
- resolve conflict;
- are consistent;
- trustworthy, happy, friendly, have a sense of humour;
- tactful;
- diplomatic.

Activity 7.6 Your qualities of leadership

Reflect on your qualities of leadership in respect to the two dimensions (task and people) outlined above. Consider your performance on the 14 'people' points above. Record your thoughts in your reflective journal.

Challenge and support

Leadership involves supporting staff, particularly those who are having difficulties. The support can be in the form of an informal chat or the offer of advice. There could be more formal support such as the provision of some training, consultancy or the involvement in a school-based project.

The need for support and the development of a supportive culture has to be balanced by challenging poor performance as a teacher. There is a need to set clear expectations and standards of behaviour and to set clear but achievable targets for improvement for those who are under performing. The room the middle manager has for challenging poor performance is largely dependent upon the support they are likely to receive should the situation continue to be poor.

Another aspect of challenge is the degree to which even high performing staff are set new goals. Establishing intellectually challenging tasks is a key characteristic of transformational leadership. Clearly, in an improving school more will be expected of staff, whether it is higher levels of achievement or whether it is taking on new roles and responsibilities. The middle manager needs to decide how much challenge and support to give each individual member of staff. The issue of challenge and support is developed in Chapter 8.

Directing and supporting

Another dimension to consider is the degree to which you as leader direct and the degree to which you support. If you are highly directive, you are likely to be giving detailed instructions and keeping a close eye on activities. Your close supervision allows little room for error and you take the responsibility for ensuring success. You are probably controlling every action staff take by giving instructions of what to do and how to do it. This may be appropriate for some staff on some occasions. With new staff, particularly those with little experience, you are likely to be more directive.

The downside to being directive is that you are probably allowing little room for staff to take responsibility, to do it their way or to think through their performance. The skills of staff are not being developed.

Staff who show that they can be relied upon, even with little experience, may be given more freedom and you adopt a more supportive role, perhaps coaching or outlining objectives but withdrawing to allow staff to perfect their own approach. You know what needs to be done and how performance can be improved. Instructions are given clearly and targets set. For some, a less directive stance is provided, perhaps being more of a supportive 'mentor'.

At the extreme you may be directing very little and supporting very little too. This would be delegating. You consider your colleagues able to get on with it themselves. It would be a mistake to assume that no support is required, however. Most staff will require at least an acknowledgement of their efforts. Too frequently managers exclaim, 'Why should I praise staff for doing what they are paid to do anyway?'

Assertiveness and cooperation

The way in which the middle manager approaches conflicts within the team is important in defining leadership and the effectiveness of the group in achieving its goals. Conflicts occur because of differences in opinion over goals, tasks or judgements. The leader needs to develop cooperation, yet must also assert themselves to ensure things get done. In a context where staff are empowered and involved, this may bring about others asserting themselves. Conditions are, therefore, ripe for conflict and ways need to be found to collaborate.

The work of Thomas (1976) is useful in analysing conflict positions. Thomas describes two dimensions, assertiveness or the desire to satisfy one's own concerns and cooperativeness, the desire to satisfy the concerns of others. He then describes five positions.

The first is a position where assertion is high but cooperation is low. This is the resolution of conflict through competition and the most forceful or most powerful wins. Other parties lose. Where time is short, where the final outcome is crucial, this may be an appropriate style.

Where there is no assertion the group may be avoiding or accommodating. Avoidance of an issue implies that there is no cooperation, since the issue is not being faced. If the issue can be left avoided, this makes sense but this is rarely possible. Accommodation involves one party sacrificing their own needs and not asserting themselves. This might lead to some sort of resolution of the conflict through cooperation.

Higher levels of assertion by all concerned are required to achieve true collaboration. This is where people are asserting themselves and cooperating. Frequently, this may involve a position of compromise where assertiveness and cooperation are moderated. High levels of collaboration occur where there is trust and openness, where differences are discussed and resolved, and where there is a search for common ground, particularly in the pursuit of common aims, goals and strategies to achieve them.

Activity 7.7 Your qualities of leadership

Reflect on your qualities of leadership in respect to the various dimensions outlined above. Record your thoughts in your reflective journal.

Conclusion

Leadership from a middle management position is a complex issue, not least because there are a number of potentially conflicting tensions. There is no safe position where you can be in a perfect position on all these dimensions. What is required is that you know where you are and can find reasons for being there or working to be somewhere better. These dimensions, then, provide a fruitful framework for reflecting upon your own performance.

Chapter 8

Getting the Best out of your Staff

A key task for middle management is to work with staff as individuals and to forge them into an effective working group or team. This involves both motivation and encouragement of staff to achieve more and concern for the health of the team as a whole. You will be dealing with staff who may be new to teaching, those that are looking for experiences to support their future promotion and those approaching retirement.

You will need to develop or sharpen the skills of staff, particularly with regard to their work in the classroom, and to motivate them to give high performance. In many schools, staff development has traditionally been a whole-school issue, managed often by a senior teacher or deputy head teacher. Clearly senior management can take responsibility for the whole school issues and develop a coherent policy for staff development. It may not be possible or appropriate for them to involve themselves in the detail of promoting and developing effective teaching and learning. This is a task for middle managers.

The chapter outlines a number of important issues to consider in your attempts to get the best out of staff through motivating them and supporting their development. You are invited to reflect upon your own work as a middle manager and propose strategies for improving your skills of getting better quality work from those you manage.

Developing people: the key resource

The talents and skills of the staff are the key resource of the department. The middle manager is responsible for ensuring that the time staff spend working for the department or team is used as effectively as possible. Continuous development of the skills of staff is essential if school and departmental goals are to be achieved. Although you may never see the money in the department budget, possibly over 80 per cent of the financial inputs into the department are effectively taken up in terms of paying staff salaries. All the other resources used in the department are dependent upon the skill and enthusiasm of the staff themselves, for we are yet to create 'teacher proof' resources.

Peters and Waterman (1982) emphasise a number of points to enhance the performance of staff including:

- working in a collaborative team;
- working as a family;
- avoiding rigid chains of command;
- knowing what is going on;
- sharing information on performance openly;
- ensuring communication;
- respecting individuals;
- making people winners;
- treating people as adults.

Activity 8.1 Making people winners

Look at the list above and reflect upon how far you are able to 'make people winners'. How far is the Peters and Waterman philosophy similar to your own? Identify strategies that might help in the future. Record your thoughts in your reflective journal.

Investing in people

In the UK, many schools have used the 'Investors in People' standard as a means of raising achievement of pupils. The standard outlines 26 indicators or bench marks for ensuring that the skills of people are developed. The standard was developed across industrial sectors but is a useful tool to use in developing the systems to support staff in schools. Whether your school is involved in 'Investors', or not, the standard provides useful insights into the indicators of effective systems for getting the best out of staff. The standard is based around four key areas:

- *Commitment:* ensuring that all staff are aware of the commitment to develop people, the aims and vision of the school, and the plan for achieving them. The plan identifies development needs and 'specifies how they will be assessed and met' (Employment Department, 1991).
- *Planning:* 'how the skills of individuals and teams are to be developed to achieve organisational goals' (Speller, 1994). The plans identify specific targets and development actions, and where possible lead to the achievement of external standards such as NVQ or other qualifications. The indicator also places emphasis on the competence of managers in carrying out their responsibilities for developing people.
- *Action:* to develop and use the skills of staff, and to provide opportunities for development. The indicators emphasise the introduction of new staff to the school and that managers are actively supporting the training and development needs of staff.
- *Evaluation:* ensures that the development is contributing to the goals of the school, and that development achieves its objectives.

Achieving 'Investors in People' status is the responsibility of senior management. However, the standard provides a useful guide to what managers should do to develop people. Clearly, in schools, the middle manager is in a prime position to develop the skills of staff to achieve the department's and the school's objectives. The standard implies development 'on the job', through the leadership and advice offered by managers, as much as attendance at in-service training. The responsibility for development is placed securely on the manager, who must ensure a number of precise conditions, including those suggested in Table 8.1:

Table 8.1 *Middle management and investing in people (Suggestions derived from Investors in People)*

The Middle Manager should ensure:
Commitment, ie that:
    staff understand the commitment to development;
    staff know the aims of the school;
    staff know the goals and development objectives of the school;
    staff are familiar with the development plan for the school;
    staff are aware of the contribution that they can make to school development;
    the department's development needs are identified;
    the development needs of the current staff are identified;
    the future staff requirements are noted;

Planning, ie that:
    there is a written plan identifying the resources that will be used to meet training and development needs including the staff responsible;
    training and development needs of the department are regularly reviewed;
    training and development needs of staff are regularly reviewed;

your own training needs are reviewed, particularly with regard to developing staff;

development targets and standards are set for the department and for individuals;

wherever possible targets that lead to academic or vocational awards are set.

Action, ie that:

Newly Qualified Teachers are effectively inducted into the department;

other new staff are effectively inducted into the department;

the skills and knowledge of staff are developed;

staff are made aware of the development opportunities open to them;

staff identify their staff development needs and plan to meet them;

effective training and development takes place;

you actively support training by briefing, follow up, coaching and debriefing.

Evaluation, ie that:

training and development activities are evaluated against the goals of the department;

the achievement of development objectives are evaluated;

the costs and benefits of training and development are examined.

Activity 8.2 Self-assessment

Use the checklist in Table 8.1 to evaluate your contribution to developing people. What are your strengths and weaknesses? Is there anything that you would wish to add to the list? Are there things that you couldn't be responsible for? Record your thoughts in your reflective journal.

'Investors in People' does not identify middle managers as the staff to take responsibility for the development. It is clear, however, that the managers of departments and curriculum teams are in the best position to focus upon development that has impact upon classroom effectiveness. The case has been made in Chapter 1 that as subject experts, middle managers are the leaders of the curriculum area and pedagogic experts in their particular field. They have control over the immediate resources which affect performance in the classroom and the supportive frameworks such as the scheme of work. The middle manager is in a prime position to ensure that institutional gaols are planned for and achieved within the remit of the work of the department.

Some may feel that the financial and time costs of development are too expensive. Yet, as one management adage goes, 'If you think training is expensive, try ignorance'. The moral argument is that the benefits of higher standards of achievement for individuals and the school are worth paying for. For the middle manager, the 'investment in people' model provides both an indicator of good management practice and a framework for effective departmental organisation to raise achievement.

Another way of looking at the 'Investors in People' framework is to say that the work it identifies is probably already going on to some degree. Meeting time is used in planning development actions which are taking place and so on. The investors' framework, however, provides a useful checklist of criteria about quality management that enables the middle manager and the department or team to evaluate and identify processes that could be improved. It may be, for example, that the department identifies the need for clearer targets, or that through evaluation it becomes clear that development has not achieved the intended goals or that the in-service provided had increased people's 'awareness' rather than their specific skills at doing the job.

Motivating staff

The key management task for the middle manager is motivating staff. To do this you need to establish what factors and conditions are necessary to encourage staff to want to achieve more. In answering this question you need to consider both members of the department under your leadership and, in keeping with our concept of self in context, you need to consider what motivates you, and your colleagues, including the senior staff and support staff.

Implicit in the Investors in People model is a set of assumptions about what motivates people. The model almost implies that clarity of goals, working together to achieve development, and investment in people themselves, motivates staff.

Table 8.2   *Theory X and Theory Y*

Theory X	**Theory Y**
Work is inherently distasteful	*Work is as natural and enjoyable as play*
People:	People:
are not ambitious	need to set and achieve goals
are not creative	are creative problem solvers
do not wish to solve problems	need the recognition from peers that success brings
must be coerced	need to enhance their self-esteem
desire to be told what to do	through successful achievement can be self-directed
need to be controlled	need the space to create and learn

McGregor (1960) suggests that managers fall into two groups, those that think people need to be controlled and coerced, and those that think that the manager's role is to ensure the conditions are right for their development, growth and improvement. These types he calls Theory X and Theory Y. Table 8.2 gives more details of McGregor's theories.

Herzberg (1966) outlines a series of 'Hygiene' factors that need to be 'cleaned up' and sorted out as a prerequisite for keeping people satisfied. These are:

- organisational policies and administration;
- management;
- working conditions;
- interpersonal relationships;
- money, status and security.

In addition, Herzberg argues that there are 'motivators'. These are outlined in Table 8.3 below.

Table 8.3   *Herzberg's motivators*

Achievement
- to attain the goals set for quality of learning
- to use your full range of talents and to achieve more
- to try to test new ideas

Responsibility
- to make one's own decisions
- to control the quality of one's own work

Recognition
- to receive positive feedback from pupils, staff and managers
- to identify and share problems and concerns

Advancement
- to be promoted in terms of status and position

Work content
- involvement in work that is interesting and personally significant challenge

Personal growth
- learning and maturing

Handy (1976) outlines a motivation theory which emphasises the choices staff have. While he accepts certain needs and aspirations being essential human characteristics, there needs to be clarity of purpose and competence to achieve these purposes. Recognition and feedback are also essential. These factors can encourage what he calls the 'E factors' of effort, enthusiasm, excitement and the expenditure of energy.

Table 8.4 *Handy's motivation factors*

Needs and aspirations
   Affiliation
   Appreciation
   Achievement
   Influence
   Ownership

The E factors
   Effort
   Energy
   Enthusiasm
   Excitement
   Expenditure

Purpose and end result
   Clarity about
   Commitment to
   Recognition of
   Feedback about

For middle managers, the implications of these theories of motivation are considerable. All three provide ideas about factors in the work environment that can enhance motivation. You need to think about the team of people that you work with and what motivates them and how far you are able to create the factors which motivate staff.

Activity 8.3 What motivates you?

Read the description of motivating factors above and identify those which motivate you. What ways do you try to motivate staff? How far do the theories explain why Investors in People motivates staff? Record your thoughts in your reflective journal.

Celebration of success

One of the tensions you will need to manage is the degree to which you celebrate success and the degree to which you attend to failure. There is a popular adage that nothing succeeds like success. Success is motivating and where it is recognised and celebrated can inspire further successes.

Management Story

A manager met regularly with each member of staff. The discussion centred around the success that was being achieved. The success was analysed and the key factors behind the success were analysed. Failures were rarely explored. When the manager was asked about this strategy, he explained that little can be learned from failures. What staff needed was to understand what made them successful and to repeat those conditions in future work.

There is a danger, however, that celebration of success can become an end in itself, leading to an uncritical acceptance of poor performance. There should be, at times, some attention drawn to failures or underachievement. This can be achieved in a positive way by looking at the factors that cause failure and seeking strategies for improvement.

Challenge and support

Implicit in the Investors in People standard and the theories about motivation is the need to establish challenging goals and targets for staff. The word 'challenge', however, has a number of meanings including:

- to invite or summon someone to do something;
- to call something into question;
- to make demands upon;
- to stimulate;
- to make a formal objection to;
- a call to engage in a fight, argument or contest;
- questioning a fact, statement or act;
- to establish a goal or target for someone.

Perhaps rather too much emphasis has been put upon the robust and aggressive interpretation of this word, in the cause of an argument or contest. The view that 'they are not doing what they should be' pervades the blaming school of management. However, there are other alternatives. Inviting staff to act is challenging, particularly where goals and targets are established. These can be negotiated collaboratively.

In several senses of the word there is an element of 'confronting', yet this does not necessarily have to be achieved in an aggressive manner. Confronting staff needs to be objective and focused on actions and outcomes. It can be non-judgemental, in the sense of presenting evidence of differences between:

- what staff say they do and what is actually done; or
- what staff think they do and what is actually done; or
- the implications of a course of actions and the intentions; or
- the impact a course of action is having and the intentions.

'Confronting' is a process of feeding back information. Clearly, this has to be done sensitively and even so can lead to strong emotional feelings. There does not have to be conflict because there is not the sense of competition and the sense of winning, but there is more a sense of supporting the achievement and development of agreed goals by collaborative action. In this case the action involves giving feedback.

If you need to reprimand staff for something they have done badly you may consider some of the following derived from the work of Blanchard and Johnson (1983):

- tell people beforehand that you are going to let them know how they are doing;
- tell people clearly and straightforwardly what they did and why it was poor;
- be specific and concentrate upon the actions and events;
- tell people about how it makes you feel;
- allow people to appreciate your feelings;
- reaffirm your positive regard for them as people;
- reaffirm that you think well of them as people but not their actions in this specific case;
- show warmth;
- confirm that the reprimand is over.

Individual differences

Both support and staff development needs to be tailored to the needs of individuals. Rather too much staff development at the whole school level focuses on the needs of the school rather than of the individual. If all staff meet on an inset day for a session of 'awareness raising' on some whole-school issue, this is the antithesis of good practice, wasteful of a scarce commodity and patronising to experienced staff.

Middle managers, taking on the role of facilitators of staff development, are working with a small enough focus to ensure that the individual teacher's needs are not lost within a whole-school priority.

One of the most obvious ways of conceptualising individual differences is by using the idea of stages of career suggested by the work of Leithwood (1990). This suggests four stages, each with particular support and staff development needs (see Table 8.5)

Table 8.5 *Leithwood's stages of your career*

Launching your career
> putting into practice the ideas derived from training
> taking sole and continuous responsibility for the first time
> searching for resources and ideas
> making sense of experience

Stabilising
> developing mature commitment
> feeling at ease
> seeking more responsibility and promotion
> new challenges and concerns
> diversifying, seeking added responsibilities

Reaching a professional plateau
> reappraisal
> sense of mortality
> ceasing striving for promotion
> stagnation
> cynicism

Preparing for retirement

Activity 8.4 Support and Staff Development

How does your support and approach to developing your staff vary according to the career stages of your staff? How do you vary your approach according to other individual differences? Record your thoughts in your reflective journal.

What needs developing?

There is a surfeit of terminology about staff development. Here we shall distinguish between three terms:

- personal development;
- personal professional development;
- professional development.

Where 'personal development' is supported, teachers attend courses or training to meet their own personal needs and agenda. The idea of sabbaticals fits into this mould. In the late 1990s, perhaps with increased accountability, interest in measuring the impact of staff development on training, or perhaps because of the need to be more careful with resources, 'personal development' is more difficult to justify. You may want to question this view, however. It is sometimes difficult to identify clearly the impact of any single activity on the quality of teaching and learning in the department.

Observation of one teacher's lessons, for example, showed that there was a consistent pattern of making derogatory remarks about pupils and their work. Often these were unnecessary asides or thoughts in passing. To one student, for example, the teacher opened with, 'We know what your problems are Samantha, but can you tell me what the problems of Germany were before the First World War?' The class were often told that the work they were doing was much simplified and reduced to meet their needs. Clearly, the teacher was reinforcing low expectations. Although the teacher may have had a range of skills, her own personal development had created a style that was not conducive to effective teaching.

It may be that there are members of your department who would benefit from activities that seem far removed from classroom life, and yet which would impact on the quality of teaching and learning, perhaps in the knowledge that may be brought to the classroom, or perhaps the skills that may be transferred into it, or perhaps because of the refreshment and energy gained. It could be argued that the teacher was not in need of skill development but a change of attitude. New attitudes might well be developed as a result of personal development programmes.

Personal professional development is about the development of an individual's skills and qualities for their personal professional life. While this may have an impact upon the department it also covers the development of skills beyond the department, such as the acquisition of management skills in order to take up future posts of responsibility.

Professional development in a more general sense is concerned with the development of knowledge, skills and attitudes which may in the main be focused upon the needs and goals of the school, department or team. Such development assumes that the school and department are clear about their development priorities and the staff development needs. Often these may be clear in the general sense of knowing the department is not good at, for example, using IT in the learning process. How this is developed with individual teachers however, is a different matter. It may be that some teachers are aware of the uses of IT, but need time to work through some examples and plan their use in the classroom. It may be that some teachers don't know how to switch the machines on or are fearful of damaging them. The kind of staff development may vary according to individual need but under the general heading of improving the use of IT.

Managing the development of staff is about finding the right balance between the different forms of staff development so that the needs of the department are maximised. The impact of staff development activities is not always easy to measure immediately.

Developing classroom skills

Despite our previous emphasis on providing a balance between personal and professional development, our immediate concern and emphasis must be upon the professional development of staff that has impact upon classroom practice. The immediate skills required are identified in Chapters 9 and 10 of this book, which deal with improving the quality of learning and teaching.

Dean (1991) suggests the following agenda for staff development focusing on the classroom:

- terms and conditions of employment;
- school information;
- child development;
- theoretical knowledge of learning;
- classroom practice;
- the motivation of pupils;
- content knowledge;
- communication skills;
- ability to observe children and young people;
- skill in recognising the stage the pupil has reached;
- the ability to plan and organise;
- the ability to help pupils structure their learning;
- the ability to help pupils develop cognitive skills;
- the ability to coach pupils in skills;
- skill in problem solving;
- skill in controlling children and young people;
- evaluative skills.

Some of these are directly used in the classroom. The suggestion that content knowledge should be a focus is apt for two reasons. First, in the UK, OFSTED inspection uses the extent of subject knowledge as a major criterion for assessing quality of teaching. Secondly, in some subjects, particularly, we can no longer take subject knowledge for granted. Subjects like geography and science change. Other subjects are often taught by specialists in specific or different fields. Within science faculties, biologists may be called upon to teach chemistry and physics. English teachers may be called upon to teach drama.

However, there are other skills which impact upon the quality of teaching and learning, such as competence as managers of aspects of the work of the department or personal skills such as communicating with colleagues. These competences have been listed in Chapter 2.

Effective staff development activities

Joyce and Showers (1988) have outlined the results of their research into the effect of training components. This illustrates that the most effective training is that which has an impact upon the knowledge, skill and transfer of the training to practice. This is achieved through providing information and theory, demonstration and practice, and feedback on practice and coaching. It may be suggested that, only if all components are present will in-service training have a real and continuing impact upon practice.

The middle manager is in a key position to ensure that theory is outlined, demonstrated and practised, and to provide coaching and feedback on practice.

Table 8.6 *The effect of training*

Component	Outcome
Information	+
Theory	++
Demonstration	+++
Theory, demonstration, practice	++++
Theory, demonstration, practice, feedback.	++++++
Theory, demonstration, practice, feedback, coaching	++++++++

Coaching and mentoring

Coaching is defined as 'to tutor, to train, to give hints, or to prime with facts'. While few use the word 'coach' with regard to education in the UK, many middle managers see themselves supporting staff by these methods. Coaching is likely to be most useful with inexperienced staff or to support the use of a new approach.

Figure 8.1 illustrates the steps to coaching, suggested by Parsloe (1992). He describes four steps of coaching, starting with analysing and assessing the situation and planning a solution. The final two steps are the solution being implemented and evaluation of the results.

Analysis involves assessing current performance and identifying achievable targets. Planning a solution involves the negotiation of appropriate learning activities and timescales. While plans are being implemented there is an opportunity for the coach to demonstrate, provide practice opportunities and feedback.

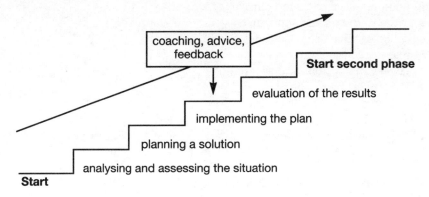

Figure 8.1   *The steps to mentoring*

Being a mentor involves working as a trusted adviser and counsellor. Parsloe defines the mentor as someone who acts as a guide, adviser and counsellor at various stages in someone's career. Mentoring may involve both career advice and support for the achieving of specific targets. Mentors need the skills to be able to reassure, to help in problem solving and with thinking up new strategies. The mentor should motivate and create the enthusiasm for success, while being challenging.

Consultancy skills

Under the heading 'Who needs consultancy skills?' Cockman *et al.* (1992) state: 'Anyone who is in a role where the main emphasis is on helping individuals, departments or organisations to be more effective in whatever they do, can be considered to be a consultant.'

They go on to outline a process and approach to consultancy that is client centred. This approach, when applied to middle managers, is largely based upon:

- starting where the member of staff is;
- allowing staff to diagnose their own problems and to suggest solutions;
- helping staff make their own sense of what they see going on;
- assisting staff to set their own plans for action.

The key to client-centred consultancy is supporting the client to take responsibility for their own problems and solutions. The process has a formal cycle composed of:

- making initial contact;
- establishing a clear contract;
- collecting data;
- making sense of the data;
- generating options and planning;
- implementing the plans;
- disengaging and arranging any follow-up activities.

Client centred consultants use different 'intervention styles' to facilitate learning and development. The four intervention styles that Cockman *et al.* distinguish are called acceptant, catalytic, confrontational and prescriptive. The acceptant style involves listening with empathy and providing emotional support. The style is non-judgemental and supports the client in exploring the emotions which often block our ability to deal rationally with situations.

The catalytic style allows the client to gather and explore their own observations and to analyse them for themselves. The style allows the client to find their own solutions. The confrontational style seeks to confront staff with the gap between what they say and do, or the gap between two conflicting statements. Prescriptive consultancy is probably the most commonly used. Here the solution is offered as a 'quick fix'. As long as the diagnosis of the problem is correct the answer may be the correct one. However, the member of staff must be able to accept, understand and implement the solution. A problem of prescription is that it allows the member of staff to relinquish ownership of the situation and become dependent upon the consultant's solutions. Table 8.7 lists types of questions using different consultancy styles.

Table 8.7 *Consultancy styles and questions*

Prescriptive
    You need to...
    You have to...

Catalytic
    Tell me about...
    What happens if...

Who else does it affect...
What have you tried...
What are the options...

Confronting
You say ... but you (do)...
You say you want ... although you seem to...

Acceptant
How does it feel when...

Activity 8.5 Questioning as a consultant

Look at the questions in Table 8.7. Which sort of questions do you generally use? Which is your preferred style of consultancy? Do you find this is as successful as you would wish? How do you feel acting as a consultant to staff? Record your thoughts in your reflective journal.

Classroom observation and feedback

Considerable literature exists concerning the observation of classrooms and giving feedback for instance in the work of Hopkins (1985), West and Bollington (1988), and Terrell *et al.* (1996). The authors of these works report that classroom observation can be a major factor in improving the quality of teaching and learning. Objections to classroom observation often revolve around lack of time. Nevertheless, classroom observation has such a considerable impact that you should find some time to support your colleagues in this way.

We propose, following the work of Cockman *et al.* (1992), a five phase model for planning classroom observation, including:

1. gaining entry to your colleague's classroom;
2. making a contract with your colleagues;
3. collecting data;
4. analysing the data;
5. making plans for improvement.

In the gaining entry phase, you will need to establish your reputation as a collaborative, supportive and trustworthy leader and manager. You will have made clear, by your actions in the past, that all evaluative exercises are processes that reveal learning points for both you, as the manager, and the classroom teacher. All observations are likely to have many different interpretations and to be only partial attempts at portraying what goes on in classrooms. This needs to be understood by all parties concerned. The need for classroom observation will have been established by you before attempting the next phase.

The second phase is to make a clear agreement about the purpose of the observation, the focus and the process. The purpose of the observation, which will need to be discussed, will centre around improving practice and making a significant impact upon the quality of the teacher's working life. You will need to discuss what issues concern the teacher and what they think would help them. Suggested focal points for the observation can be selected from:

- the teacher's suggestions;
- the good practice statements in Chapter 10;
- the OFSTED handbook;
- development priorities.

Once agreement is made about a focus, you should agree what data to collect and how it should be collected. Using audio or video tape should be considered, although, frequently, observers make notes on some form of observation record. Terrell *et al.* (1996) and Hopkins (1985) are two sources of format for such observation records.

The third phase is to collect the data using the method which has been agreed.

Phase four is to analyse the data to decide what it means and to establish target areas for action. The first part of this process is to provide feedback to your colleague of the events that have been observed. Wherever possible, it is wise to remove any judgements or explanations. The second part of this discussion needs to be a discussion about possible judgements of quality, noting the good and the bad. There should be some discussion of cause and effect. The last phase is to identify the key areas for development.

Once the key areas are identified, more detailed plans can be made to establish, by negotiation, more specific targets and plans for supporting the achievement of these. The good practice statements in Chapter 10 will be of help in describing the exact nature of the practice that needs to be achieved. Use these as a model to be adapted by you. Remember to include actions by both you and the teacher. Agree activities that will support the achievement of targets, such as a period of experimentation, or observation of another teacher's classroom, or the opportunity for further feedback.

In some cases, it may be possible for you to tie in classroom observation into the system of appraisal operating in your school.

School teacher appraisal

School teacher appraisal is now a statutory requirement in the UK following The Education (School Teacher Appraisal) Regulations 1991 and DES Circular 12/91. These regulations call for all schools to have a policy for appraisal to meet a set of central government requirements outlined in the regulations. There are, therefore, differences in approach between schools within a common framework.

Appraisal regulations cover all school teachers and teaching staff must be appraised within the two-year cycle established by the regulations. Managers themselves are appraised and this may be an opportunity for your own management development. Non-teaching staff ought to be part of an appraisal process.

The appraisal cycle includes an initial planning meeting between appraiser and appraisee. A session observing classroom practice is planned and other information gathered. At a professional development interview, a two-way discussion can take place reviewing the achievements of the teacher, the support offered within the school and identifying targets for future action. Normally a review meeting is arranged to complete the first appraisal cycle and embark upon the second.

An official record is a requirement of the legislation. This is a statement about what occurred during the appraisal and the identified targets for action. The record is normally confidential to the head teacher, the appraiser and appraisee, although the targets for development action may be shared more widely with, for example, a school in-service training coordinator.

Appraisal can provide a major opportunity for professional development and the improvement of teaching and learning within the department. However, to be effective the process requires:

- commitment and enthusiasm of the middle manager;
- commitment through involvement in the process and personal interest in the outcomes by the teacher;
- understanding of the nature of development and the part played by appraisal;
- selection of 'SMART' targets;
- development actions supporting the achievement of personal targets;
- that the process is challenging but supportive.

'SMART' targets are those that are *specific, measurable, achievable, realistic* and *targetable*. In some appraisal schemes, middle managers are not the appraisers of staff within the department. This may make using appraisal as a means of supporting the development of your staff more difficult.

Activity 8.6 Teacher appraisal

You must read the school appraisal policy. How do you see your role in terms of appraisal? How will you be able to establish this role with colleagues? How will you create a comfortable atmosphere which is also challenging? Record your thoughts in your reflective journal.

Getting the best out of your team

Throughout this book, we emphasise the importance of understanding the staff with whom you work. In particular, we highlight the importance for the middle manager to understand the different beliefs and values held by staff, and how these influence the way they approach their work. We also emphasise the importance of adopting a style of leadership and management appropriate to the individual context of the institution. The effective functioning of teams depends on the extent to which these different factors – values, beliefs, management and leadership styles – are complementary.

Handy (1976), outlined four stages of development of groups.

- *Forming* is where the group is a collection of individuals. The purpose of the group, its composition and organisation is discussed. Individuals establish their positions in and towards the group.
- *Storming* is where the group is in conflict as purposes and roles are worked out in practice. There are many individual agendas and some personal hostility.
- *Norming* is where the group establishes a set of norms and ways of working, including how decisions are made and carried out, how each member should behave and so on.
- *Performing* is where the previous three stages have been successful and the group starts to be really effective in achieving its goals

While the Handy categories are most relevant to the creation of new teams, some long-established teams may be locked into an early phase of formation. You can use the Handy description to assess where your team is in its internal development. Handy goes on to outline several characteristics of effective teams including the following:

- *Goals:* which are clear, shared, and important to the individuals in the group;
- *Participation:* where all participants are active and listened to in discussion;
- *Feelings:* which are freely expressed and responded to;
- *Group problems:* which are diagnosed and remedied, acting on the causes;
- *Leadership:* where leaders emerge to meet particular needs;
- *Decisions:* that are made through consensus, yet discerning voices are used to improve decisions;
- *Trust:* team members trust one another and can express negative reactions without fear;
- *Creativity:* the team seeks new and better ways of working.

Activity 8.7 Team analysis

Analyse the health of your team using the descriptions above. Indicate what you think are the main priorities to work upon and strategies for doing this. Record your thoughts in your reflective journal.

Conclusion

In this chapter the focus has been upon getting the best out of your staff. We have concentrated on ways of motivating people and approaches to developing their professional skills to get higher standards of performance from them. The next chapters look at ways of raising achievement through getting the best out of pupils.

Part IV   Teaching and Learning

Chapter 9

Talking about Good Teaching and Learning

'I have come increasingly to recognise that most learning in most settings is a communal activity, a sharing of the culture.'

(Bruner, 1986, p. 127)

Think back to the last few department meetings that you have attended or led. What were the major agenda items at each of these meetings? What proportion of time was allocated to discussing pedagogy, to sharing subject knowledge or exploring notions of good teaching and learning? Many departments feel under constant pressure from internal and external sources to improve the standards of pupils' work and this pressure is often translated into tensions concerning administration or lesson content. Each colleague, working within a department, has a clear, if unstated, notion of what constitutes sound teaching and learning practices. If all these individual, unstated conceptions match, the department may be providing consistency of approach and of expectations of the learning and teaching processes. If, however, these perceptions do not match and the conceptual differences are not shared or explored, a potential source of genuine improvement for the department is not being tapped. Research undertaken by Harris *et al.* (1996) revealed that effective departments are able to establish, organise and manage effective teaching and learning. It is the process of defining and establishing effective teaching and learning that is sometimes omitted from the departmental agenda.

The major focus of this chapter is the notion of improving the quality of teaching and learning within the department through finding time to talk about good teaching and learning. The chapter, therefore, aims to revisit explorations of what constitutes effective classroom practice, to explore ways of managing and enabling the sharing of ideas and good practice across the department, to examine potential means of communicating departmental practice to others and to discuss possibilities for monitoring practice across the department.

The threads running throughout the chapter are that of the learner's active involvement with the learning, the teacher's role in enabling this to happen and the middle manager's role in facilitating the whole process. Clearly, a key issue within this framework is that of communication.

Exploring and developing models held by colleagues

'To be asked to talk about the ordinary, everyday familiar things one does spontaneously, routinely, habitually in the classroom, is to be presented with a very difficult task. The things which are done automatically, even unconsciously, are the hardest to articulate and, in normal circumstances, teachers are rarely required to make them explicit.'

(Brown and McIntyre, 1993, p. 34)

In schools, initiatives can fail simply because it is assumed that the teachers share a common vision of teaching. Time spent within the department exploring and sharing individual visions of what constitutes good teaching and learning practices in your particular subject may well bear fruit in terms of improving practice across the team. Such exploration, coupled with a brief examination of individual pupils' preferred learning styles, could form a sound basis for a department in-service session. An exercise for the department to undertake initially as individuals and then to share could be to think back to a significant 'learning event' in their own lives and start to examine what constituted the significance. Table 9.1 might act as a prompt.

Table 9.1 *Significant learning events*

---

1. Talk about a time in your education where you felt that you learnt something well – that you had a positive learning experience.

   You might wish to discuss the experience in terms of the following:
   - skills
   - knowledge
   - attitude
   - personal development
   - self-esteem.

   Was the model of teaching/learning based on

   TRANSMISSION or CONSTRUCTION?

Some additional questions:
   - What was the teacher doing?
   - What was the learner (you) doing?
   - Were there any relevant factors?

2. Think back over your personal history of learning. What were the different types of learning that you were exposed to? These might vary between the different phases of your education or may well have altered according to the different styles of different teachers.

You could describe your experiences in prose, in chart form, in a diagram or pictorially.

Activity 9.1 Significant Learning Events

Look at Table 9.1 and undertake this exercise on your own. Record your thoughts in your reflective journal.

Further exercises designed to enable exploration of individual understandings of teaching and learning are provided in Chapter 4.

Undertaking such a task as outlined in Table 9.1 can prove problematic for the department and/or the manager for a number of reasons. Practical issues such as lack of time can prevent such discussions from taking place. Teachers' reluctance to expose their thinking on potentially sensitive areas such as professional practice might also erect barriers. Once the discussions are under way, there might be interesting, but potentially sensitive issues of difference due to cultural background, ethnicity or class. The manager needs to be aware of potential pitfalls so that the discussions can be empowering rather than debilitating. Cultural background can have a profound effect on the way in which teachers view children, the processes of teaching and learning, and their own professional role in the classroom. Cullingford (1995, p. 165) cites the work of Osborne and Broadfoot, noting such cultural differences between primary classrooms observed in France and England. The differences include such dimensions as seeing knowledge as content or knowledge as process; learning as social or learning as individual; the teacher in control or the child in control. In each of these examples, the first were apparent in French classrooms, the second in British classrooms. Of course, such differences may not be due to the country in which we are educated, but the culture of teaching and learning in which we work.

As discussed in Chapter 4, teachers' personal understanding of their role in these processes of teaching and learning can have an impact on their effectiveness in the classroom. We would wish to argue that regardless of the personal view held by teachers, it is the level of expectation of the pupils which is paramount to the pupils achieving and gaining a genuine sense of success.

Cullingford (op. cit.) reinforces this view when he states, 'what characterises success in teachers most of all is the expectation of success'. Expectations of pupils, both as individuals as well as groups, must be explored across the department, along with positive strategies for raising expectations where necessary.

On a practical note, teachers will sometimes report that they have little time to engage in professional discussion. This includes talking to colleagues within the school and even in the department. However, clearly there are some departments which often find time to talk over coffee, at lunch break and after school. Some of these have the advantage of a departmental base or a place to work in when not in the classroom, which can act as a suitable meeting room. Such helpful environmental conditions can encourage staff to talk about their work on an informal basis which can then ease the process of discussions about teaching and learning at a more formal level.

Exploring other models of teaching and learning

Having explored personal and departmental views and beliefs about teaching and learning, it might be useful to revisit some of the models that we were presented with when in our initial training. Many colleagues will remember major theorists from such training, but a revisit is sometimes useful in order to examine how our own practice reflects or rejects such theories. Do we set up our classrooms so that a constructivist model of learning can be played out? Do we value and encourage independent/individual learning or are our efforts centred on enabling and encouraging pupils to talk to each other, working collaboratively and learning through and with each other? Discussing such practices via exploring the major theorists such as Piaget, Bruner, Vygotsky or Feuerstein also has the advantage of taking the debate away from the individual. Claxton (1984) is of interest in his work about how people learn. The checklist in Table 9.2 is derived from his ideas and again may be used as a prompt for departmental discussions.

Table 9.2 *Teaching and learning checklist (adapted from Claxton, 1984)*

Thinking back to your own schooling…
- Were you encouraged to discuss what mattered to you?
- Were you encouraged to evaluate your own solutions?
- Were you encouraged to experiment with who you were?
- Were you encouraged to collaborate?
- Were you allowed to be vague and hazy?
- Were you encouraged to give up?
- Were you taught that play is valuable?
- Were your powers of mental play – fantasy, imagination – expanded?

- Were you given time?
- Were you taught the techniques of relaxation and meditation?
- Were you encouraged to be unconventional?
- Were you encouraged to look inside yourself for answers?
- Were you listened to attentively?
- Were you encouraged to test and question what you and others had taken for granted?
- Were you taught how to understand things?
- Were you taught how to remember things?
- Were you shown models of resourcefulness and flexibility?
- Were you helped to become a good learner?

From their research into effective teaching and learning, Cooper and McIntyre (1996) listed important common aspects of approches to teaching and learning that were perceived to be effective:

- clear goals for pupil learning;
- clarity of communication of lesson goals and agenda to pupils;
- use of preview and review of lesson content;
- helping pupils to contextualise content in terms of their own experience and knowledge, as well as in terms of other teaching goals and learning experiences;
- some willingness to allow pupils to have input into goal and agenda setting;
- supportive social context designed by teachers to help pupils feel accepted, cared for and valued;
- ability and willingness to allow for different cognitive styles and ways of engaging in the learning process among pupils, through multiple exemplification, the use of different types of illustration and mode of presentation, and offering pupils a choice from a menu of possible ways of engaging;
- willingness to take account of pupil circumstances and to modify/pace/structure learning tasks accordingly.

Taking this 'list' and comparing and contrasting it with current practice in the department might be of value to the department. It is sometimes easier to explore thoughts when presented with a concrete model against which to compare own thinking. When looking at the above model, the department might like to consider the following questions:

- Are there any points that we would like to incorporate into our own practice?
- If so, what would need to change?

- What would be the implications of such change?
- Are there potential conflicts between our individual model and that of colleagues?

There is a role here for employing action research in our own classrooms. Those colleagues who have actively undertaken small-scale enquiries into their own/departmental practice have reaped enormous benefit to both their teaching and ultimately the pupils' learning. The following comments were made by teachers after undertaking a higher education module entitled 'Raising Achievement Through Improving Teaching and Learning', using an action research process:

> 'I believe the undertaking of this module has helped me to improve my teaching skills by increasing my awareness of the need to acknowledge pupils' achievement and the use of rewards.'

> 'Achievement raised!! I feel more confident in my approach to maths.'

> 'I have started to implement some strategies to improve the boys' reading.'

> 'Enabled me to have a better understanding of the relationship between theory and classroom practice.'

> 'New improved lessons on refraction have resulted from undertaking this module.'

For additional material on effective teaching and learning, parts of an Australian document entitled 'Principles of Effective Learning and Teaching' are included in the Appendix to this volume. This has been produced by the Queensland Department of Education and sections could prove useful as prompts for discussion.

The purpose of identifying good teaching and learning

So why identify and share our visions of quality teaching and learning? Chapter 10 explores the issue of raising attainment through improving practice. It is essential that there is a sense of shared understanding by members of the teaching group as to what good practice entails. We need to communicate with each other about our goals, expectations and methods. In addition, these notions of good practice need to be communicated to colleagues in other departments and to outside audiences. Developing a policy for teaching and learning in the department might enable such communication to take place. Such a policy should:

- clarify expectations of staff and students;
- form the basis for evaluation and development of the department;
- form the basis for staff development;

- form the basis of in-depth discussion of learning in the department;
- link with school aims, policies and practice.

Suggestions of ways of identifying and agreeing good practice in the department can be found in the OFSTED Handbook and Guidance and, of course, within the literature and models of teaching and learning. Table 9.3 may be of some help, as a checklist, in establishing current and desired classroom practice.

Table 9.3   *Checklist of classroom practice*

☐ Collaborative groupwork
☐ Experiential learning
☐ Resource-based learning
☐ Role play
☐ Active learning
☐ Discussion groups
☐ Student-centred learning
☐ Use of IT in learning
☐ Teaching styles and strategies
☐ Classroom tasks
☐ TIme on task
☐ Talk in the classroom
☐ Asking questions
☐ Using texts
☐ Teacher behaviour and types
☐ Teacher expectations and self-fulfilling prophecies
☐ Involving the pupils in their learning
☐ Involving pupils in monitoring their progress

You may find it helpful to use the headings in Table 9.3 to discuss current and desired practice. If the group decides to implement new practice, it might be appropriate to develop a mini 'action plan' for each initiative. Basing the discussion around the following questions may be of use:

- Why do we wish to incorporate this?
- How might we incorporate this?
- What will we need to do?
- Where and when will we implement this?
- What is our preferred timescale?
- How will we evaluate our success?

It would be useful to begin to collect together examples of good practice from elsewhere, not simply within the subject area, but also in terms of developing skills within the classroom. One example would be the discussion of best practice with texts which can be found within the 'Directed Activities Related to Texts' (DARTs) materials (Lunzer and Gardner, 1984).

Communicating good practice to a wider audience

The arguments above have outlined the need to communicate visions, values and beliefs of the department to each other and to those outside the department. The scheme of work has a key role to play here. Not only should it communicate the aims, but it is also one way of ensuring that the department is an integral part of the whole school. The essential tool for planning the contribution of the department is the scheme of work. This can be used as a tool for recording the contribution of each department to the whole curriculum and for ensuring that everything is covered. The scheme of work can also be used to ensure curriculum entitlement for all pupils. Constructing the scheme of work is an essential task for the department and one that emphasises its focus on teaching and learning.

Harris *et al.* (1996) report that, 'the real success of the effective departments lay in their ability to organise the key elements of the teaching and learning process in an optimum way. All the effective departments had detailed and agreed schemes of work that had been collectively approved'. They go on to emphasise that the scheme needs to be consistent with the general vision of the department, be detailed, clear and accessible, and agreed through departmental discussion.

Members of the department need to be actively involved in the creation of the scheme of work and to create a scheme that they feel is appropriate for their preferred ways of working. In addition, staff need to be convinced of the appropriate contribution that their subject makes to the whole curriculum. They may feel that there is not enough time to do it all and that it isn't part of their role in delivering their subject to make such a whole school contribution. Staff may resent being constrained by the scheme of work, arguing that it is inflexible. These feelings and concerns need to be explored and answered.

Monitoring the quality of teaching and learning within the department

> 'Teaching, like nursing, engineering, journalism... is an activity which entails reflection on what one has done in order to become more accomplished. This kind of reflection on doing has been called "practical reasoning". It is a form of reasoning in which envisaged ends and practical means are considered jointly in order to improve practice. Whatever our criteria for judging effectiveness, such practical reasoning cannot be spelt out in operational terms, but only in terms of teachers' reflective understanding of their own practices with regard to specific areas of the curriculum, assessment and pedagogy.' (Adelman, 1989)

Regardless of the processes involved with monitoring and evaluating (see Chapter 12), the importance of individual teachers maintaining and improving their own expertise in their broad subject base is of real consequence.

They need to have access to current thinking and developments both in their subject base and within the broader framework of changing practices. Within a national framework of decreasing funds for in-service work, ways of sharing and encouraging knowledge expertise need to be constructed. One possible way of doing this would be for a group of schools to come together within a geographical area, to share subject knowledge as well as methodology. There is a real problem with this suggestion in areas where schools are in direct competition with each other and are reluctant to share expertise. Ensuring that the department is affiliated to a national subject body (ALL – Association for Language Learning; NATE – National Association for Teachers of English; ASE – Association of Science Education would all be examples of such national bodies), and has access to its materials and conferences, might be a way round this.

Staff need access to educational libraries. It is useful and highly appropriate to establish and update a teacher resource area in the department base, where possible. If the school works in partnership with a university education department, there may be ways in which teaching staff could have access to the university library. As part of a mentoring scheme, some universities offer in-service modules at reduced rates for mentors, with full library membership as part of the package. Once relationships between school colleagues and university staff are established, there may be possibilities for collaboration with courses and in-service work, once again broadening the knowledge base for all parties. Such potential sources need to be tapped.

Using meeting time for raising the issues of teaching and learning has been discussed at length, but using such time for collaborative monitoring and evaluation also needs to be highlighted. Once the debate has been opened, further discussion will need to take place in order for colleagues to continue with a sense of ownership. This is crucial if improvements to the quality of the teaching and learning are to take place. Once again, the possibility of using action research methods to monitor progress collaboratively might be considered. A potential starting point may be to provide the opportunity for colleagues to observe each other, following an agreed framework. This probably works best when undertaken informally and within a shared notion of support. It could also link in with aspects of appraisal if this was felt to be appropriate. However the monitoring takes place, it is clearly useful and important for the internal monitoring to reflect external foci such as the OFSTED framework. The overall aim of monitoring and evaluating practice within the department must be that of empowering the individual teacher to 'do the job better', and to lead to a greater sense of satisfaction and self-worth, without placing yet more stress on the teacher in the classroom. Talking and sharing expectations, concerns and evaluations should help with this process.

Conclusion

The key focus throughout has been on communication; reflecting on one's own values, visions and beliefs; communicating and sharing these values with immediate colleagues; and communicating our aims and intentions to those outside the department. Pupils' active involvement in their learning – and teachers' active involvement in their learning and teaching is crucial. In order for active involvement to take place, the learner, be it teacher or pupil, needs to have intrinsic interest in the subject/content, or she or he needs to be interested in the process or approach of the 'teacher'. The learner needs to feel motivated by either intrinsic or extrinsic outcomes. We feel strongly that the role of learner remains remarkably similar, whether it is a pupil learning French in year 9, or a teacher being encouraged to reflect on their methodology. For both situations to achieve successful outcomes, the middle manager's role in enabling and facilitating the process is of the utmost importance.

Chapter 10

Raising Attainment Through Improving Teaching and Learning

Many schools are concerned to raise the level of attainment of pupils, particularly with regard to the attainment of external standards such as GCSE in the UK, or National Curriculum tests. Our view is that middle managers need to be concerned with the attainment of pupils at all levels of ability. In some schools, the major task is to raise general levels of attainment. In others it is to focus on the relative under-performance of the least able or the more able. The ideas we report here have been developed and used in a number of schools and are outlined more fully in an In-service Training Pack published by Framework Press entitled 'Raising Achievement at GCSE'. The pack is designed for use by middle managers as a training resource.

The reasons for pupil under-attainment will vary from school to school, department to department and teacher to teacher. Hence, there is a need to reflect upon the exact circumstances you are in now and to address the issues you feel are most important. Our experience has been that successful improvement, at departmental level, involves certain requirements. These include:

- the process should be collaborative, involving all department members;
- departments should be able to select the most appropriate strategies, from a range of alternatives, according to need;
- departments need to pay equal attention to the teaching of the subject, the learning experiences of the pupils and the structuring of pupils' written notes;
- departments should make the maximum use of information provided by examination boards;
- curriculum planning should be precise and targeted upon assessment criteria;

- the process of improvement should be led by the head of department, with the active support of senior management;
- teachers need to talk and think about the process of teaching and learning in their classrooms.

The most powerful and effective tool for improvement is to allow teachers to reflect, critically and systematically, upon their methods and approaches, as well as on their own attitudes and values which support their approach. Teachers then need to plan their own strategies to put things right. The process needs to be a learning experience, which may challenge long-held assumptions and beliefs and values about what works best.

Laying the foundations

The department must resolve a number of issues, as a precondition to successfully raising the level of attainment. These are developed from the work of Hopkins *et al.* (1994) outlined in Chapter 1. They include the following:

- staff believe the level of attainment can be improved;
- staff really want to raise levels of attainment;
- planning is collaborative;
- the teaching skills of staff are developed;
- there is leadership and coordination;
- staff are involved and participate in raising attainment;
- there is an emphasis on evaluation, enquiry and critical reflection.

Opinions may differ within the department about whether standards of attainment can be improved. Some may feel it can be improved and others not. Some staff may be prepared to attempt to raise achievement and others not. You need to develop the notion that the potential of your pupils is untapped. The evidence for this lies in the large numbers of people who didn't do well at school, yet go on as adults to achieve success, even in academic work. The success of the Open University, in the UK, is evidence of this.

Identifying good departmental practice

You need to create a discussion of what good teaching and learning practice looks like in your department and your curriculum area. This may enable the development of a consensus and the establishment of departmental priorities to work on, in order to raise attainment .

We begin here by looking at statements drawn from LEA and OFSTED inspection reports (Table 10.1).

Activity 10.1 Readiness and commitment

Consider the conditions outlined above. How far are these evident in your department? What strategies can you use to improve the conditions? Record your thoughts in your reflective journal.

Table 10.1   *Good practice in teaching and learning*

1. The department is aware of which groups of pupils are under-performing and has strategies for addressing their difficulties.
2. Assessment comments relate primarily to the subject content and concepts taught.
3. Pupils always know how their current level of performance stands in relation to the standards expected of the year group.
4. Pupils are knowledgeable about the structure of the course.
5. Pupils are regularly exposed to examples of good quality work.
6. Standards of work expected, and the depth and detail of syllabus coverage, should be the same for pupils of similar abilities in different classes.
7. Schemes of work accurately reflect the weighting of examination assessment criteria.
8. Pupils' books and files are uncluttered and have clear sections for information, notes, practice exercises, etc.
9. Pupils work from a wide range of texts and learning materials.
10. Teachers are sufficiently confident to devise their own pupil tasks without excessive reliance on textbooks.
11. Teachers' lesson planning should emphasise learning objectives, including desired outcomes in terms of pupil performance.
12. Pupils understand clearly, in each lesson, what they are expected to learn and in what detail they should demonstrate it.
13. Different tasks and targets are given to pupils of different abilities.
14. Wherever possible, pupils are allowed to explore tasks independently.
15. Pupils are encouraged to take a more active part in lessons, for example by taking rough notes or keeping their own records.
16. Homework is regular, varied and relevant.
17. Pupils are given adequate opportunities to talk about the subject in more depth.
18. Pupils are expected to demonstrate, retain and recall relevant background knowledge.
19. Teachers actively instruct pupils in revision techniques.
20. Teachers actively instruct pupils in how to devise strategies to help them apply prior learning to unfamiliar situations.

Activity 10.2 Good practice in teaching and learning

Consider the 20 statements in Table 10.1. Add your own if you wish. Consider how far these characteristics are displayed in your department. Devise possible focal points for improvement. Select the key areas which need to be worked upon in your department. What possible strategies might you employ? Record your thoughts in your reflective journal.

Assessing pupil progress and setting targets

A major key to raising the attainment of pupils is through regularly assessing pupil progress and setting targets for future achievement. If you know what grades individual pupils are likely to achieve, or ought to achieve, then you can measure whether they are performing sufficiently well or under-performing according to your estimates. Under-performance can be put right by investigation and targeting development. Inaccurate estimating, particularly underestimating future performance is pernicious, since it not only conveys low expectations to pupils but also is likely to be the basis of planning learning activities which are too easy for pupils and don't challenge them sufficiently.

In practice, monitoring performance is not easy. There may be few standardised assessment records that you can use which don't change frequently so that you can compare them over time. You will need to establish your own system if standardised or national systems do not exist. You will need to be careful that your system of assessment really identifies specific knowledge and skills that need to be developed.

Establishing base-line performance

It is important that you have some base-line against which to measure progress. You may be fortunate in being able to use assessment records from national testing such as the National Curriculum tests in the UK. Many secondary schools use non-verbal reasoning tests on entry. At worst you may need to devise your own assessments early in the pupil's career.

Prediction

You need to predict what you expect the attainment of pupils to be at the end of your courses, given your best estimate about their existing levels of ability and your experience of attainment achieved by pupils in the past. Although your estimate is not going to be precise, you do have some evidence on which to work. The expectations of teachers themselves is another starting point. The prediction needs to be for each individual pupil, as well as for classes and year groups.

In Figure 10.1, the whole of a previous cohort of pupils can be plotted on a graph showing your predictions for their grades and the grades they actually obtained. Ideally all pupils should attain the grades that you predict. Predictions may be higher than actual results or lower. There may be many reasons for this, however, systematic over-prediction of groups, or by particular teachers, may be symptomatic of a problem of low expectation or lack of support for some pupils. Poor prediction may indicate insufficient knowledge of the pupil's abilities or poor grasp of the criteria for assessment.

The graph, with the appropriate additional information, may identify under-performance compared to expectations of different ethnic groups or of different genders.

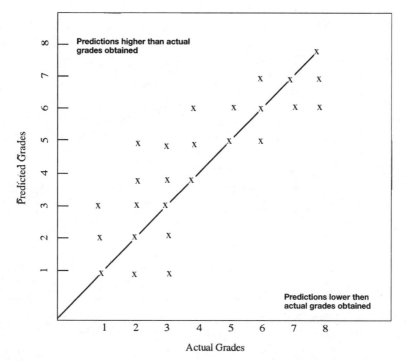

Figure 10.1   *Predicted and actual grades*

Review attainment

Teachers need to have a precise idea about the attainment of pupils and their progress so that they can give accurate and detailed advice to pupils. When attainment records are collated, they need to be reviewed. We have already shown how they can be reviewed against predictions. Attainment also needs to be compared to other subjects or the same subjects in other schools, particularly those with similar intake profiles. You need to know if pupils in your area under-perform compared to other subject areas. You need to know that at another school, doing the same subject, pupils would probably have achieved a different grade. Again, there may be many reasons for this. Some of these reasons can be put right by you. Some, such as differences in base line attainment, may be beyond you.

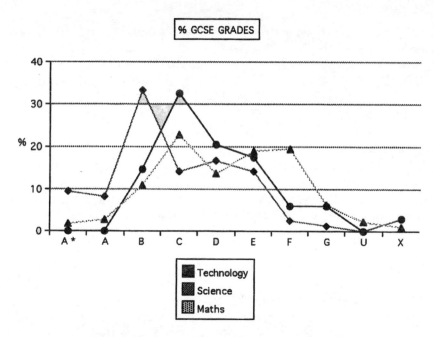

Figure 10.2 *Performance in the subject does not match performance in other subjects or other schools. (% of cohort entered for exam plotted against grades)*

In the above graph, you will see that a number of candidates are not achieving the same levels in one subject compared to other subjects. A graph drawn using the data from a similar school may show you that your pupils are not achieving what a comparable department in a comparable school is achieving.

Activity 10.3 Reviewing assessment

How do you review assessment scores? How might you review scores more systematically? Which departments would you be able to use as a comparison within the school and beyond? Record your thoughts in your reflective journal.

Establishing targets

Targets need to be set for pupils and staff, and for groups and individuals. These need to be based upon the predicted grades, plus a small but achievable addition to recognise improvement. Improvements ought to be targeted with particularly problematic groups such as the least able or underperforming boys. The targets should be recorded in study guides or on assessment records kept by pupils. Targets need to be frequently monitored, and pupils and teachers should use all formative assessment data as feedback on progress towards targets.

Pupils need a great deal of help understanding the meaning of targets and criteria. Teachers have to be very specific and performance needs to be measurable. It will be helpful to have level descriptors written for different performance levels. These are clear descriptions of what work should look like and what quality criteria are to be met at specific levels. Pupils can then be given a clear idea of what to aim for. Sample work at a corresponding level of attainment is also useful in target setting.

Activity 10.4 Establishing targets

How far do individual pupils understand the criteria for work they produce? Do they understand the criteria for work above the level of work they currently produce? How explicit are the comments teachers make about the actions students should take to make their work better? Record your thoughts in your reflective journal.

Curriculum planning

The starting point for high achievement is good curriculum planning for teaching and learning. If pupils and teachers are clear about the learning objectives of the teaching programme, they can then undertake activities to learn those objectives. Curriculum planning is essential to:

- provide a basis for planning individual lessons;
- provide a basis for ensuring lessons meet the needs of all levels of ability;
- ensure that all pupils have access to activities that maximise their grade potential;
- ensure that the whole of the syllabus is covered within the required period;
- plan for assessment exercises at appropriate points;
- plan resource use and allocation;
- balance the time spent teaching knowledge, skills and attitudes.

Plans should be at two levels. First there is the general scheme of work. This should specify the key ideas, concepts and skills that will be assessed. It should specify the units of work to be covered and the timescales available. It should indicate when and how assessments will be arranged, so that staff and pupils can work towards those dates in their target setting.

Plans should identify the knowledge which needs to be memorised, the ideas and concepts which need to be developed and understood, and the skills which need to be acquired. A key to successful planning is to think of the end of the statement, 'Pupils should be able to...'

It may be, for example:

- list the key features of a glacier on a photograph;
- name the parts of the heart on a diagram.

Alternatively, the pupil should be able to:

- explain the working of a steam engine;
- describe the process of making rubber;
- evaluate the causes of the First World War;

These require a degree of understanding and the learning activity associated with these objectives should be different to those for simply memorising.

Similarly, skill acquisition should have precise objectives and activities that enable the skill to be perfected. For example, pupils should be able to:

- draw a straight line graph accurately from a table of figures.

The best schemes of work will identify pupil activities and assignments, including homework which will be linked to assessment criteria. Resources and classroom activities should be suggested, so that staff are not left to fend for themselves. Too often this leads to over-reliance on textbook activities which may not necessarily focus on assessed knowledge or skills. All activities, whether self-produced or those found in textbooks, must be selected to achieve the specific learning outcomes which are required.

At the second level there should be detailed lesson plans. These need to be specifically tailored to individual lessons or blocks of time. They need to be tailored to the needs of specific groups and individuals. Based on the scheme of work the learning outcomes of the activities in the lesson need to be specified and to match the activities. For example, a class that is expected to remember information needs to undertake some activities that enhance memory, whether this is through repetition, keeping a set of notes for revision or whatever.

Detailed and specific planning that focuses upon the knowledge and skills that pupils are expected to acquire provides a framework which individual teachers may need to adapt. Schemes of work and lesson plans are not a strait-jacket or recipe. However, where individual adaptations are not focused upon better ways of working with individual pupils they can blur the focus on attainment. The 'Learning to Teach in the Primary/Secondary School' texts produced by Routledge Publishers (New Fetter Lane, London. UK.) provide detailed advice about the planning of classroom practice.

Activity 10.5 Planning in the department

To what extent is planning adequately focused on the specific knowledge, skills and attitudes you want pupils to achieve? To what extent is there variation between teachers' approaches to the subject and how far does this enhance the achievement of pupils in the subject? Record your thoughts in your reflective journal.

Study guides

Study guides for pupils and parents can be used to convey the essential elements of the scheme of work and be used as 'advance organisers' by pupils. They will need support from the teacher to use the advance organiser so that they understand the structure of the learning programme and the expectations you have for them. The expectations should be both at a general level and specific to each pupil's level of work. Pupils should, therefore, know what their current level of performance is, what the likely future performance is to be and what aspects of their work would improve their performance to at least the next grade above what is expected.

Lesson Plan

Topic: **Date:**

Title of lesson: **Class:**

Abilities and needs of group/individuals

Learning objectives:
At the end of this lesson pupils will be able to:

Knowledge

Skills

Attitudes

Learning activities
1.
2.
3.
4.

Extension activities/homework

Resources required

Evaluation
Strengths   Weaknesses

Figure 10.3   *Suggested lesson plan format*

Table 10.2 *Suggestion for a study guide*

Past examination papers	Course work topics
Syllabus	Key skills
Course content	Examples of good quality work
Learning activities in class	List of terminology covered
Homework	Topics covered and timing
Assessment dates	Class activities
Self-assessment exercises	Action planning activities
Library materials	Description of work at different grades
Assessment criteria for work	Mark recording sheet
Criteria and grade descriptors	
Local places of interest connected to the syllabus	

Information to parents

You need to provide adequate information to parents about the learning outcomes and activities necessary to achieve them in your department. Clearly, parents do not want to be bombarded with large quantities of information from all departments in the school, and information needs to be understandable and usable. The information need not simply be about 'assessment' but also what help and what activities would be useful for pupils to engage in with their parents. Such activities may be part of any suggested homework plan.

Parents need to be encouraged to become co-educators. You may find that teachers will say parents are not interested or do not have the time, but parents often do not know how to help. Providing some guidance for how to help learning in your subject will be useful to them.

Table 10.3 *Information to parents checklist*

Examination dates	Past examination papers
Syllabus	Course work topics
Course content	Local places of interest connected to the syllabus
Key skills	Local museums that have materials connected to the syllabus
Assignments	Local galleries which have items connected to the syllabus
Assessment dates	Learning activities in class
Homework	List of terminology covered
Topics covered and timing	
Assessment criteria for work	

Activity 10.6 Parental support for learning

Consider how far you think parents could support the learning of their children in your subject. What help and support might they need to be able to do this? What activities could parents help with? How might you go about developing this work with parents? Record your ideas in your reflective journal.

Learning activities

You need to be sure that the learning activities in the department match the planned learning objectives. To do this you need to be very clear about the factual knowledge pupils are expected to recall, the understanding they need to develop and the skills you wish them to acquire.

Recall

Activities that promote recall emphasise:

- repetition and practice at recalling;
- association with pleasurable experiences;
- making relationships and connections with items of information;
- association with action;
- association with visual images.

According to recent research the left and right hemispheres of the brain have been found to perform different functions, and different people have different left and right brain abilities (Dryden and Vos, 1994). The left side emphasises language, logic, numbers, mathematics, sequence and words. The right side emphasises rhyme, rhythm, music, pictures, imagination and patterns. Some learners are more accomplished at using one or other of the hemispheres.

Hence, you need to ensure that activities use a variety of techniques, eg:

Lists	Alphabet Lists
Mnemonics	Stories and Rhymes
Rules and Patterns	Diagrams and Pictures
Action Stories and Songs	Concept or Mind Maps
Soft Background Music	Relaxation Exercises

You should also ensure that pupils are left with sets of notes that they can use to revise from. Extended pieces of writing are not the best form of notes to revise from.

Activity 10.7 Focus on memory

To what extent are the activities that pupils undertake in your department focused upon memory? To what extent do you use the approaches in the above list? How else do you develop memory? To what extent are the notes of pupils in your department useful in practising memory? Record your observations in your reflective journal.

Developing understanding

Understanding develops through the building of concepts. The idea that we perceive new information through our previous understanding and then develop new insights is found in the work of Piaget, Vygotsky, Ausubel and Dewey. Bruner (1960) emphasises returning to previous understanding in a spiral curriculum.

The process of developing understanding begins with identifying current understanding, and presenting activities and experiences that challenge the pupil's frameworks and allows them to rethink. This is termed 'transformation' because it describes the way in which old ideas are transformed into new understanding. This can be achieved through activities that:

- develop understanding through using talk and the use of subject language;
- develop understanding through manipulating text and diagrams.

Pupils must be given opportunities to explore their understanding through talking. They must be encouraged to use the language of the subject wherever possible. Some will do anything to avoid using the 'technical' terms appropriate to your subject. Vocabulary dictionaries may be helpful but practice is essential.

Talk should be organised in pairs, fours and larger groups. Opportunities for talk should be both short and extended. Some subjects, such as English, use talk extensively. Others use talk relatively less. You may be able to borrow ideas from other departments. How many pupils have an opportunity to talk about your subject for longer than say two minutes at a time?

Talk activities are suggested in Table 10.4.

Table 10.4   *Talk activities*

Discussions in twos and fours
Two discuss a problem and compare their answer with another pair
Standpoint taking
Two pupils are given two opposing views to argue
Just-a-minute games
Pupils talk for one minute on a given subject
Presentations
Pupils present their answer to a problem
Role play
Pupils act in role discussing a particular problem
News bulletins
Pupils prepare a short news bulletin
Radio programme features stories
A taped 'feature' is presented on a selected issue or problem
Interviews with 'experts'
Pupils prepare themselves to be interviewed as 'experts' on a subject
Interviews with 'witnesses'
Pupils act as eye-witnesses to an event, explaining what happened or is happening

Text and diagrams need to be worked upon so that understanding is developed. Reading figures from a table is a skill but it does not necessarily develop understanding. Converting a table into a short piece of descriptive text, which then has to be explained to a small group, requires understanding of what the table means. Similarly, taking a piece of text and converting it into a flow diagram or a hierarchy of concepts requires understanding. Reading and answering some simple comprehension questions often requires pupils to do little more than scan and copy the right words. The pupil may not need to understand the text at all but merely lift the appropriate text using the cues in the question. (For further information see Lunzer and Gardner, 1984; Capel *et al.*, 1995, 1996.)

Activity 10.8 Developing understanding

To what extent do the activities in your department develop pupils' understanding of the ideas and concepts you have planned for them to develop? What strategies can you use to improve the understanding of pupils? Record your thoughts in your reflective journal.

Conclusion

This chapter has focused upon some aspects of raising attainment through better teaching and learning. The chapter has been based upon observations of practice, including in OFSTED inspections.

The chapter has invited you to reflect on the current approach of the department. You now may have two issues to contend with. The first is that you have this view of what needs to be done but how do you involve others in this? The second is that you know the problems, but what are the solutions and how do you put them into action? Our suggestion, again based on experience, is that departmental collaborative action research provides a useful approach for collecting data about what is happening, so that the discussion in the department about what needs to be done is based upon a team approach to the issues under scrutiny. You may consider using a facilitator from outside, such as an LEA adviser or consultant, but make sure that they are able to facilitate a collaborative process of learning that involves all the department.

Part V   Management Tasks

Chapter 11

Turning your Vision to Action: The Planning Process

How do you think the quality of the current work of your section can be improved? You may have a clear vision of how you want things to be or a vague inkling that your section could be more effective, but be unsure about where you should start.

The planning process offers a framework which you can use to guide your analysis of problems, your thinking about the solutions and the monitoring of any changes you decide to put into place.

If you are in a school where the whole-school development process is well understood by all members of staff then your task in developing a departmental/team plan may be relatively easy. On the other hand, if understanding about the process is weak then you need to make decisions about the best way to introduce the process to staff.

By the end of this chapter, you should understand how development planning and action planning can help you achieve your goals, and have analysed the conditions for development in your area of responsibility. The general process of development planning is discussed, as is the rationale of establishing your own private strategic plan for the development of your work.

Your (private) strategic plan

Plans for the development of your area of responsibility are built on the foundation provided by you as a manager. Your ability to analyse successfully the conditions inhibiting and supporting development is crucial to the achievement of goals for improvement. In addition, your ability to provide solutions to problems, as well as resources to support change, enables development to take place. Your management skills provide the environment which supports or stifles development and improvement.

Your private strategic plan (see Figure 11.1) is your personal plan for managing the development of work in your area. The ideas in this private plan are introduced over time, as appropriate, to discussions about the department/team's development plan. This is the development plan which details the section's priorities and which is produced by all staff working together to develop a shared and agreed sense of direction to the development, as well as a rational framework for the allocation of resources.

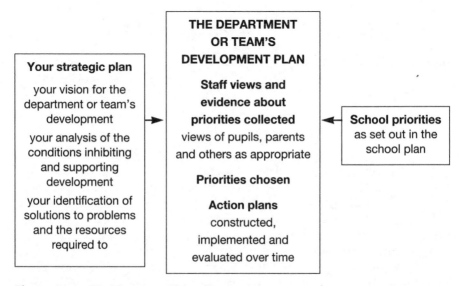

Figure 11.1   *Turning your vision into action*

Chapter 2 introduced the idea of structured reflective practice as a means of systematically examining your practice. The reference to your reflective journal throughout this book is linked with this strategy of reflective practice. Recording the results of your reflection and linking this with strategies for improvement provides you with the basis of a personal strategic plan. If you envisage considerable change in the work of the department or team, you will have to make a decision about your strategy for implementing this change. This may involve telling staff everything at once or it may require you to introduce ideas gradually, and ensure these are implemented and embedded in practice before you move on to the next goal. Decisions about how to implement change have to be taken by you and the implementation process required to ensure that change actually takes place is discussed in Chapter 12.

Therefore, your strategic plan may be a private document or you may use it with others for particular purposes, eg when making a case to senior management for resources of a particular type – a new staff member with a particular specialist area. Chapters 15 and 16 provide advice about resource and staffing plans.

The strategic plan may consist of a series of notes under key headings (material resources, staffing, curriculum, communication strategies, staff development) to which you add comments over a period of years or it may be more formally written up. The important part of the plan is that it is kept on hand to guide your work. The document itself is likely to be brief. You may consider keeping it in your reflective journal or along with other important records and notes of other key decisions in a ringbinder, a file or a hardcover notebook.

Why do you need a strategic plan?

You are the person responsible to the head and governors for work in a particular area. Carrying out that responsibility means that ultimately you can be required to justify any decisions which are made about the running of your section eg about the curriculum, the staffing, the resources. The final responsibility cannot be delegated. This means that in becoming a middle manager you are accepting a different role to the class teacher. Head teachers have a similar responsibility for the whole school. In our experience, staff sometimes criticise decision making procedures in schools for not being sufficiently democratic. However, an examination of the responsibilities of the head and middle managers indicates that these are the staff who ultimately are held responsible. Class teachers do not carry this responsibility; they are not accountable for the work of the whole section. Therefore, although a democratic approach to decision making can be helpful in giving staff 'ownership' of ideas, because you carry the final responsibility, you may consider that you must have a final veto on decisions. How decisions are made in your department or team is, in itself, a decision you make as a manager.

Producing your strategic plan

The stages to be gone through in producing a strategic plan are similar to that for development planning in general (see Figure 11.2). However, the purpose of your strategic plan is different – in that it is your personal guide to development – so the planning process as it relates to the stages of review/audit, prioritising, implementation and evaluation is likely to be informal and private. Reflection on what needs to be done in the four management dimensions identified in Chapter 2 may provide a useful starting point. (The dimensions are: management tasks, ways in which you work with people, who you are in the context in which you work, your philosophy of teaching and learning.)

The stages in development planning are discussed more fully in following sections.

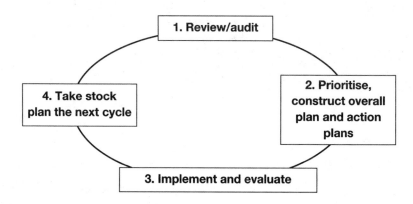

Figure 11.2   *The planning cycle*

Development planning

In 1989, in the UK the Department of Education and Science provided advice about the process of producing a school development plan to schools in England and Wales (Hargreaves, *et al.*, 1989). This advice was drawn from practice developed in schools in a number of LEAs. Originally the planning process was seen as a way of involving staff (and parents, pupils and governors) in decisions about the priorities for school development. But inevitably practice in schools has varied and in some schools the experience of managing the planning process may be confined to the senior management team. Experience since 1989 suggests that in large schools while the school plan sets out overarching goals for development, this plan needs to be underpinned by detailed planning at department or team level. In this section, we focus on planning at the department or team level.

The planning process can, in itself, promote discussion which brings about change. However, if development planning is seen by staff as an administrative duty, ie something to be produced to satisfy senior management or inspectors, then the potential of the process to promote development is lost. In the right circumstances, the planning process provides a tool for team building, for developing consensus about priorities for development, and the means of achieving and evaluating development.

What is a department/team development plan?

Effective development plans are those which are actually used by staff to bring about desired changes. The department or team development plan needs to be a short working document which gives those reading it an understanding of:

- the priorities pinpointed for development;
- the tasks to be done;
- proposed timescales for implementing change;
- the resources required;
- the people responsible;
- how progress will be evaluated and reported.

The relationship between the department or team plan and the school plan is shown in Figure 11.3.

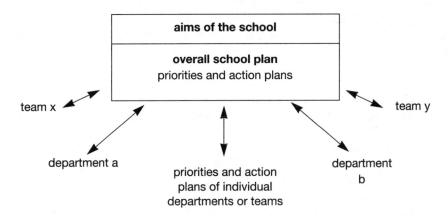

Figure 11.3 *The relationship between department or team plans and the overall school plan*

Why have a department/team development plan?

While you may have a vision and a strategic plan, without the support of your staff you will achieve little. Development planning provides a process which enables you to couple the vision you have with that of the staff so that together, in a planned and managed way, you are able to translate the shared vision into action. Discussion about priorities for development allows this generating of a shared vision.

Planning in a systematic way may:

- guide your section in developing and improving aspects of your work in a steady way over time;
- provide a focus for decision making about the allocation of resources for staff development and materials;
- provide a structure which encourages the staff to discuss their values and to develop a shared philosophy of teaching and learning issues;
- support the development of an ethos where staff share common goals and have a shared sense of direction;
- support staff in working systematically to solve problems and improve;
- provide professional development for staff about approaches to middle management;
- provide a clear rationale for delegation of responsibility within the department or team.

However, there can be a downside to planning:

- expectations of what can be achieved are too high and frustration or disappointment may result;
- some staff may never participate fully in the exercise.

Strategies for dealing with conflict are discussed in Chapter 8 and the text *Handling Conflict and Negotiation* provides further advice (Manchester Open Learning, 1993). When you wonder whether planning is worth the effort, consider the alternatives:

- there may be no agreement among staff about shared goals;
- your effectiveness as an advocate for your section is lessened as there is no evidence that your demands have staff support or are thought through fully;
- reviews of the section's work are not linked to overall strategies for improvement.

Table 11.1 lists some of the views middle managers hold about the process of development planning.

Table 11.1   *The development plan: for and against*

The following accounts are fiction in as much as no one said all of these things...
But the sentiments have been expressed by different people. They are both intended
to provide genuine perspectives but they are reflections rather than images.

Jo

There is no point in writing a DP. It has no useful purpose. It is merely an
administrative task – a complete waste of time. The only function is to keep those
above you off our backs and keeps the LEA happy.

We cannot plan in our department because there are lots of factors beyond our
control. Things keep changing so rapidly, I don't even know who is in my
department next year.

I write the DP myself based upon what I know. It's intuitive. None of the
department are interested and they don't want to do any Inset. There is not enough
time to do the job of teaching.

The school DP itself is turgid. It's too large to be useful and everyone is heading
off in different directions. It's just not cohesive.

Joanne

I have found writing the DP a very useful exercise. It has helped me to clarify my
plans and set targets and goals that are attainable. I have been able to establish
priorities for the future.

I try to involve as many people as possible so that all of my department know
what needs to be done, where we are going and why. Some of the department
draft bits of the DP and we all get together to amend their drafts before I put it all
together. I speak to every member of the department about their individual Inset
plans for the future year.

DP writing provides a good opportunity to put together fresh ideas. On the other
hand, we are able to plan something that is really manageable. I use the DP as a
checklist of events and activities and it keeps us on track for the rest of the year.
We use it to form a framework for department meetings for the rest of the year. We
are able to monitor and review our progress. When things don't go right, we can
reflect upon why and try not to make the same mistake next year.

Next year I think I might try to meet with senior staff to sort out difficulties and try
to liaise with other departments in my area more.

(from Terrell, 1989)

It seems apparent that the usefulness of the process depends very much on
the context in which you find yourself. One middle manager reported that
when she found resistance to planning from staff, and no support for the process from management, she managed the development of the department
through a private strategic plan. In spite of the lack of involvement from staff,
there was enormous change in the section over a three-year period as she
managed to implement her vision – because goals and achievements had
been noted in staff meeting minutes, it was easy to track the development
which had occurred.

The planning process is a tool to enable you and the staff to work more effectively. Beware of a tendency to try to do too much too soon so that staff become disillusioned. Focusing on small, achievable goals is a realistic way to improve, given the demands of the normal daily work of teachers.

Four stages in the planning process

The stages of preparing a department/team development plan are the same as for a whole-school plan. One way of looking at these stages is to consider the questions which have to be answered at each stage:

Stage 1 Review/Audit	Where are we now?
Stage 2 Prioritising and constructing the plan	Where do we want to be? How are we going to get there? What is realistic within the resources available? Who is going to do the work? By when does the work have to be done? How are we going to check how our plans are going in practice? (planning evaluation)
Stage 3 Implementation	How do we ensure that the changes actually happen?
Stage 4 Evaluation (evaluation should take place during as well as at the end of the implementation stage)	Have our plans had the effect intended? If not, what went well and why, and what did not go well and why?

Before undertaking planning in the department, you need to ensure that the process is linked appropriately with any school review/development planning processes which are taking place.

Stage 1 Review/audit

The ideas from your strategic plan feed into the development planning process at the review/audit stage.

The review (audit) stage is used to establish strengths and weaknesses in order to choose the priorities for development. All those connected with a department/team have different perspectives. Younger pupils have different viewpoints to older pupils, parents different to teachers, the head and governors too will have individual perspectives.

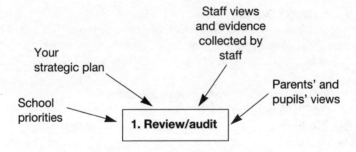

Figure 11.4 *Review/audit*

At department or team level, it may not be appropriate to gain parents' views. Parents' views can be gained at parents' evenings or through letters home. Pupils' views can be collected via the School Council, or through questionnaires or small group interviews. Pupils often come up with perspectives which enable staff to understand how the school functions at the pupil level.

There are a number of short effective strategies for analysing the work of the department or a team which can be used with small groups or you may find them effective to use yourself in establishing your priorities for your area of responsibility. Details of two of these – SWOT exercises and the nominal group technique – are given below.

The SWOT exercise

The initials SWOT stand for Strengths, Weaknesses, Opportunities and Threats. Table 11.2 provides an example of a simple planning proforma for this exercise.

Table 11.2 *SWOT analysis proforma*

Issue to be analysed	Strengths	Weaknesses (eg pupil motivation, staff knowledge, resources)	Opportunities (for improvement)	Threats (limiting improvement)
eg pupil attainment in examinations at age 16	● girls perform well ● average grades are rising	● boys' motivation seems to be less than girls	● enlisting parental support ● raising pupil aspirations	● poor attitudes to homework ● community experience of lack of employment

Nominal Group Technique

'The technique aims to protect the expression of individual views while permitting any consensus of view to be identified. It consists of the following phases:

1. Presentation of the task (question or problem).
2. Individual (silent) nominations.
3. Round-robin listing (master list construction).
4. Item clarification.
5. Evaluation by rank ordering items.
6. Discussion and subsequent action.

The group leader's role is governed by the following instructions:

1. Do not re-interpret a person's idea(s).
2. Use the participant's own wording.
3. Do not interject your own ideas – you are not participating.
4. Give people time to think.
5. This is not a debate – do not allow participants to challenge each other.
6. Do not try to interpret results – do not look for a pattern.'

(Elliott, 1982, p. 68)

Priorities identified in this way are fed into stage 2 of the planning process which results in the construction of detailed action plans for achieving change.

Stage 2 Prioritise, construct overall plan and action plans

Priorities

It is easy to come up with so many areas for development and improvement that the task of accomplishing anything can be daunting. Priorities need to be organised into those that are urgent, those that need attention in the short term and those that can be attended to in the longer term. They also need to be considered in terms of demands they will make on the staff resources you have available.

Action plans

Action plans provide the working guide to action. Action plans are drawn up to include details of what is to be done, the timescales involved and the criteria for judging success. An action planning format, such as that in Table 11.3, provides a concise and clear method for setting out your plans. Filling in the action plans needs to be carefully managed if you are to achieve commitment to development from other members of the section. The establishing of 'success criteria' or 'performance indicators' needs to be done in such a way that goals are achievable.

Table 11.3 *An action planning proforma*

Priority	Key tasks? What exactly is to be done?	Person responsible? Who is to do the work?	Timescale? By when does the work have to be done?	Success criteria? What are our criteria for the successful achievement of this priority?	Reporting? – of findings: to whom and when?
to develop collaborative environmental work with science departments in schools in different environments using the Internet to facilitate communication focusing on the investigation of water quality in rivers near the schools	• identify schools interested in such collaborative work by consulting with LEA staff or by searching schoolnet/schoolhouse web sites in the USA, Germany, Australia or Canada • some staff will need induction into running Internet projects	year 9 teachers teaching the module will plan the work supported by the IT coordinator in the school	end of summer term	quality of learning outcomes including collection of comparative data from three different environments, the analysis, discussion and reporting of findings, etc	review in departmental meeting at the end of the summer term

Success criteria

Success criteria (column 5, of Table 11.3) are simply statements about what standards have to be achieved, by when. These are planned at the early stages to provide a clear focus for those who are undertaking the work. The precise identification of criteria for success helps in evaluating whether goals are realistically achievable or not and what evidence must be collected by when, so that the judgement about success can be made (further details about success criteria and their application are provided in Chapter 12).

Stage 3 Implement and evaluate

This is such an important area that we have devoted a whole chapter to the issues of maintaining the momentum of the work as planned and then collecting data about how things are going, the analysis and reporting of the findings. Chapter 12 provides these details. It is worth noting at this point that those staff who are undertaking MA study will often have assignments or will be undertaking dissertations which can, if focused on the work of the section, be designed to evaluate progress in achieving development plan goals.

Stage 4 Take stock and plan the next cycle

At some point, termly or yearly, one cycle should end, and the next begin. This gives the opportunity to examine and record what has happened – formally in a staff meeting – and to move on. While there will be some successes there will also be failures. It is important to recognise the successes and to put the failures behind the section. A formal 'taking stock' provides this opportunity.

Conclusion

Planning offers the opportunity to choose between crisis management or strategic management: the choice is yours. We have little sympathy with those who see planning as constraining development. Take the analogy of two car drivers who both wish to get to the same destination. One has no map, the other has an incomplete map requiring the driver to ask directions occasionally. We feel the second option gives the driver more chance of arriving at the desired destination within a reasonable timescale. Similarly, an imperfect plan is likely to be more use than no plan at all. The effectiveness of any plan produced does depend on the creativity and commitment of those involved. Inflexible planning clearly straight-jackets development and we would not recommend such an approach. In addition, where the development plan becomes part of the inspection process development may be stifled. The commitment of staff is vital – improvement through planning involves not just the achieving of tasks and targets, it also involves working with people, within the constraints of the work environment, to allow all to work towards improvement.

Chapter 12

Keeping up the Momentum: Evaluating and Monitoring Your Plans

Planning is the creative part of the development process. If the department development plan is to be more than a wish list, then the process of implementing and evaluating the plans must be thoroughly worked out. A central aspect of your role as a middle manager is to sustain the implementation and evaluation phases so that planned changes actually happen. If you do not take on this role then the chances of your plans being brought to fruition are severely impaired and, importantly, you run the risk of the process running out of steam and staff becoming disillusioned. Inevitably this will make it more difficult for you to motivate them to plan development in the future. Diversions too can easily take staff off to other tasks. If you, as middle manager, consider the work important enough to monitor progress regularly, to allocate resources where these are needed to support the plans, and to support and encourage staff, then staff too feel able to give the work a high priority.

This chapter outlines the crucial role of the middle manager in sustaining work on development plans. A variety of terms used to describe work in the area of monitoring and evaluation are discussed, as are time effective strategies for monitoring and evaluation. The history of developments in educational evaluation are outlined, including the introduction of performance indicators.

Definition of terms

Staff may have different understandings of the terms listed below. At the outset of any evaluative exercise we suggest that you clarify the meanings of the terms used. For example, the differences between monitoring and evaluation and evaluation and assessment in particular may need to be clarified.

Evaluation

Evaluation 'is a general term used to describe any activity... where the quality of provision is the subject of systematic study' (Department of Education and Science, 1985, p. 7). The term 'evaluation' encompasses formative processes (monitoring, appraisal) and summative processes (assessment, review), but it also goes beyond these when it is used to describe a more formal process of collecting and analysing data and reporting of findings. In this form, the evaluation process is akin to the research process, a major difference being the purpose of the exercise – evaluation is undertaken in order to provide information on which professional judgements are based. Research does not have this focus on the collection of data for the specific purpose of informing professional judgements. Collaborative action research, classroom action research and reflective practice are activities which fit within this definition of evaluation.

Monitoring

Monitoring or keeping an eye on how things are going is more informal. However it is an important part of the middle manager's role in checking standards in the department. It involves and provides information which then leads to corrective action on an ongoing basis.

Review

Review 'indicates a retrospective activity and implies the collection and examination of evidence and information' (Department of Education and Science, 1985, p. 7). Review is a more formal process – checking how things are going – and is undertaken at a particular point in time such as at a department meeting. Criteria for review should be clear and the changes indicated in the outcome of the review should be incorporated into the development planning process, perhaps, for example, through an amendment of the action plan.

Appraisal

Appraisal 'emphasises the forming of qualitative judgements about an activity, a person or an organisation' (Department of Education and Science, 1985, p. 7), but in practice is usually used to describe the process of evaluating staff performance.

Assessment

Assessment 'implies the use of measurement and/or grading based on known criteria' (Department of Education and Science, 1985, p. 7), but in practice it is usually applied to the evaluation of pupils' work.

Performance indicators

Performance indicators (PIs) are

> 'any piece of information that helps you know how well someone or something is performing. In practice the term is often reserved for factual information (examination results, class sizes, attendance figures, costs per pupil) which is fairly easy to obtain and can stand proxy for professional judgement. PIs directly measure something which may or may not be important in itself; they "indicate" – point to – something else that is significant but harder to measure.

> 'A school's examination results, for example, measure the standards pupils have reached in public examinations. As PIs they may provide pointers to the quality of teaching in each subject and the "success" of the school as a whole.

> 'These quantitative PIs on their own, rarely provide definitive answers to the really important questions, however. The temptation is to over-value what is measurable, simply because it is measurable. Examination results may say where pupils have got to in particular subjects at particular times – but not how far they have progressed, how hard it was for them to get there or why they have not got further; still less, what they have gained from school that public examinations do not test.

> 'Despite this, PIs can be a valuable support to audit and evaluation, because of the questions they raise. They draw attention to issues that deserve a closer look.

> 'Comparisons between one year and another, between subjects, or with local and national norms, should prompt you to ask three sorts of question:

> - Are we (they) doing as well as could be expected in the circumstances?

> - Even if the answer is "yes" are we (they) doing well enough for our pupils in absolute terms?

> - If not, what needs doing to change the circumstances, and who needs to do it?'

> (DFEE, 1991, p. 23)

Success criteria

Success criteria are a form of performance indicator. In devising them, staff have to define what would be a realistic successful outcome of work being undertaken. Success criteria as they are used in departmental action planning:

- provide specific guidance about the goals and standards to be achieved;
- indicate the evidence needed to judge success;
- relate to a specific priority for improvement;
- are chosen by those who choose the priority;
- influence the focus for development in a priority;
- emphasise success rather than failure;
- can be used to shape further planning.

(adapted from notes from the School Development Plans Project)

Evaluation

The purpose of evaluation in development planning is to provide feedback so that modifications can be made as work in the chosen area progresses. If evaluation is carefully planned, you will have sound evidence on which to base decisions. To provide such evidence, your evaluation strategies need to be systematic and draw on a range of sources and view points. So the evaluation strategy for your development plan should:

- involve the collection of evidence;
- focus on the investigation of an area in a systematic way;
- give rise to findings which are used to improve outcomes.

Members of professional groups have a responsibility to be self-monitoring and the term 'reflective practice', to describe the processes used, is found not only in education but also for example in the health service and police force to describe the cycle of collecting and analysing evidence about the quality of provision which is followed by implementation of changes and ongoing evaluation. This process forms an 'improvement cycle' which has, as its focus, the quality of professional practice.

Sustaining the implementation of plans

That the implementation and evaluation phases are difficult to sustain has been borne out by research in the area (Hargreaves *et al.*, 1989, p. 10). Planning is the easy part, ensuring change happens is much more difficult.

Keeping the progress of action plans as an item on the department meeting agenda is one way of sustaining and monitoring implementation. Planning and implementing ongoing evaluation strategies for each priority is one way in which you can ensure that evidence about how plans are going is collected and that implementation is sustained.

In the case study, one head of faculty discusses her experience of monitoring and evaluation in the departmental context.

Head of faculty: reflection on monitoring and evaluation

I have been in this role (as head of faculty) for one year, and covered the post in an acting capacity for six months previous to that.
During these 18 months I have become very aware of the need to
allow staff the space to create their own classroom environments
but I am also aware of the need for consistency and standards within
a faculty to ensure the highest quality teaching, accurate and efficient assessment and record keeping, and effective teamwork. The
area of monitoring and evaluation is clearly the key to guiding and
shaping these elements of faculty practice.

In my own experience I found monitoring to be most useful when
everyone in the faculty actively participates. This then makes evaluation a shared experience, and gives ownership to all members of
the faculty when the time comes for acting upon the issue raised by
it.

The head of faculty has overall responsibility and should never
shirk this when monitoring and evaluation leads to the more awkward areas such as individual staff performance, but the majority of
the experience will be more useful if it is shared.

However, I have found monitoring and evaluation to be the most
intangible area of my responsibility and the most fraught with pitfalls… This is one reason I want to explore the theory and practi-
cality of this area thoroughly.

Following a discussion with an OFSTED consultant, who convinced me of the complexity of the nature of monitoring and evaluation, I then attended an Inset course to look at the more practical
aspects. Both experiences were useful but they did not seem complementary and this led me to experiment with a range of methods.

There are a variety of methods which can be used to collect information for
monitoring and evaluative purposes. Some of these are introduced in the
next section. The choice of method must take into account the staff time available – it is better to build up a picture of the functioning of the department by
systematically focusing on a series of small aspects than to attempt a large
comprehensive evaluation which drags on for a long time, because staff have
not the time to devote to it.

Collecting evidence for evaluation

In evaluating progress on priorities for development, the action plan format (Chapter 11, Table 11.3) allows 'at a glance' reminders of timelines, priorities and the criteria to be used in judging success in the achievement of goals. The success criteria you have identified will point to the evidence needed to judge whether you have achieved a specific goal. To fit evaluation strategies into the time available may mean that you have to be satisfied with collecting more limited data than you would like. This limitation of scope is a reality which has to be faced and accepted. However, careful assessing of the quality and meaning of the data collected is essential if unsubstantiated generalisations about what is happening are to be avoided. Once you have identified success criteria, the next stage is to decide who has or where is the evidence you need to show that success has been achieved. This then leads you to consider how is the evidence to be collected and by when does it have to be collected. The form of analysis of the evidence to be undertaken must be considered at this stage. It is very easy to collect data – for example, the administration of questionnaires to all children in a school is easy – the time taken to analyse such a mound of data could be months and months. Being faced with such a task is demoralising for those involved. Start small and build expertise on the basis of success is the advice we would wish to give! A number of examples about how pupils can be involved in evaluation are provided by Clinton *et al.* (1994, pp. 54–61). These include course evaluations, providing positive and negative statements about a course (these can be written or developed as a group exercise), sentence completion (eg 'The most useful part was…'), discussions, questionnaires.

Monitoring should be focused for example on standards and achievement so that effective use of time is made. Middle managers often use strategies such as analysing assessment results across a year group and discussing differences with staff, casual observation of lessons, ie in passing through, observation of pupil behaviour in corridors, of book work, eg randomly looking at pupils' work to monitor marking and feedback, asking for lesson plans. If standards in these areas are set with staff beforehand then establishing a professional dialogue about the results of monitoring is easier. Sharing views about aspects of teaching and learning in staff meetings gives staff an understanding of the expectations of the middle manager.

Collaborative action research may provide an effective way of examining the work of a department. Within this approach, a team of staff undertake mini-research projects targeted on a specific area. Evaluation carried out in this way may mean that staff themselves identify ways of improving practice rather than changes having to be imposed from the top-down. Thus the evaluation strategy which you adopt for your development plan can fulfil two purposes – it can provide evidence of how changes are being implemented as well as provide evidence of changes that are needed. Staff who are undertaking MA degree study will usually find that they can undertake action research as part of the assessment of their course. Issues related to ethics, including confidentiality, must be considered if this work is being undertaken. Hopkins (1993) provides detailed advice about the conduct of such work.

Sources of evidence

Evidence can be collected from a wide range of sources and examples which may be available to you are shown in table 12.1. Research on school development plans shows how evidence can be effectively used at each stage of your planning process. For example, at the audit/review stage, evidence is used to define strengths and weaknesses. When action plans are constructed, the success criteria indicate what evidence needs to be collected and when. At the implementation stage, reviews in departmental meetings draw upon evidence to guide further action. At the final evaluation stage, accumulated evidence indicates how successfully plans have been implemented (adapted from Hargreaves *et al.*, 1989).

Table 12.1   *Sources of evidence for evaluation*

Individuals	The views of anyone with a contribution to make may be helpful: pupils, teachers and support staff, peripatetic staff, parents, members of the community or local industry
Documents	Any papers related to the area under scrutiny: examination and test papers, minutes of meetings, staff handbooks, prospectuses, pupil work. Statistical information will also be available in a number of forms and this can provide useful information for example when analysed over a number of years to show changes
Observations	Of pupils in classrooms and in other areas of the school, through pupil shadowing, of teachers – paired observation can be helpful. This is the process where two teachers observe each other teaching and then debrief about each other's practice. Usually a sharp focus is identified, eg the use of open and closed questions
Processes and procedures within the institution	While some of these will be documented, others will need to be observed and then recorded for the purposes of the evaluation: for example, communication processes, management processes, assessment processes, development processes, resource allocation procedures

Evidence is collected by questionnaire, observation or interview. *A Teacher's Guide to Classroom Research* (Hopkins, 1993) is recommended as a starting point for those new to these activities.

Recognising the nature and value of evidence

Hargreaves (*et al.* 1989, p. 2) made the point that:

'evidence informs the planning process in two ways: highlighting areas for consideration and throwing light on solutions. In the audit, for example, pupils' under-achievement in reading might be identified through an analysis of reading scores, teachers' observations of pupils, and the numbers of books being borrowed to take home. Asking staff and parents for their views provides opportunities for suggestions about ways to solve the problem.

In collecting evidence staff should consider qualitative information, such as views, opinions and judgements, as well as quantitative information in the form of statistics. Both kinds of evidence are very important. The distinction between the two types of information is not a sharp one – counting the parents' views transforms qualitative opinions into a quantitative summary of their perceptions.'

The development and dissemination of new practice in the UK

In the late 1980s and early 1990s, while there seemed to be widespread acceptance of the importance of teacher involvement in the evaluation process, the adoption of evaluation processes as routine in schools was poor, as the findings of the School Management Task Force confirmed:

'*Monitoring and Evaluation:* This was the area in which least was apparently being done but which most people considered a priority for future action. Recognising the desirability of performance indicators as benchmarks and more systematic approaches to evaluation, both primary and secondary schools called for more training in evaluation methods. Most LEAs were only just developing their own monitoring and evaluation structures and strategies, and had yet to devise formal systems for supporting evaluation in schools.' (School Management Task Force, 1990, pp. 11–12)

Lack of knowledge among the profession of cost and time effective evaluation strategies was a stumbling block to the monitoring of the effectiveness of development plans (Wilcox, 1992). While schools may be successful in producing development plans, implementation and evaluation strategies may be less well understood:

'Evaluation

This too, is a problematic area. Many schools have examples of policies, thoughtfully produced and attractively presented, which are, nevertheless, of little value as nobody appears to read them and few apply them.

The Head must hold accountable each group or team responsible for an aspect of development and ensure that regular discussions of progress are built into the process. The result of these discussions should be conveyed to all parties involved.' (ILEA, 1988, p. 10)

The evaluation strategies proposed as a result of the research in the School Development Plans (SDP) project were designed to be fitted into the routine of the school. Wilcox (1992, p. 15) considered that the evaluation approaches espoused by the SDP project were a useful contribution to the problem of effective school-based evaluation:

> 'The merit of the proposals (for development plans) is that they focus self-evaluation on to very specific priorities and targets. The approach is therefore likely to overcome both the unrealistic comprehensiveness and general vagueness of purpose which characterised some of the early efforts in self-evaluation.' (Wilcox, 1992, p. 15)

At the time, pressure for the use of quantitative performance indicators to judge schools was growing (DES, 1988; OECD, 1988). The School Development Plans project advice went against the drive for quantitative indicators, making the case for qualitative indicators to be used alongside quantitative indicators (Hopkins and Leask, 1988; Hargreaves *et al.*, 1989). The use of the term 'success criteria' instead of 'performance indicator' to give a positive focus to goal setting was adopted by the SDP project.

Conclusion

Educational evaluation strategies used in schools in the UK are considered a cause for concern (TTA, 1995). As a middle manager you can expect to have responsibility for the approaches adopted in your area of work. In developing your own and your staff's skills in this area, focusing on achievable goals in terms of data collection and subsequent evaluation is necessary to build experience and confidence about the usefulness of the process.

Chapter 13

Making Time for Management

Being a middle manager in a secondary school is certain to raise a number of issues concerning time management. Demands are made on the middle manager's time from a number of different directions, from senior management, from members of the department, from pupils, from parents and from agencies outside the school. There are a wide range of tasks and responsibilities to be undertaken, including planning and delivering one's own lessons, drafting a scheme of work, managing the department's budget, providing support and encouraging the development of newly qualified teachers (NQTs), dealing with the local inspectorate, writing reports, observing the lessons of colleagues, monitoring the progress of the department, ensuring record keeping, managing change and innovation.

The middle manager in schools is constantly having to deal with interruptions. Time is arranged in 35-minute, 40-minute or 1-hour chunks, depending on the length of a teaching period. Tasks have to be left in order to teach a lesson. The middle manager could be asked to cover for an absent colleague, sometimes at short notice. A pupil could be sent to them to deal with. Some middle managers do not have an office and only have access to a telephone in the school's general office. Administrative support has to be shared, causing most middle managers to do their own word-processing and photocopying. Necessary meetings are not easily arranged as colleagues may not be free, or may have teams to run after school. Most meetings necessarily have to take place either at the end of the school day, at lunch time or even in the school holidays. Middle managers are forced to rely on the goodwill of others in order to get the job done.

All of this, and more, has to be managed within a limited amount of time. In the UK, teachers are contracted to work 1925 hours of 'directed time' per year and many voluntarily work more than this. Since 'time' cannot be created we need to think carefully about the efficient and effective use of the time we have. Time management is crucial to the middle manager. The aim of this chapter, therefore, is to explore a time management model particularly relevant to the middle manager. By the end of this chapter you will have explored a number of strategies that will assist you in managing your time more effectively, and dealing more effectively with people who make calls on your time and in the process enable you to feel more satisfied with your professional performance.

The complexity of managing time

Time management is a very complex activity. Partly it is about being organised, prioritising tasks and working in the most time efficient ways. These are described in many management books (see Adair, 1988; Donnelly, 1990; Capel *et al.*, 1995, 1996).

We asked a number of middle managers to give us an account of their own experiences of time management. Some case studies are now described.

Case Study 1

I have never actually worked harder than in my probationary year – with marking and preparation practically every evening. The second year was hard too with new classes and syllabuses and the second year for each exam course to prepare. In addition, I began to take on school teams and other extra-curricular activities – with very few free periods.

However, although I was always busy and often exhausted, I never felt that I needed time management help. I had expected to work hard and, aside from the stress of the classroom, the work was quite enjoyable.

My own problems began with the starting of a family. Having married a colleague I had been accustomed to spend long hours after school with much of our conversation about school activities and evenings spent marking.

With a young family at home, however, after-school activities were less attractive and evening hours not so freely available to do what had to be done. More things had to be done during the school day, but with promotion to a pastoral post, much of my free time was taken up with talking to kids, parents and colleagues. Few of these conversations were concise, many were spontaneous, the day became bitty and impossible to plan.

It was difficult to give things up, especially work with sports teams. People seemed to expect me to carry on doing the voluntary things which took up valuable administrative time. It seemed that if I wanted time for myself and my family it couldn't be done without disappointing other people, cutting corners or giving a bad impression. Recent changes in education, of course, have made things harder still.

Case Study 2

I had always dreamed of being a teacher and playing an important part in the life of the school should I be lucky enough to get a job. I was lucky on leaving college, I found no difficulty in getting a job in what I considered to be a good school. In college, I had always been able to manage my time and was fanatical about getting my papers in on time – I hated being late.

This fanaticism for punctuality and being 'on time' with reports and marking was still with me and was now beginning to eat into me as I fell further behind other members of staff who, being more experienced, managed to complete on time. I was also teaching PE and was, therefore, required to spend time after school and during Saturday mornings with clubs and school teams, again placing more pressure on me just at the only time in my life when I was feeling pretty disorganised. However, as I became more experienced and more organised I gradually managed to rise above the disarray and muddle and again felt in control.

Promotion was very welcome and the new responsibility exciting and challenging, but could I really cope with actually arranging fixtures, teaching, being a tutor and marking as well? I made sure that I was organised and everything went like clockwork. Two years later, I suddenly realised that everything was running well but it was all standing still. How was I going to move things forward? I was working as hard as I could just to keep things stable. I decided to make a list of urgent jobs and a list of long-term tasks to work towards in order to develop the department. The list of urgent jobs eventually became my biggest problem, it never seemed to decrease, as fast as I dealt with the jobs new ones kept coming along. The long-term tasks became longer and longer and longer.

How could I have managed to do the long-term tasks when people were making demands upon me, how could I refuse them?

Case Study 3

Although I can honestly say that I never felt as physically exhausted as I did during my probationary year, there were so many other elements which seemed to help counteract the tiredness.

Everything was new and exciting. I was keen to be involved in the whole life of the school to prove that I was a good teacher. I liked the people that I worked with. I wanted to be with them socially. I enjoyed their company. My whole life centred around the school. I never missed a school function. I actually wanted to be there. No wonder I was tired!

My enthusiasm did not wane for quite a while. I can remember criticising older, higher status colleagues for their seeming lack of support for extra-curricular activities. I didn't truly understand their position.

I gained a few promotions and picked up a lot of extra responsibility over the years. I was still fairly enthusiastic but I was beginning to question whether there were enough hours in the day. Was everybody else juggling six balls in the air at one time? Why did people come to me with still more things for me to cope with?

I really began to question the nature of the job with the teachers' strike. It was actually rather nice to have a lunch hour like people in other jobs. Why should I spend my hard-earned holidays with the kids? Who thanked me for it anyway? If my husband hadn't also been a teacher in virtually the same situation, although in another school, I might have come to these conclusions a lot earlier on, but invariably, if I was working late at school, so was he. We seemed to both be fairly happy in our chosen profession.

The real crux came when I became pregnant. Before I left to go on maternity leave the amount of pressure put on me was tremendous with people saying to me 'Before you leave will you just do...' 'That needs to be ready before you go on leave.' I actually left work only a week before my daughter was born and I had work sent home!

After the birth of my daughter I actually discovered that there was life outside school! I worked to earn money. This came as a great surprise to me. I returned to work in a different frame of mind and discovered that I could do a great job without the job being the be all and end all of my life. I actually believe that my life is now much richer.

Activity 13.1 Professional Autobiography and Time

Write your own account of your professional life and how time has been an issue. What have been the stresses on you and how have you been able to resolve them so far? Will these things work in the future? Record your thoughts in your reflective journal.

The accounts reveal that people feel anxious about other people's opinion of them, about disappointing other people, and about not moving forwards quickly enough for themselves and others. People adopt a number of different strategies to assist them in coping with a challenging job. The most common of these is to spend more and more time at school in order to get the job done. They find themselves arriving earlier and earlier in the mornings to complete tasks before school and leaving later and later in the evenings in order to complete tasks after school. People take work home to complete in the evenings and spend time at the weekend working in order to keep their heads above water.

This happens even with the most efficient, including those with excellent skills at organising their time efficiently. Occasionally overload can occur where time ceases to be used well because people are 'jaded' or 'burnt out'.

Much of the writing on time management starts with the premise that efficiency will solve all problems. Actually the accounts reveal that middle managers are often in the position where there is not enough time because there is too much to do. Yet they have to cope with their own feelings of falling behind or of not keeping up the pace. In addition, they have to work with other people. At times, this means saying no. At other times, it means saying yes, but within an extended time period.

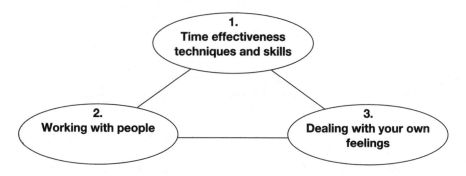

Figure 13.1 *The time management model*

Time management is about three components:

1. time effectiveness skills and techniques which one can develop in order to save time, make time and use time more effectively;
2. working with people;
3. handling your own feelings.

The time effectiveness skills and techniques

The school calendar

Planning is a major issue in time management. If we are aware that something is going to take place and are given a long period of notice before the event, the more prepared we can be and crisis management is avoided. Although in a school setting there will always be things happening about which we have very little warning, there are a number of events which are known well in advance and are a regular features of the school year, eg open evenings, parental consultation evenings, presentation evenings, deadlines for capitation bids, dates for mock examinations, dates for the start of GCSE examinations, etc. Some of these dates are fixed and some are negotiable within the organisation. The school calendar is a vital time management tool.

Middle managers in most secondary schools will be asked to contribute to this and usually asked to make comments on a draft before it becomes finalised. Schools should put as much information as possible on this calender. These are the 'knowns' and can be planned for. One of the first tasks of the middle manager is to interpret that information and use it as an aid to more effective planning.

Diaries

We find it unhelpful to keep separate social diaries and work diaries as we believe that good time management requires one to keep a 'whole life' picture. It is useful for the middle manager to write down dates from the school calender into personal diaries, along with other important dates such as family birthdays, etc.

As a next stage, we recommend working backwards from the dates given on the calendar and writing into your diary set times to plan for the event. For example, if the school calendar says that option booklets will be distributed to year 9 on 14 February and that heads of department need to complete their contributions by 16 December that is the deadline to which you are working. It is up to you to plan when you are going to write your contribution in line with that deadline and to decide whether or not you will invite members of your department to contribute. If so, time must be made available for that. The deadline for information for a number of such items is usually before or just after the start of the autumn term, allowing adequate planning to take place. We have found that writing in planning time is an excellent strategy as it allows one to see the whole picture before undertaking other tasks and also juggling tasks, so assisting the decision making process.

However, some things cannot be planned for in advance, eg cover for a colleague who has suddenly been taken ill, so middle managers in schools always have to be be prepared to reschedule when necessary. This does not have to be problematic, it merely involves another set of decisions being taken. It is useful for the middle manager always to have their diary with them. People will often make demands on you while you are moving between classroom and staff room. *Write it down.*

Deadline erosion

When you know that you have a deadline to meet and that other members of your department have to get information to you in order that you can meet that deadline it is important that they are not allowed to operate what we have termed deadline erosion. One person being late can put your planning out a great deal. Be prepared to issue reminders to people and to check whether they are on target as well as to check your own progress. It is also important to discuss the issue if members of your department fail to meet agreed deadlines. Getting things out in the open can be very useful.

Lists

Lists can also be a great aid to planning the term, the week and the day. A week-to-view diary is a useful tool as is a year planner or term planner displayed on an office wall. We advise dividing lists up into urgent and important items. A daily update of this list or a daily task sheet is necessary in order to have a clear picture of demands on your time. These lists change frequently sometimes in minutes in response to a telephone call, eg from an exam board requiring clarification about a candidate. If these lists are not updated it is very easy to forget something of great importance in your busy schedule. There is nothing more satisfying than crossing items off the lists. However, beware of becoming depressed if the lists rarely get shorter as new items are added, often on a daily basis. As a middle manager you will never be in a position where you have nothing to do! It is important that this is recognised.

Time budgets

Time budgets are a useful strategy for time management. As well as creating lists it is useful to allocate a nominal amount of time which you think should be spent on various tasks, eg writing a departmental description for the school handbook – half-an-hour to create a first draft. It is also useful to allocate a portion of time each day for various tasks, as some may be done at better times than others, eg write letters to be typed – half-an-hour 8am to 8.30. This will enable you to get letters to the school typist before the start of the school session. There is a well-known phrase that is used in school staff rooms, ie if you give someone a day to do something they will take a day. Some thought as to how much time things take realistically is a useful tactic in time management. Recording how long particular tasks take may assist you in this exercise.

Time budgets are particularly useful for meetings. We have all been to meetings that have seemed to be endless and got nowhere as a result. A time limit on meetings helps to focus the minds of the individuals involved. In our experience departmental business meetings need to go on for no more than one-and-a-half hours. Obviously planning meetings when working out a new scheme of work and meetings for which the focus is staff development will need to take longer. Sometimes a whole day is exactly what is needed to do the job properly! It is also important that meetings are planned in advance. It is vital to be clear about the purpose of the meetings which may be to inform, to discuss, to negotiate, to plan, to create, to evaluate or to monitor. People should receive the necessary papers and agenda in order that they can be read before the meeting and enable everyone to be prepared. It is also helpful to ask people to put items on the agenda in advance in order that you can be prepared, particularly if there is a delicate matter to be discussed, eg the fact that not all members of the department are carrying out agreed procedures. Meeting time is a scarce but necessary resource to ensure the development of the department. However, one really crucial question to ask is whether a meeting is essential or the best way of managing a particular issue. Would a memo suffice? Would a discussion paper with room for comments be more appropriate?

It is also important that an accurate record of every meeting is kept. We recommend minutes that highlight, and by whom, and by when as the most useful. Once things are written down and shared with all concerned, there can be no excuse for people failing to carry out agreed tasks. The meeting record is the evidence. This record not only aids everyone's time management but also provides useful data to show OFSTED or local inspectors as evidence of effective middle management. Chapter 14 provides further advice on managing administrative matters

Proforma

The use of proforma can also be time saving. These include a printed memo sheet, a meetings record sheet with action points and a pre-printed check list of departmental stationery for people to tick. All of these cut down on the amount of time spent writing.

Emergencies

With emergencies, you must ask yourself what action should be taken and the effect that this action will have on your time management. Three alternative but linked questions are possible:

- Emergency or non-emergency?
- Action or no action?
- Action by self or action by others?

Making sense of these and acting upon them involves the skills of decision making and prioritisation, interpersonal approaches to how you deal with others and time management skills relating to rescheduling.

Activity 13.2 Time efficient techniques

What approaches to being efficient with your use of time do you employ? How far do they work? What might make you work more efficiently with your time? Record your thoughts in your reflective journal.

Managing your own feelings

One of the most important aspects about the decision making process that middle managers have to go through when organising their time is their own feelings about the decisions they have taken. It is useful to explore one's own way of working. If you ask colleagues when they set about completing a task that is set for them to do – do they do it at once to get it out of the way, do they leave it until the last possible moment as the higher level of anxiety enables them to complete the task with greater motivation – it will be interesting to note that people work in a number of different ways. Some people can only deal with one task at a time, others may well leave a tasks for a few minutes to make some telephone calls and then get back to it with greater concentration. Knowing yourself is the first step in being able to manage your feelings.

Much of the way we feel about our actions is to do with expectations. The expectations that others have of us and the expectation that we have of ourselves. These two can be quite different. This is an issue well worth exploring. When you set a time budget on a task you may be allocating much more time to it than the senior manager who delegated it to you expected you to allocate in order that you do a good job. On the other hand, something to which you attach little importance, so allocate little time to it, may, in the eyes of your line manager, need more time, perhaps because the success of the task is seen as very public. It is important to check out this expectation with the person allocating the tasks to you. Some of the tasks may be part of a job description and can be discussed at line management meetings, while others may be tasks that have been delegated to you. It does not take long to check out beforehand what is expected of you. Doing this will eliminate feelings of frustration at time wasted and will assist your overall time management.

Being realistic is also important. Most middle mangers have what appears to be an impossible job. They have to manage the department and meet all deadlines and all of this on five free periods a week which are not guaranteed. You need to realise that this is what you have to work with. You are not going to get five more free periods. Don't waste time lamenting over this. The parameters are set and these are what you have to work within. If you don't feel that you can work within these parameters then maybe you should consider alternative forms of employment. However, you may be able to negotiate task parameters which will assist you in completing the task, eg not having to attend assemblies with your tutor group for a period of time.

We wrote earlier about seeing the whole picture by keeping only one diary for both work and social life, and by writing down planning for events and time for tasks. This provides one with the whole picture when making decisions about additional, unplanned tasks which one is asked to undertake. It is helpful to use this information to either say no to undertaking additional work by giving a valid reason for you not being able to complete the task satisfactorily or to be able to say 'yes, but...' and negotiate the parameters within which you are prepared to work. Our experience is that people are only able to feel comfortable with saying either of these if they have the relevant facts to hand.

The middle manager needs to assert themselves over additional tasks, take control and make informed decisions about how the task can be done and how long it will take. It is important to remember that there is nothing wrong with saying no to a task that one is invited to undertake, if one feels unable to complete it successfully. In addition, there is nothing wrong with negotiating parameters to undertake a task that one is directed to do at short notice by senior management. There may also be situations in which you will be able to ask for time to think about undertaking a task before you agree to do it. The most important thing is to be able to say no to the deputy head or head teacher and feel comfortable with doing that because you have shown that you are a good professional manager who has considered all the issues.

Working with people

The middle manager role, as mentioned earlier in this book, is like the filling in the sandwich. People will constantly make demands on your time. Phrases like 'Have you got a minute?' or 'Have you got time to...?' are frequently heard on school corridors, in the staff room, in the loo! It is important to clarify tasks you ask others to undertake. It is important for you to seek clarification about tasks that you are asked to undertake. Be open with people about the parameters within which they have to work, including the time parameters. Develop negotiating skills to assist you in creating optimum conditions within which to get the tasks completed.

People calling on your time

Ensure that all discussions have an agreed time limit and agenda. You need to be clear about the purpose of meetings. Ask people how long they think it will take. Plan an appropriate time and stick to it. Give yourself preparation and thinking time before meetings if you need it. Agree to adjourn meetings to give you time to think if you want it. Be careful of just stalling though. This is merely putting things off.

Just say no

You will need to say no to some people. Saying no is preferable to putting people off by delaying tactics. However, it may be more difficult for you. Make sure that those who have earned your time have it. Some people, particularly your own staff, may need a lot of time to talk and for you to support them. Others may waste time with fanciful ideas which rarely get off the ground. Often you might remind them of the last scheme, on which you spent some time, but that didn't go anywhere.

Managing their feelings

People will have their own feelings about your time together. You will need to ask them if they feel OK about the use of the time.

Pleasure time

Teams of people who work hard together need pleasure time together. In fact, they probably get more done in pleasure time. This might happen in the pub on a Friday night, at the bridge table in the staff room or over a cup of tea after school.

Energising time

There are periods when people run out of steam, particularly towards the end of term or the end of the year. Make sure that you monitor this. You have two options. Either take the pressure off and let people rest or energise them until they reach the end of term and a well-earned holiday. You will add to the feeling of 'lowness' if you yourself are low in energy. Get lively: crack jokes, get louder, keep them at it.

Deadlines

People need firm deadlines and as manager you need to keep them to them. There is no point of a deadline if no one sticks to it. People will merely take advantage. However, you need to be flexible and fair. If the deadline causes people problems because it is genuinely too tight, then change it. Set targets for staff who always miss deadlines.

Delegation

A well-known phrase given to managers from all walks of life is 'Don't do, delegate', indeed this is the title of a book by Jenks and Kelly (1985). We delegate for a number of different reasons: to get the tasks done by the division of labour involved; to give others an opportunity to develop their own management skills; to get out of something we do not want to do ourselves. The latter is of course the worst possible reason for delegating anything!

People react differently to delegation. It is worth considering how you as a middle manager decide what to delegate. Some managers will not delegate anything for fear of the tasks not being done. Others delegate but then shadow every move that the person makes. Some people delegate only the low status, routine, predictable, easy task. Often those tasks that are not delegated are those that are unpredictable, require experience and are high profile with a risk of public failure. Some people do not want to let go. It is worth spending some time thinking about what type of delegator you are. It is then worth exploring how delegation can assist your time management. It is also worth considering what safeguards you want to build in – regular updating of progress made, etc.

On a note of caution, the department is often made up of a number of individuals who have their own area of responsibility. You could have a deputy head or even a head teacher as a member of your department, you could have a year head or the person responsible for examinations and assessment. People with posts of responsibility will be most reluctant to undertake additional tasks when they already feel themselves to be struggling to complete what they perceive as their own. You may yourself feel resentful at being asked to undertake pastoral tasks as a form tutor when you have your own department to run.You could have a number of Newly Qualified Teachers with little experience. It is also important to remember that you can delegate tasks but not responsibility. Delegation of tasks must be negotiated with care. Once people have agreed to carry out a designated task it is important to provide support for them to undertake it but not to do it for them. We believe that true delegation is empowering people within the department.

Conclusion

The management of time is, like all aspects of management, about being 'good enough' to get by and reflective enough to improve, wherever possible. This chapter has outlined several areas for consideration under the three key areas of skills and techniques, working with people and handling your own feelings.

Chapter 14

Administration

'The paperwork hit me like a ton of bricks. I'd inherited a department with no records about anything – just the sheer amount of stuff to be done overwhelmed me. There was no induction or process of support. At a simple level, in the filing system nothing was in place, there were no class lists or records of stats or averages for classes. There was no framework or skeleton of events – a timetable of what had to happen. I felt I was too late in carrying out the work all the time – for example, in preparing the staff timetable, in submitting details of pupils being entered for examinations. There were no job descriptions in the department.'

This is how one, now experienced, middle manager described his introduction to the administrative side of his new post. In his first post as head of department he was left to find his own way of working with staff, and to establish his own routines and procedures.

Even if you are working in a supportive environment, you may consider that you have to undertake administrative tasks (filing, letter writing, record keeping) which could be dealt with more efficiently by administrative staff who are not juggling teaching with administration and management tasks. To a certain extent that will be true. The amount of administration which has to be done is often the subject of complaint by teachers at all levels of the education system. Deputy head teachers too often spend their time undertaking tasks which could be done by less well qualified staff, for example on statistical returns, cleaning and caretaking matters. Different schools respond to the need to provide administrative support in different ways – some allocating more of the budget to this area than others. Such decisions about allocation of the budget are taken by schools on an individual basis.

Whatever the support in your school, when you move into middle management, you will have much more 'paperwork' to do than before. If you develop procedures for dealing with the administrative tasks early on, rather than hoping they will go away, then you are more likely to be running a department or team where staff feel there is an organised framework of support for their teaching. This chapter addresses issues related to the administrative tasks faced by the middle manager.

By the end of this chapter you should have an understanding of the range of administrative tasks you are expected to deal with, considered forms of communication appropriate to the needs of the department or team and given some thought to the systems which need to be in place if you are to be an effective and efficient administrator.

Management and administration: the differences

Management is concerned with the effective and efficient operation of all aspects of the work of a team. The manager needs to be aware of his or her own strengths and weaknesses and those of the staff, to understand the nature of the organisation, to be able to set high standards and establish conditions which motivate staff and pupils to achieve such standards. These issues are covered in earlier chapters. Another aspect of effective management requires the establishment and evaluation of procedures and routines which facilitate the work of the department or team. The operation of these procedures and routines constitutes the main administrative task in the department or for the team.

The administration of a department or team requires work in two main areas:

- the maintenance and preparation of documentation related to planning future development and record keeping in general;
- the establishment and operation of routines and procedures providing the framework within which the work of the department is carried out.

The discussion of the tasks related to these two key areas is the focus for this chapter.

Planning and record keeping, routines and procedures

Careful planning and the establishment of systems for dealing with paperwork will enable the administration of the department or team to run smoothly. The establishment of routines and procedures enable all involved to understand what is required and when it is required. Planning and careful record keeping enable the focus on development to be maintained and provide documents by which progress in achieving goals can be judged.

In the following sections, administrative demands related to routines and procedures, and planning and record keeping, are considered. The issues discussed below are examples of what may be expected, but bear in mind that each school and each department or team will vary.

Requirements for general record keeping

Departmental records or records related to the work of a team may cover a wide range of areas. Examples are listed below.

Pupil related:

- class lists/pupil allocation to classes;
- pupils' records of achievement, reports, profiles;
- details of pupils' special educational needs and how these are being met;
- assessment results and their analysis (see Chapter 10);
- assessment moderation processes;
- equipment/books on loan;
- attendance;
- letters home and to other agencies.

Staff related:

- timetabling – year on year/staff workloads;
- professional development undertaken and requested;
- appraisal goals;
- staff development materials.

Curriculum and general assessment issues:

- schemes of work – what is taught when, to whom, and how, using what resources;
- coverage of the National Curriculum;
- assessment strategies;
- entries for option booklets and school prospectuses;
- evaluation records;
- examination syllabuses, past examination papers.

More detailed coverage of responsibilities in this area is included in the 'Curriculum and assessment' section on page 195.

Material resources:

- budget and expenditure details (see Chapter 15);
- materials for classes requiring cover where a teacher is absent;
- stock available – videos, texts and other resources to support the curricu-

lum – storage, retrieval and access are aspects of stock control;
- stock maintenance issues (eg servicing of equipment, maintenance of texts, consumables).

Departmental/team development related:

- records of meetings;
- department/team development plan;
- polices (where needed to supplement whole-school policies);
- procedures governing the work of the department or team.

The administration related to extra-curricular activities is not covered here but that is another aspect of administration for which the middle manager may be responsible.

Activity 14.1 Record keeping

Review the current record keeping procedures covering your department/team's work. To what extent do you consider these are adequate? In what ways might they be altered in order to support the work of the section more effectively?

Ways of communicating information

Poor communication within organisations is often a source of complaint from staff. What procedures are appropriate in your department or for your team? In most departments or teams, meetings rather than memos or newsletters will be the usual way of communicating information to staff.

As middle manager you will be organising meetings within your department/team, as well as attending meetings with the senior management team together with other middle managers. Chapter 13 covers some of these issues from the time management perspective. There are, however, a number of administrative approaches which if implemented ensure that meetings can be managed effectively to the benefit of the staff and the department or team.

Meetings

You may feel, as you see staff every day, that the informal meetings at lunch and coffee times keep everyone well informed. Memos can be useful in ensuring that all staff get the same message but be aware that some staff definitely prefer the personal approach. However formal meetings are essential as they fulfil a number of purposes (such as identifying ideas, promoting discussion, team building, consultation and decision making. Agendas should provide clear indications of the purpose of meetings). The minutes of such formal meetings provide a documentary record of decisions taken, as well as providing a reminder to all involved about the tasks to be undertaken (using the subheading 'Action' after items in the minutes and identifying what is to be done and who is to do it helps ensure that it is quite clear to all what action is required). Just as you need to keep staff informed about issues raised in meetings of middle managers, so too should staff be able to use you as an avenue of communication with senior management. The formal meeting provides a medium for formal discussions about the work of the school. It also provides a forum in which staff report back on professional development undertaken and debate current issues in the subject area.

Staff time is costly and limited so meetings must be managed to ensure that the time is used effectively. The management of meetings affects how staff feel about working in the department or team. You will no doubt have sat through meetings which were poorly managed and will want to avoid this situation in your area of responsibility. The environment in which meetings are held can also affect staff feelings about attendance. The provision of refreshments may help staff relax after a busy day.

While it is good practice to establish a cycle of regular meetings, meetings should be cancelled where they are not necessary and they should normally finish within the specified time. Meetings which drag on in a rambling, disorderly way may not be the best way to achieve your goals. Agendas should be circulated beforehand and staff should be given the opportunity to add items to the agenda. Allocating time to agenda items can ensure that business is finished on time. The chair should summarise decisions and the action to be taken. Well-managed meetings can promote good communication, collaborative working and a sense of ownership in the management of the department/team's work. You will of course need to be sensitive and supportive of the personal contributions of all colleagues – personality issues and 'hidden agendas' can destroy the functioning of groups.

Meetings with the senior management team and other middle managers

You are the advocate for your department or team at these meetings and how you manage this role requires you to think strategically. Your behaviour in such meetings will influence the views held about your section. As a middle manager, while you have responsibility to the staff in your department or team, you also have a responsibility to work within a whole-school framework where the whole curriculum experienced by pupils is the focus for attention. Chapter 7 provides an opportunity for you to analyse your leadership style.

Activity 14.2 Running effective meetings

Make notes in your reflective journal about how you plan to ensure meetings for which you are responsible are run effectively. What in your experience should be avoided? Do your plans for meetings provide an opportunity for staff to share in the decision making about the way in which the budget is spent, about the allocation of pupils to classes, about the syllabuses to be followed? Will staff feel included or excluded in the processes you establish?

Planning to support curriculum and assessment activities

A number of planning and record keeping tasks are associated with the curriculum and assessment aspects of the department/team's work.

Schemes of work provide the foundation for the work in a curriculum area. Chapter 10 discusses what might be included and detailed advice is provided in Capel *et al.* (1995). Schemes of work need to be drawn up, circulated and copies kept.

Schools adopt different approaches to testing, for example, some test all pupils on entry to the school. As a middle manager, you are responsible for ensuring that school and national tests are conducted under the conditions required by those setting the tests. In Chapter 10 the issue of establishing base line assessment of pupils on entry is discussed in the context of raising pupil achievement. All approaches to testing have associated administrative tasks – rooms and test papers have to be organised, tests have to be timetabled, student lists produced and results recorded, analysed and filed so they are readily accessible. Forms of assessment (of year groups or modules of work) will usually be discussed and agreed with staff. However the responsibility of administering, recording and analysing the results ultimately rests with the middle manager.

Documentation for inducting staff and recording plans

The middle manager has a central role in ensuring that the school vision is supported and implemented by staff. The development plan, procedures and policies provide mechanisms for staff to work together to plan for high quality outcomes for the pupils and staff. The different documents which relate to the ways of working of the department/team are often placed together in a staff handbook.

The staff handbook

A staff handbook related to your area of responsibility should complement any school staff handbook. If a handbook does not exist for your section, then the compilation of it can be done over time, as papers come to hand, as policies are developed and as procedures are confirmed with staff. Such a staff handbook is an invaluable source of reference for new staff, supply staff and visitors (like governors and inspectors), as well as a working document for existing staff.

Three substantial sections in such a handbook are those covering the following:

- *The development plan:* this provides a record of your hopes and achievements over the years and its evaluation provides a useful indicator of progress.
- *Policies:* where these are needed to supplement school policies, eg on staff development, marking and assessment policies, pupils borrowing resources, safety, ways of working in the classroom, loss or breakages of equipment.
- *Procedures:* staff energy can be released by the establishment of clear guidelines for carrying out routine aspects of work, eg assessment and recording of pupil work (in class, at home and in tests), moderation of assessed work, use of resources, decision making about resources, submission and storage of examination work, appraisal, induction of new teachers, meeting routines. Some staff may feel that formally recording these procedures is too bureaucratic but others will find such structures supportive. As a manager you need to learn to work effectively with staff with their different preferences.

Activity 14.3 The staff handbook

Consider the contents of the staff handbook for your area of work. How useful is it as a staff resource? How could it be improved? What in your view should a staff handbook include? Record your views in your reflective journal.

Financial plans, lists of staff and their areas of responsibility, meeting schedules, appraisal and evaluation procedures may also be included.

Chapter 11 provides more information about the process of effective development planning.

Organising contacts with external groups

Departments and teams are increasingly required to maintain contacts and links with groups outside the school. For these to operate smoothly, a significant amount of administration must be undertaken.

You will already be familiar with open evenings and parents' evenings. Now, as middle manager, the organisation of your section's role in these becomes your responsibility (this is not the same as saying you have to do everything).

You may need to meet prospective parents during the school day – letters have to be written and records made if appropriate. Governors may visit or be permanently allocated to the department or team so that they can develop their knowledge of the work of the school.

School–industry links are well developed in many schools but you will need to ensure this work is sustained in the area for which you are responsible. Careers' guidance goes beyond any information pupils get from interviews with the careers officer. Your section has an obligation to provide information for pupils about the possible career outcomes of work they are undertaking. Pupils will be motivated by being able to set goals for their futures. Children often follow their parents' footsteps, possibly because this is the information which is easily available to them. Teachers are able to provide to pupils, or through omission to deny them, knowledge about career paths.

Staff with pastoral responsibilities need to be kept informed about pupils' progress, attitudes and attendance. The Education Welfare service will usually liaise with staff with pastoral responsibilities but heads of subject departments may also be required to provide information. Each school will have established procedures of which you, as middle manager, should be aware.

Inspection of the school by externally appointed staff will occur from time to time. The middle manager is responsible for providing the documentation required about their area. Inspection reports on English schools are published on the Internet.

Liaison with examination boards about pupil entries and assessment may be part of your role, as may the organisation of moderation of pupils' assessed work.

You may also have contact with university or college staff. Many schools play a part in the education and training of student teachers. Such links may require you, or another staff member, to allocate time to plan and discuss lessons, as well as to inform the student about the functioning of the department or team and how to teach effectively. Written feedback on lessons observed is also normally required.

Some universities enter into compacts with schools. These schemes (compacts) provide close links between university departments and school departments. Such links may improve pupils' chances of gaining university places.

Records of quality assurance procedures

Quality assurance procedures are an important part of the middle manager's responsibilities. If records are kept in the areas outlined above, information should be available to fulfil these requirements. However institutions vary in their requirements.

Activity 14.4 Quality assurance

Find out what quality assurance procedures are considered to be good practice in your current school. Consider the points made in Chapters 11 and 12. Note in your reflective journal the methods which you use now, together with those which you wish to use. Outline a brief action plan for achieving the desired results.

Information about evaluation and monitoring procedures is provided in Chapter 12, and methods which can be used to monitor pupil achievement are included in Chapter 10.

Procedures for ensuring compliance with health and safety requirements

In some subjects the middle manager carries more responsibilities for health and safety issues than others. Managers of physical education, science and technology sections in particular must ensure that staff are aware of health and safety issues in their work. Schemes of work will usually include reminders of health and safety points to be considered with particular lessons. Again, the middle manager must check that their section is conforming with school requirements.

Filing and retrieving information

There is little point in establishing clear routines and procedures, and ensuring that planning and record keeping are well done, if your filing system does not allow you to retrieve such information as and when it is required. The maintenance of efficient systems for the filing and retrieval of information is part of the middle manager's role.

Processing paper-based information

Some texts suggest that managers handle a piece of paper once only. Do you, for example, need to look at catalogues that you are sent if you are not planning to spend money at the moment? It may be appropriate just to skim through these and then file them immediately for easy reference when decisions about purchasing have to be made. What procedures do you use for processing paper? How can they be improved?

Information retrieval

You can only do this effectively if your filing system is set up in such a way that you can find the papers you need immediately. If you feel there is scope for improvement in your methods of filing and retrieving information ask secretarial staff and other middle managers about the methods they use.

Assisting your memory

Staff and pupils often tell you quite important pieces of information in passing. If, however, you find can't fully recall such conversations later (worse, you find out you didn't even know you had forgotten), then carrying a notebook for recording jobs needing doing may help you. Keeping lists of jobs can also enable you to work more efficiently if you deal with similar tasks together as a block, for example telephone calls, filing and letter writing. Similarly, keeping a notebook by the phone for recording phone calls, both ingoing and outgoing, allows you to check messages have been dealt with.

Chapter 13 on time management provides details of other strategies for managing your time efficiently.

Conclusion

We hope you will see the need to step back from the immediate pressures of teaching and plan how you are going to manage the administrative demands of your post. Setting up easy-to-use filing systems and noting administrative demands on a calendar of events for the year will save you time in the long run. Everything does not have to be done at once; you can build procedures over time as the need becomes apparent. Efficiency in the area of administration is worth aiming for as efficient systems provide a supportive framework for the work of the team.

Chapter 15

Finance and Material Resources

In the UK, a large secondary school receives a budget (formula funded) of something, say, in the region of £2 million. The LEA will already have taken its share of the funds allocated by government to the local area in order to provide various support programmes and initiatives. Having drawn up a budget based on a centrally approved formula, the LEA presents a sum to school management which construct the school budget, allocating funds to departments, pastoral teams and faculties.

School management start by stripping away the fixed and variable operating costs, which include a catalogue of expenditure starting with staffing and working its way through premises, exam fees, general maintenance and so on. The usual scenario is for a meeting to be held some time in February or March at which the various budget holders of the school are:

- told that they have so much money for the year; or
- competitively bidding for their share of the money; or
- engaged in some other process which results in the distribution of the funds available.

The amount of money, the same in all three versions of the 'consultative process', is an extremely small percentage of the total budget, but none the less provides the funds to support the classroom practice. Although in many, if not most cases, the funds you are allocated are inadequate to fulfil your vision, the process of applying for allocation of funds is a yearly task for the middle manager. You are held responsible for the spending of this money and dependent on the spending of this money is the delivery of quality education to your pupils.

Leaving aside the national and local contexts, there follow suggestions and strategies for increasing your share of the budget as well as dealing with the day-to-day, weekly, monthly and yearly demands on the budget holder in a school. What must be borne in mind throughout, however, are the facts that the delegation of funds to schools in the UK takes place in an atmosphere of ever-increasing accountability and visibility in which the survival of the institution is left more and more to so-called 'market forces' and in which, in the UK, notions of cooperation between schools are more and more threatened by competition for the hearts and minds of the client group and their parents.

By the end of this chapter, you should understand the constraints related to the school budget and the ways in which money may be allocated, as well as procedures for bidding for development funds for the department in which you, as a middle manager, may need to participate.

The school context

The variety of school management styles in operation are legion. Senior management teams may exhibit styles ranging from the purely machiavellian to the openly democratic and, mirrored in departments and faculties and teams, may be the same traits and characteristics which are found at the top. Understanding a school's professional ethos as well as the procedures and structures which stem from it, is the starting point for your consideration of how to achieve what you want in budgetary terms. The allocation of the school budget itself in the UK is ultimately determined by the governors of the school. Their participation, or not as the case may be, will be significant in the final allocation of funds to the various competing elements of the school community. Middle managers are well advised to examine the processes and procedures leading to the allocation of resources in the school and to locate the centres of decision making where who gets what and for what reasons is determined.

At its simplest, the school will receive a sum of money which will be indicated to the school early in the calendar year to enable planning for the financial year which, in the UK, does not coincide with the academic year. The head or deputy or the finance committee of the governing body, or a combination of the three, will produce a proposed budget for the full governing body. Local authorities generally provide a consultative service for this process although some schools have dispensed with a deputy or two and hired in a bursar either on a full or part-time basis. The governing body will examine the proposed budget, hopefully in conjunction with the school development plan and with some idea of what needs to be done to improve the quality of education in the school. A budget will be ratified, notified to the authority and expenditure for the year is thus set.

The budget itself will be based on precedent but should also, in financial terms, give an indication of the future development of the school. The balance between the two is critical.

The constraints on budget setting are many, and the simple fact is that most of the money is gone before it gets to the client group. The yearly, termly and day-to-day running costs of the school account for most of the budget. Governors are required to pay the staffing costs of the school – teachers, support staff and any others. They are required to allocate money for the projected use of supply and possibly long-term sick colleagues and maternity costs. They will be looking to secure the maintenance of the premises, pay the various rate charges, utilities and any insurance demands. Governors will have to consider the funding implications arising from both short and long-term decision making, and then allocate money to 'supplies and services', as it is called in some authorities. Into this latter category will be placed the 'nuts and bolts' day-to-day running costs of the school which will include anything and everything from the cost of telephone calls to the payment of licence fees, examination fees, recruitment costs, subscriptions, hospitality… the list is endless, or potentially so.

The focus for allocating the budget is, of course, the teaching of children but this has to be done within the confines of a building that needs maintenance, and with the need to pay teaching and support staff and all the other fixed and variable costs of the institution. The inescapable truth is that the delivery of resources to the 'clients' expressed in more books, better facilities, better teacher/pupil ratios, in short the delivery of the National Curriculum, takes place in the context of demands for limited resources within a fixed budget which is set by parties who have a greater say in the decision making process of that budget allocation than any middle manager who is given a contract to deliver the vision of the institution itself.

Decision making and the budget process

If school management styles can be seen to occupy a place on a continuum ranging from the purely machiavellian to the openly democratic, consultative procedures, processes and structures can and do fall into the same patterns. The means of influencing budget decisions will depend on the day-to-day working practices in place within the institution. It is up to the middle management to locate those possibilities for influence and exert that influence where possible. It is not always easy.

At national and local authority levels the scope for influence by middle managers is virtually non-existent. Nonetheless middle managers should be aware of the constraints imposed on the school by the formula as expressed in the local authority's allocation of funds to schools. Certainly the head and governing body will have an interest in the budgets of other schools in the area. In a wider political context, a most informative figure is the percentage of the total education budget retained centrally by the local authority; the simple observation being that the higher the percentage retained centrally the less is available to schools on a yearly basis, but that has to be balanced against the value of the services provided by the local authority.

At school level, the personnel involved in budget decision making are generally a combination of one, some or all of the following. Here again the particular combination can be seen as an extension of a particular management style and the school's view of the consultative process. The governing body must be involved but may delegate much of its finance work to a subcommittee which may or may not work closely with the head and the senior management group. Middle management will have an interest, as will professional associations, a premises subcommittee which may incorporate a health and safety committee, and any other formal groups which lay claim to regular meeting time in the yearly calendar and need a budget to carry out their work.

In a rational view of budget construction the school development plan will occupy a central place of influence. Ideally, it will have been constructed after an extensive audit and consultative process. HMI, OFSTED and the local inspectorate and advisory service will probably have had an input and the developmental agenda of the school may have been set for anything up to five years. If this is the case, then the primary expenditure for the school is set in advance and much of the debate which takes place at the time budgets are set becomes an act of fine tuning. The forward development of the school is set and the cyclical process becomes one of evaluating, monitoring and reviewing progress towards fixed goals and the achievement of performance indicators. The fine tuning is to reaffirm and re-establish priorities and allocate funds accordingly.

The elements of making a case

For a budget holder to secure funds, at some point a case will have to be made for any proposed expenditure. An institution with clearly defined budget policies and open procedures will make life easier for the middle management. Competition for scarce resources will take place in a structure which is visible to all and thus less susceptible to the all too common special treatment available to some. Whoever the case has to be made to, whether it be the head, the senior management group, the resources committee or the finance committee of the governing body, a number of questions will set the framework for making that case:

1. What have we got at the moment?
2. What do we need to do the same as we did last year?
3. What do we need to do better?
4. How will we keep track of what we do this year?

The questions allow for a departmental audit of resources in hand, the construction of what might be called a basic submission (see Figure 15.1), a consideration of proposed development in the department and the putting into place of a monitoring system for expenditure for the year.

Budget Centre: _____ **Financial Year:** _____

Proposal for Spending:

		Previous Year/Actual	Current Year Proposal
1.	Printing/stationery		
2.	Photocopying		
3.	Computer software*		
4.	Educational equipment*		
5.	Materials (general)		
6.	Books*		
7.	Curriculum-related travel		
8.	Other*		
	TOTAL (B)		

*Starred items (3, 4, 6, 8) require itemisation and costing.

SIGNED: _____ DATE: _____

Figure 15.1 *Form 1 Yearly Budget Basic Submission (Maintenance)*

What have we got at the moment? The audit

If the notion of a departmental audit is expanded from a yearly counting of pencils and boxes of chalk, and the concept of resources widened to embrace the human element, the task of determining what we have at the moment becomes more demanding but potentially more rewarding both for the professional development of staff and also for the development of the pupils. Most departments will have some form of record keeping and cataloguing procedure for books and consumables, and on the basis of this the middle manager will lay claim to a budget for the continuation or maintenance of the work in the classroom. This will be a non-contentious set of items and because the cost will not vary substantially from year to year, the money will most probably be made available. Similarly, a well-kept stock book following the standard format of what you have got, where it is, what condition what you have got is in, what repairs have taken place and so on, will usually result in replacements being allowed because you've been a good housekeeper. The audit, however, must be conducted so as to include those obvious but often unseen items which determine the working conditions for staff and pupils alike; such as flooring, decoration, notice boards, tables and chairs, window cleaning, lighting.

Similarly with Inset. The construction of school timetables is often thought to be a mystical affair with a nominated deputy disappearing into the clouds for anything up to a month and returning with a magic formula for the lives of staff for the following academic year. The middle management will have been consulted at various points during the proceedings and, by and large, most are moderately happy with the result. Assuming the needs of the department have been met in respect of the allocation of classes and teaching time, a primary consideration becomes the in-service training (Inset) needs of the staff. Are the Inset needs of staff in the department to be met from a central school fund or does the department have a budget allocation for Inset?

What do we need to do the same? The basic submission

Form 1 (Figure 15.1: Basic submission) indicates a possible format for making a case for a basic submission. The principle is that a department will need a certain amount of funding to provide the same service to the students as for the previous year, allowing for inflation. The assumption is, of course, that the numbers have remained constant; if not, a prorata adjustment is made up or down. The basic submission is governed by the end of year audit to prevent duplication and simply provides for consumables and replacements to existing stock and hardware. The target person or group for the basic submission will depend of course on the budget forming procedures in the particular school but the basic submission can in any case assist you in keeping a running record from year to year. The form itself can be adapted for individual departmental idiosyncrasies in the form of additional items and can assist you in weighing up proposed expenditure against the department's development plan.

Minor works feature on most school budgets. Paradoxically, the major nature of these 'minor' works is expressed, for example, in doors that won't open or close, cabinets that are falling to bits, shelves that get stuck, windows that won't close or open, damaged whiteboards, obsolete and non-chalk friendly blackboards. In-house procedures for dealing with such items of disrepair will exist and may well be the responsibility of another budget holder. It's a question of finding who the budget holder is and in many cases negotiating responsibility for the cost.

There is often a fine line between the minor works programme proposed by middle management and a health and safety issue or issues. The advice here is that, if in doubt, consult someone who knows, such as the health and safety representative! And do it immediately.

What do we need to do better? Submitting a development bid

Forms 2 and 3 (Figures 15.2 and 15.3: Development bid) indicate a possible format for making a submission for a development bid. The cornerstone of this bid is the departmental development plan, a document which has been informed by and contributed to the construction of the whole-school development plan. The principle here is that having achieved the budgetary allocation for the basic submission, the middle manager is now in a position to justify further spending within his or her area of responsibility which will result in increased performance of the pupils who come through the doors of the classroom on a daily basis. The development plan should be a vision of what is possible given the best possible set of conditions, tempered with a realisation that those conditions will not be met. It is a plan dedicated to the raising of the levels of achievement of the pupils. It is a plan which is laid on the table in the competition for scarce resources and as such must be clearly, rationally and, at times, passionately justified.

Budget Centre: _____ **Financial Year:** _____

Budget centres are required to submit proposals under the following headings. (Use additional sheets as necessary.)

Aims/Objectives:

Proposals:

Inset Requirements with Costings (A)

TOTAL (A)

Figure 15.2 *Form 2 Yearly Budget Development Bid (Outline)*

Proposal for Spending:

		Previous Year/Actual	Current Year Proposal
1.	Printing/stationery		
2.	Photocopying		
3.	Computer software*		
4.	Educational equipment*		
5.	Materials (General)		
6.	Books*		
7.	Curriculum-related travel		
8.	Other*		
	TOTAL (B)		

*Starred items (3, 4, 6, 8) require itemisation and costing.

Total (A) + (B) =
Financial Implication

SIGNED: —————————————— DATE: ——————————

Figure 15.3   *Form 3 Yearly Budget Development Bid (Detail)*

The departmental development bid is based on the assumption that if it does not succeed, that the department will manage to struggle through the next 12 months with no significant changes, that the status quo will prevail and that there will be no significant and/or awkward questions for you to answer. It will be assumed that there are no pressing health and safety issues to be resolved.

The development bid process assumes the middle manager can and should be making decisions about the development of the department. It invites a consideration that the person in charge of history or mathematics or science is aware and cognisant of the school development plan, has kept abreast of developments within his or her subject area, is aware of the numerous budgetary restraints operating and is capable of and prepared to justify extra expenditure in the department against real and measurable targets. As such, it is a source for continuing revision and expansion of the school development plan and, used properly, within supportive and sympathetic structures, and processes a vehicle for improving the working conditions of departmental members and increasing the quality of learning experience in the classroom. What is encapsulated in the development bid is the vision of the middle manager of what is possible educationally in their area of responsibility.

Form 3 (Figure 15.3) can be adapted for development bids ranging from simple and inexpensive items to the more elaborate, costly and extensive changes of direction stemming from major policy decisions at either school, local authority or national levels. An example of the former would be an English department's bid for a new set of books to expand the range of poetry available to pupils at Key Stage 3; of the latter, funding to support a policy decision taken at senior management level in consultation with the maths department to move to more teacher directed learning programmes. In either example, you are required to 'make the case' for the bid justifying the extra expenditure in professional terms, costing the bid, not only for consumables and hard items, but also for the Inset requirements arising from the development proposal.

As stated above, the target group for the receipt and consideration of basic submissions and development bids will vary from school to school. Depending on the systems in place and the size of the bid the middle manager can expect to have to present the case which he or she has laid out on paper to bodies, formal and informal, ranging from the casual chat with the bursar/finance deputy to a full presentation to the whole governing body. Preparation for these events is obviously crucial; a clearly presented case backed up with the appropriate paperwork and costings standing a much better chance of success. The key task here is to develop a presentation based on the school ethos, its development plan and the findings of any recent inspectorate reports at either local or national levels. It should fit with the direction that the school has decided for itself. (If the submission or bid argues for a change of direction, the task is that much more difficult.) Whatever the level at which the bid is presented, the guiding principles are to demonstrate that the proposed expenditure will result in enhanced provision for the pupils, that the quality of the teaching and learning experiences in the classroom will be improved and, as may be required in many cases, that the results will be measurable against performance indicators. Governing bodies are increasingly aware that in the current climate the 'value for money question' is one that not only forms part of the OFSTED brief but is also posed by HMI and the local authority inspectorate teams. Heads, who are placed in the position of having to justify expenditure in replying to the value for money question, will need to be well and fully briefed to defend decisions on items of major expenditure and development recommended by their middle managers.

The mechanism, whatever it is, for sorting and prioritising bids and allocating funds may result in stress and disappointment. In any event, whatever the emotions, the middle management will then have the responsibility of spending the allocation, accounting for the spending and preparing for the next round.

Keeping track: budget monitoring

The fixed nature of a departmental budget makes accounting for expenditure extremely simple. The accounting may be computerised and centrally located or operate out of a Victorian roll-top desk. It doesn't matter.

For the purposes of the middle manager a simple, easy to use form for keeping track is given in Form 4 (Figure 15.4: Proforma for Recording Expenditure). The department is allocated a sum of money for the year in two categories: basic and developmental. Two separate records of expenditure need to be kept (basic submission and development bid), and expenditure deducted as and when it occurs. If a bonus occurs, extra money for a project for example, the bonus is simply added to the left-hand column and adjustments made. Spread sheet maestros could play with and improve on this simple format, but all that is necessary is to record how much money is spent and how much remains.

Centralisation in the school of accounting procedures may negate the need for departmental accounting of this nature to take place. However, you may feel the need for a form of hands-on control.

Keeping track enables you to prepare for the next budget round and historical spending records can not only inform future spending and stock control procedures but also can serve as useful information in preparing the case for subsequent years.

Shopping around is always advised but can result in counter-productive, time-consuming activity for the saving of a few pence. Bulk buying with other departments or the whole school is a possibility but the middle

Budget Centre _____   **Basic submission or development project** _____

Year _____

Balance	Description	Date	Printing/ stationery	Photocopying	Computer software	Education equipment	Materials general	Books	Curriculum	Other	Inset	Checked by Date

Figure 15.4   *Form 4 Proforma for Recording Expenditure of Annual Financial Submissions*

manager should acquaint him or herself with standing orders in relation to expenditure on major and costly items, and the rules and regulations governing expenditure over certain local authority cash ceilings. Authorities may require verbal or written quotations and for major developments a tendering process may have to be adhered to.

The purposes of financial record keeping are internal to the department and preparation for external audit or monitoring either by the school, the local authority or the national inspectorate. It should not be an onerous task but a simple administrative procedure, within the school's guidelines, carried out regularly and summarised half-termly. It may be as simple as asking for a print-out of the current state of affairs from the bursar.

Unless a mechanism for savings exists, clearly stated in school policy, money should be spent according to the timescale requirements of the bursar or deputy in charge of finance. Panic spending in February or March is not to be recommended. (In the UK a budget is for a financial year ending in April.) Low expenditure may indicate to some that the money was not needed and this may have a bearing on future requests.

Other budgets

The amount of money coming into a school for the financial year will not be fixed solely by the centrally approved local authority formula. You may need to find out what extra funds are available and how they may be accessed. You should be prepared to duplicate the bidding process to other persons or groups who carry responsibility for these potentially hidden sources of income. Again, if sympathetic, open and supportive structures and processes exist, the distribution of the funding will be equitable and will address the clearly stated aims and objectives of the school development plan.

There are a number of extra sources of income to which UK schools may have access. These are listed below, together with questions which will need to be answered about each one:

1. For inner city schools, the single regeneration budget (SRB) may provide funds. Has the school applied for funding under this category?
2. Government grants for in service training/professional development. How much is coming into the school per year and under what categories are we receiving money? Who controls this Budget in the school? How can I bid for it?
3. The school fund. Does it exist? How much is there in the fund? What is the mechanism for laying claim to it?
4. The trigger mechanism for increased rolls. Are we receiving money for an increased roll intake in any particular year? If so, how much and what happens to it? How can I bid for it?

5. Training of student teachers. Do we have students in the school? How much are we getting for them? How can I bid for this extra source of income?
6. Other sources. Is there anything else I should know about?

Conclusion

The attention you pay to financial management will have an impact on the resources available to maintain or develop your work. In this chapter we have described some of the processes which you may need to understand if you are to be a successful advocate for your department when funds are allocated.

Chapter 16

The Selection of Staff

The selection of staff is a major task involving a number of skills and requiring the exercise of one's own values and judgement. We believe that the role of the middle manager in school improvement can be greatly enhanced if the middle manager is given significant responsibility for the selection of staff within their department. They know the subject area, they know the team of people in their department, and they also know their strengths and weaknesses. They are, in our view, in the best position to decide what qualities and experiences are needed to increase the performance of the department. The aim of this chapter is to outline the stages of the selection process, to encourage middle managers to be ready to participate in the process, to be able to communicate their views clearly to senior management and to be able to influence the decision making.

At the end of this chapter you will have greater knowledge and understanding of the selection process and be in a position to negotiate greater responsibility for appointing staff to your department.

Shadow staffing strategy

We suggest that there should be a strategy for staffing. Middle managers should be fully aware of the strengths and weaknesses of each member of the department, and the long and short-term tasks that need to be completed as outlined in the department development plan and schemes of work. Using this information, the effective middle manager should know exactly what qualities they would be looking for should any member of the department leave for one reason or another. For example, it may be that the department needs someone with greater experience at teaching a particular examination syllabus that you have been considering for a long time. It may be that the average age of staff teaching in the faculty is high, and some younger members might inspire the students differently. It may be that the majority of people in your department lack experience of teaching in other schools and you see appointing someone with experience of a number of schools as a way to move the department forward.

A shadow staffing structure is something that senior management teams in most schools have ready to hand. We feel that middle managers should have a view of where they would like to see the department in three or five years' time and be considering the staffing changes that would facilitate this, ie having a shadow staffing structure for the department. If you have thought about this in advance, you will be a position to present a case to senior management for the type of person you want to advertise for. You will be better prepared to have a greater say in the appointment or to fight your corner if you are told that you cannot replace a member of staff who is leaving because of financial constraints. You may not win the battle, but if you are prepared, you have the advantage. As we have already highlighted in Chapter 13 on time management, advance planning helps us to avoid crisis management. It is advisable to share your analysis with your line manager once you have completed it so that they understand your goals. It is not necessary to wait until someone resigns.

The selection process

Stage 1: Resignation

A member of staff in your department resigns and you have been informed that that person will be replaced. It is crucial to consider the position that that person held in the department. It may be that the second in the department has left to take up a head of department post in another school. It may be that a deputy head teacher in your department has left. Key decisions have to be made. If it is a deputy head who has left, the senior management team will have to consider replacing the deputy head or not. You may have no part to play in that selection process if they decide to replace! However, there will be implications for you and your team. Does this mean that you can have a full-time member of staff, will you have to try to appoint a part-time member of staff? So, the position within the school of the person who has left will greatly influence the decision making process.

For the purpose of this exercise we will assume that the person who is leaving is your second in the department. You have to consider a number of issues. Do you need a second in the department? What role did the previous incumbent fulfil? Was it satisfactory? How would you change it? If you decide that you do need a second in department, but feel that there is already someone within your department who would do an excellent job, you could argue for their promotion and the appointment of someone on a lower scale. You may feel that the department would be greatly energised by appointing a newly qualified teacher. Whatever you decide the department needs must be the result of a detailed analysis of the department team by you. You will never convince senior management to agree to your ideas if you have not done your homework. A position paper on the state of the department would be useful to present to your line manager or the head teacher.

The amount of time you have to do this depends upon when the person hands in their resignation. Some people hand in their resignation at the last possible moment, often through no fault of their own, making it difficult for you to secure an appointment for the start of the next term. You could be faced with a temporary teacher covering absent staff for a term! This is an issue that will not be discussed here, although it is of great importance. We will assume that the decision has been made to go ahead with a replacement from outside the school.

Stage 2: Drafting the advert and arranging for its placement

The wording the advert is very important. You want to attract the right sort of people to apply, also you want to have a 'field' of candidates from which to choose. You also don't want to waste your time and the time of others through lack of clarity. Different schools have different experiences. Some find it very difficult to attract a good number of suitably qualified staff for one reason or another – bad public press, position of the school, etc. Other schools find that whatever post they advertise, they are inundated with responses. Some are in between. Whichever applies to your school, the wording is important.

The wording of the advertisement should be the responsibility of the head of department where possible. You need to ensure that the advert is clear about what the post is, when the post is available, how much it will pay, how and from whom further details can be obtained, the closing date for receipt of applications and any other attractions the school can offer, eg the possibility for an additional scale point for an outstanding candidate, the opportunity to participate in a national project of which the school is part, the opportunity for specialist retraining, etc. It is a useful exercise to look through the variety of adverts in the professional journals. Which do you think are the most attractive? Analyse your reasons for choosing particular adverts. Apply similar wording to the drafting of your own adverts. It is also useful to put yourself in the position of prospective candidates. You have made applications yourself and there must be things that you liked and things that you did not like about the advertisements.

It is important to check how much notice the newspapers and journals need before the placement of an advertisement. You must also make sure that all the paperwork you want to send out to candidates is prepared well in advance of the advert being published. Most interested applicants apply for the information on the day that the job adverts are published. Your office staff will have to have the materials at hand to send out as soon as possible in order to give applicants the maximum amount of time to complete their applications.

Stage 3: Information for candidates

It may be that this stage is completed before the advert is drafted. So long as it is ready to go out as soon as the advert is printed, the order in which these two stages are carried out is of no real importance.

Applicants should receive a clear description of the post for which they are applying. This should, of course, be based on previous discussions between yourself and senior management. Ask yourself the question whether it is clear what the responsibilities are. A person specification is also vital. You know best what sort of person you are looking for in your department. Some of this will obviously relate to qualifications and experience. Some will relate to personality, eg a sense of humour, an enthusiastic person etc. We have found it helpful to indicate whether these traits are essential for the post or desirable. This helps the applicant to decide whether they would fit in to your department or not.

An application form may or may not be sent out. Some schools automatically use the local authority standard application form if it is available. Some schools have created their own application forms. Increasingly, head teachers are not asking candidates to complete an application form, but ask them to send a curriculum vitae and a letter of application. This decision may well be out of your hands as a school policy may apply. However, it is worth thinking about your own views on the best way to gauge an applicant's suitability for a post. It is also useful to send instructions for applicants in order to ensure that applications are completed correctly.

Other relevant papers to send should, in our view, include information about the school, eg position, school population, number of staff. Some information about the department is also valuable. Even if you are not responsible for the advert and drawing up the person specification you will most probably be asked to provide information about your department. This should ideally cover no more than a side of A4. Members of staff, syllabuses being used etc should be included.

It is not essential to send each person any more detailed information at this stage. Once you have selected candidates for interview you may deem it useful to send out more information such as a recent OFSTED report, department scheme of work, school development plan, etc.

As a middle manager you should be very interested in the people who are contacting the school for information. It is useful for office staff to use a proforma to log calls, including names and addresses of people who have asked for details. It is also useful to have this information as data for analysis if few applications are received. We can then begin to ask questions about the information sent out, timing etc. How many people expressed an interest? How many people actually applied? Is there a huge discrepancy between the two figures? Why didn't they apply? If you do not get the anticipated response we feel that is useful to contact some of the people who asked for information but did not apply and ask what put them off. This will provide valuable information for future use.

Stage 4: Sifting through the applications

It is really important at this stage to remember the amount of time and effort it takes to complete a job application.

We find it useful to wait until the closing date for all applications and then to look at all the applications together. We believe that you as a middle manager should be a key player in this stage of the process. Depending upon the style of management within the school in which you work you will either get the applications first or after the head teacher and senior management team have read them and made certain decisions. Our view is that so long as you get an opportunity to see all the applications, the order in which you receive them is unimportant. It would be a great cause for concern if you did not have a chance to participate in the process at this stage.

It is only fair to view each applicant in light of the selection criteria and we would recommend sorting them initially into three piles: definite, maybe and not on your life! In our experience, there are a number of ways that people approach the sorting of applications. Much depends upon the number received and the time available. If there are a large number, applicants often are rejected for fairly minor reasons like only having three years' experience when four was stipulated in the selection material. You need to set aside a fair amount of time to read the applications thoroughly. Excellent staff can be discarded by cutting corners.

A discussion should follow between yourself and members of the senior management team to see if you have selected the same applicants or whether there are huge differences of opinion. In these discussions, you should reach a consensus, although often in practice the final decision rests with the head teacher. Once a decision has been reached three or four candidates should be selected to invite for interview.

Stage 5: References

Several policies concerning the taking up of references exist. Some schools do not take up references until they have selected a successful candidate and the post is then offered on the basis of satisfactory references being received. Some schools take up references before inviting applicants for interview and may change their views about calling them on the basis of the references received. Some people rely heavily on references, while some people do not think they are worth the paper they are written on. References are confidential and offer one person's opinion about another's professional ability.

Some people look for the so-called head teacher's code phrase 'I recommend so and so to you without reservation'. Some people place a great deal of faith in this phrase. Our view is that the reference has to be looked at in perspective. The decision to appoint or not to appoint should not rely solely on the references received. We favour using our own judgement based on the application form about whether or not to invite an applicant for interview, and then again using our own judgement on interviewing the candidate and then looking at references to see if someone else confirms our decision. Concerns about something a referee has said can be checked out by calling them on the telephone and discussing it with them.

Stage 6: The interview

Once it has been decided which applicants you would like to interview, the next stage is to set up the interview. There are a number of decisions to be made. Some of these may have already been made before the advert was placed and some may not be up to you to make. However, these decisions include the interview panel: who is going to interview? It is usual for the head teacher to want to be part of the panel and yourself as head of department. A governor and a local authority representative might be useful additions, and sometimes a deputy head will be included. Three or four interviewers are adequate for any post below head of department. If you are using people outside the school to interview you must make sure that you give them adequate notice. Time will be quite tight as most people will want to make an appointment giving the candidate enough time to resign in order to start at the beginning of the new term.

Once you have a panel, papers must be duplicated for all interviewers so that they can do their homework. They need to know what the job and the person specification is, in addition to copies of the candidates' applications. We believe that it is important to plan for the interview carefully in order that candidates will be able to show themselves in the best possible light. Decisions now include issues like do you want candidates to give some sort of presentation? Is there just going to be one interview or a series of interviews with different interviewers? What style will the interview take? What questions will give you greater insight into the ability the candidate has to do the job you want him or her to do? We do not believe that it is helpful to use trick questions. Presentations can be useful as they give the candidate an opportunity to take charge and offer great insight into the candidate's knowledge of the chosen topic and teaching ability. If you do decide that you want a presentation, it is important to ensure that all the candidate's requirements will be met, eg the provision of an overhead projector or flip chart, duplication facilities etc. For posts below head of faculty we believe that one formal interview will give all the information that you need to decide if a person is suitable for the post. But, we also believe that it is important to allow the candidates an opportunity to talk to a number of people informally so that they can really get a feel for the school and the department. They have to want to work in your school. Honesty is the best policy. Candidates should be given an opportunity to see it as it is and be given ample opportunity to withdraw if they feel that they would not fit into the school or the department.

There needs to be a planned programme for the day which should look something like the example given in Figure 16.1.

Dodge City High School
Appointment of Second in X Department
Interview Schedule

9am	Arrival (report to school office and meet with Ms Money – School Business Manager)
9.15	Coffee – Introductions – outline of the day – Head's office with Ms Evans, Head Teacher
9.30	Tour of the school and department with Mr Yew, Head of Department
11am	Coffee – staff room – opportunity to talk to staff
11.30	Presentation and interview candidate 1
12.10	Presentation and interview candidate 2
12.50	Lunch – (in parents' room) – further opportunity to meet with other members of staff
1.50pm	Presentation and interview candidate 3
2.30	Presentation and inverview candidate 4

Figure 16.1 *Interview schedule*

It is useful for candidates to receive this programme in advance in order that they know they will have an opportunity to ask questions and can compose themselves before their interview. The above programme, with one-and-a-half hours dedicated to touring the school with all candidates, will give you as the middle manager an excellent opportunity to talk informally with all the candidates together, which will help you in the decision making process.

Presentation

If you have decided to ask the candidates to present something to you, you have to be clear about the purpose of the activity and accordingly offer them a topic which will enable them to meet this purpose. It could be that you want to test their knowledge about the latest National Curriculum developments or a new syllabus. It could be that you want evidence of candidates' ability to put over their views in an interesting way.

Questions

The questions that candidates are asked should be well thought out and designed to give you greater insight into each candidate's ability to carry out the job. We believe that in order to ensure equal opportunity, each candidate should be asked the same questions. The first question should be designed to put the candidate at ease and therefore should be something that is not difficult to answer. This question should be open ended and could be something like, 'Tell us a little bit about your past experience at teaching X' or 'Tell us a little about yourself'. Further questions should be about the subject, about the candidate's teaching experience, about things like record keeping, classroom management, discipline and working as part of a team. These should give the candidate an opportunity to tell you about their professional ability. Candidates should be given the opportunity to ask any questions they have not had answered. The last question should be closed and is simply to ask the candidate whether they would accept the post if it was offered to them.

It is important to decide beforehand which member of the panel will ask which questions. We have found it useful to have a chair of the interview panel so that order is ensured. We also find it useful to allow interviewers to ask supplementary questions if they are seeking clarity.

Notes should be taken on the performance of each candidate and sometimes a proforma can help. Some schools have devised sophisticated scoring schemes for each set of interviews. At the end of the interview day you will have the following knowledge about each candidate:

- Written information about their education, qualifications and experience from the application form.
- Written opinions about their professional ability from two colleagues (if references have been taken up prior to interview).
- Their ability to present a topic in an interesting way and to demonstrate their subject knowledge.
- What they are like as a person: from the one-and-a-half hours you spent with them before the formal interviews.
- Their ability to perform under pressure: judged from the presentation and the formal interview. This is where you need to use both head and heart.

You might have really liked a candidate and built up great rapport with them but discover that their knowledge of the subject is minimal and this is confirmed by their referees. Each of the other interviewers will also have formed opinions of the candidates which may or may not agree with yours.

Before the real business of decision making begins you should have decided whether you want all candidates to remain or whether candidates can leave after their formal interview and be contacted at home or wherever that evening. We favour the latter as we believe that there is nothing worse than waiting around for a long time, only to be told that you have been unsuccessful. A debriefing should be offered to unsuccessful candidates.

Once all the interviews have finished it is useful to use a flip chart and note down the strengths and weaknesses of each candidate as perceived by each member of the interview panel. The person specification and your department analysis is important here as it will enable you to put up a good case for your chosen candidate. Using this information you should be able to judge the best fit.

Hopefully a consensus will be reached. However, you may be given the final decision or the head teacher may choose to have the final decision or, of course, it may be decided not to appoint and the whole process has to be gone through again!

If the decision is to appoint then the successful candidate should be contacted first and once they have agreed to accept the post, the unsuccessful candidates should be informed of this. Confirmation of the offer must be made in writing and is not firm until the successful candidate has replied, agreeing to the terms and conditions.

Conclusion

The appointment of new staff allows you the opportunity to develop the work of the department in the direction of your development plan. If you have a clear vision for the department backed up by a development plan then the new member of staff will have a sound understanding of your expectations and a secure foundation to build the next steps in their career.

In many countries, staff are allocated to schools and departments by the government department responsible for teaching staff. Where middle managers can have an input into the selection of staff, their challenge is to build an effective and complementary team, focused upon quality teaching and learning.

Chapter 17

Your Future

Whether you are content to stay as a middle manager, or whether you wish to move on to become head teacher, a teacher–educator in higher education or an education administrator, is very much a personal decision. Whatever your background in terms of formal training and whatever your aspirations, it is clear that regular updating must be part of your career. In a career that may span 40 years, classrooms and schools can easily change beyond recognition.

Therefore, planning for your own personal and professional development is as important as the other work you do as a middle manager. There are a number of avenues for professional development easily available to you.

Professional associations provide an excellent service for members – providing access to training, texts, conferences and international links. Higher degrees provide one route into further study and many universities offer flexible programmes designed to meet the needs of teachers by providing opportunities to carry out research and evaluation on school-based practice. Many of these programmes will provide some accreditation for prior learning (APL). Shorter courses may also be available – advertised in the educational press or through networks to which you may belong. Increasingly information useful for professional development is available on the Internet – perhaps you should treat yourself to a little 'surfing' now and then just to see what is available that interests you. Making contact with colleagues from around the world who have similar interests is increasingly easy to do using the Internet and setting up joint curriculum projects with classes in other countries is something many teachers have done already.

Industrial placements are often available to provide professional updating, and teacher exchanges in Europe and the rest of the world provide an option that many teachers enjoy. In the UK, the Central Bureau for Educational Visits and Exchanges is a good place to start if you want to find out more (10 Spring Gardens, London SW1). In other countries, the British Council will usually have an office in the capital and they will offer advice on travel schemes to the UK. Embassies will usually have education officers who provide information about opportunities within their own country.

Educational conferences where educational research is presented and discussed are an annual affair in most countries and there are also a number of international conferences held every year. These are in addition to subject specific conferences. Presentation of papers is often planned at least nine months ahead so plan early if you want to report some of your work – perhaps the results of collaborative action research which you have carried out with colleagues.

Educational journals, newspapers and publishers need a constant stream of copy. As an experienced professional you may wish to share your knowledge with others through this medium.

Activity 17.1 Planning your future

Read through the notes you have made in your reflective journal. Identify the personal and professional priorities which you wish to pursue for the next stage in your career. Set personal goals for the next five years and sketch out the methods by which you hope to achieve these goals.

Opportunities exist for you to choose personal and professional development from a range of options. The choice is yours.

Appendix: Principles of effective learning and teaching

A booklet containing this advice was circulated to all maintained schools in Queensland by the Department of Education. (Reprinted with permission: Queensland State Department of Education, Australia)

Introduction

The Queensland Department of Education is committed to ensuring that all students attending state schools are provided with the opportunity to obtain a comprehensive, balanced and equitable education. Such an education promotes the holistic development of each individual, and ensures that students are provided with opportunities to prepare them for their present and future life roles.

Central to the state education system is the continuous task of exploring ways to improve learning and teaching. The department's commitment to this task is evident in its *Corporate Plan 1994–98*, which identifies student learning and teaching as a key issue and includes effective learning and teaching as a corporate value. To further promote effective learning and teaching, five guiding principles have been formulated for the development and implementation of quality learning programs in Queensland state schools. These principles are expected to underpin learning and teaching practices across all sectors of schooling.

The principles are as follows:

- Effective learning and teaching is founded on an understanding of the learner.
- Effective learning and teaching requires active construction of meaning.

- Effective learning and teaching enhances and is enhanced *by* a supportive and challenging environment.
- Effective learning and teaching is enhanced through worthwhile learning partnerships.
- Effective learning and teaching shapes and responds to social and cultural contexts.

These principles acknowledge the complex and dynamic nature of the learning –teaching process. They are based on the premise that to learn is to make meaning from experience. They acknowledge the impact of such factors as attitudes, perceptions, expectations, abilities, gender, sociocultural background and maturity on every learning experience. They also recognise the learner's capacity to continually extend and refine knowledge. Collectively, the principles emphasise that an essential ingredient of effective teaching is the modelling of a commitment to learning.

Later in this document, each principle is listed separately with explanatory points. These points provide more detail about each principle through specific references to processes and practices. The lists are not intended to be exhaustive, nor is there any implied meaning in the order of the points.

Although stated separately, the five principles are interrelated and some explanatory points apply to more than one principle. In essence, the principles emphasise the need to:

- understand the learner
- understand the learning process
- provide a supportive and challenging environment
- establish worthwhile learning partnerships
- shape and respond to a variety of social and cultural contexts.

Assumptions

The principles are based on the following assumptions:

- Every person is a learner.
- Learning is an ongoing and lifelong process.
- People learn within social and cultural contexts, independently and through interaction with others.
- What is learned depends on the way it is learned and with whom it is learned.
- The vital aspects of teaching include identifying the ways others learn best and extending the ways they learn, creating learning opportunities, and evaluating learning outcomes.

- Principles of effective learning and teaching provide the basis for ongoing improvement of learning and teaching practices.

These assumptions suggest that the learning–teaching process is multi-faceted in terms of what is learned, how it is learned and the roles of partici-pants.

Students develop knowledge about the topics covered in the curriculum. They learn social norms and values from the ways people behave at school as well as in society. And, by reflecting on the actions and processes by which they learn, students develop an understanding about the ways they learn.

Teachers continually learn about ways people learn – the processes of learning and how individuals learn best. They learn *about* their students as individuals, and learn *with* as well as *from* their students when they seek knowledge together.

Teachers bring their own social and cultural values to the learning–teaching process. These values can be different from those held by other members of the school community. Recognising these differences in values, and developing programs and practices that respect the differences, repre-sents another aspect of learning.

Every student and teacher, therefore, experiences many different aspects of learning. The extent and number of aspects increases with the number of participants – ie when school administrators, parents, caregivers, para-professionals, specialist support teachers and other community members participate, further dimensions are added to the learning and teaching pro-cess. Consequently, the principles of effective learning and teaching should apply to all facets of the school's operations. In addition, learning and teach-ing needs to be a cooperative effort. It is not the exclusive responsibility of the student nor the teacher. Responsibility for the overall outcome is shared. All individuals and groups can contribute to the learning–teaching process, and the outcomes will be richer when more people contribute.

Definitions

As described above, the assumptions lead to the following definitions.

Learning

Learning is the process of making meaning out of experience.

Teaching

Teaching is the process of guiding and facilitating learning.

Learner

The term 'learner' primarily refers to the student; however, all individuals involved in the learning–teaching process are learning. The term 'learner' therefore applies to teachers, school administrators, parents and anyone else involved in the learning–teaching process.

Teacher

The term 'teacher' primarily refers to a qualified professional in the educational field whose actions guide or facilitate learning. There are times, however, when the role of teacher is adopted by students, school administrators, parents, caregivers, para-professionals, specialist support teachers and other community members.

Note: The term 'effective learning and teaching' emphasises the interrelationship of learning and teaching. To be effective, learning and teaching must be complementary. They are therefore considered one process and the term is used throughout this document with singular verbs.

Effective learning and teaching is founded on an understanding of the learner

Understanding the learner involves:

- identifying features of the learner's past and present experiences, and respecting the influence of these features on the learner's personal development;
- recognising factors – such as location, gender, ethnicity, ability, disability, and socio-economic and political circumstances – that place the learner within power relationships in the learning context as well as in society;
- recognising and supporting each learner's motivation and capacity to challenge and change his or her current circumstances;
- promoting continuity of experience by identifying, valuing, linking to, and extending from, prior knowledge and experience;
- taking into account relevance and meaning for the learner;
- identifying and catering for the needs, interests and abilities of individual learners and groups of learners;
- recognising and addressing the expectations and aspirations of the learner;
- recognising the impact of others' expectations on the learner;
- promoting the creative potential of each learner;
- recognising an individual's preferred learning styles, and promoting the development of other learning styles;
- recognising and supporting the holistic development of the learner –

intellectually, emotionally, socially, physically, ethically and spiritually.
- administrators, parents, caregivers, para-professionals, specialist support teachers and other community members.

Effective learning and teaching requires active construction of meaning

Learners construct meaning when they:

- challenge their own knowledge and understanding, and respond to the challenges of others;
- participate in a variety of formal and informal social and cultural interactions;
- explore, and develop an openness to, the diversity of knowledge, understanding, values and beliefs;
- take appropriate risks and learn from 'mistakes';
- reflect critically on their own and others' knowledge, actions and assumptions, including those relating to gender, race and class;
- develop a range of thinking processes including divergent, convergent, lateral, critical and creative thinking;
- achieve success and have a sense of progress in their learning;
- explore and manipulate concrete materials;
- explore practical and purposeful contexts;
- build knowledge and understanding by linking to what is already known;
- negotiate, make choices in, and take their share of responsibility for learning;
- engage in, and reflect on, learning opportunities created through the application of teachers' professional expertise and practical experience;
- reflect on and discuss the process of learning and teaching.

Effective learning and teaching enhances and is enhanced by a supportive and challenging environment

A supportive and challenging environment is characterised by:

- a climate that emphasises care, support and quality relationships based on mutual respect for all involved in the learning–teaching process;
- a climate that values effort, presents achievable but challenging expectations, builds self-esteem and encourages learners to become responsible and independent;
- effective communication among all learners;
- cooperative planning, implementation and evaluation of programs for continuity of learning;
- equitable access to, and flexible use of, quality human and material

resources which are appropriate to the needs of learners;

- experiences that are sensitive to the needs of learners and encourage timely intervention by a range of professionals;
- experiences that reflect an appreciation of different views, opinions, values and beliefs;
- diverse, yet relevant, experiences that use the school and wider community as contexts for learning;
- parents, caregivers and other community members supporting the learning–teaching process as partners or skilled participants;
- experiences that motivate learners and promote enjoyment, achievement and satisfaction from learning;
- experiences that cater for different ways and rates of learning;
- flexible procedures and predictable routines.

Effective learning and teaching is enhanced through worthwhile learning partnerships

Worthwhile learning partnerships develop in a variety of contexts when:

- learners and teachers seek knowledge together;
- teachers are active learners, and learners have the opportunity to teach others;
- learners and teachers communicate their expectations and achievements;
- learners and teachers encourage interaction and respond to the opportunities that arise from them;
- learners and teachers demonstrate their enthusiasm and commitment to learning through their actions and approaches;
- learners and teachers take time to reflect critically and creatively on their practices;
- learners and teachers review and plan together for a shared purpose;
- learners and teachers share accountability for outcomes;
- learners have the confidence and are given the opportunity and guidance to display leadership;
- learners and teachers share in planning, learning and assessment;
- school administrators, parents, caregivers, para-professionals, specialist support teachers and other members of the community participate in the learning–teaching process.

Effective learning and teaching shapes and responds to social and cultural contexts

The learning–teaching process shapes and responds to social and cultural contexts when:

- learners develop attitudes, knowledge, skills and processes which enable them to contribute and respond to change within the community;
- all learners have equitable access to and participation in all aspects of the learning–teaching process, regardless of location, gender, ethnicity, ability, disability or socio-economic circumstances;
- all groups of learners achieve success based on realistic and challenging expectations;
- learners participate as active and informed citizens in Australia's diverse society;
- individual diversity as well as the perspectives, contributions and experiences of diverse social and cultural groups is included and valued;
- critical reflection on the past and present informs future decisions;
- learners explore the impact of the construction of gender, ethnicity, disability and social class on their lives and the lives of others;
- learners develop skills for challenging discrimination arising from the construction of gender, ethnicity, disability and social class.

References

Adair, J (1988) *Time Management*, London: Pan Books.

Adelman, C (1989) 'The practical ethic takes priority over methodology', in *Quality in Teaching*, W Carr (ed.), Lewes: The Falmer Press.

Alexandersson, M (1984) 'Focusing teacher consciousness', in *Teachers' Minds and Action*, G Handal, I Carlgren and S Vaage (eds), Lewes: The Falmer Press.

Anker, B and Hauge, T E (1993) *Self-management in the Oslo-school (Selvforvaltning i Oslo-skolen Slugrapport)* Oslo: Department for Teacher Education and School Development, UiO.

Ausubel, D, Novak, J and Hanesian, H (1978) *Educational Psychology: A Cognitive View*, New York: Holt Rinehart & Winston.

Ball, S (1994) *Educational Reform*, Milton Keynes: Open University Press.

Ball, S (1987) *The Micropolitics of the School: Towards a Theory of Educational Organisation*, London: Methuen.

Bashi, D (1992) *School Effectiveness and Improvement*, Tel-Aviv: Tel-Aviv University.

Bass, D (1990) 'From transactional to transformational leadership', *Organisational Dynamics*, **18**, 19–31.

Becher, T (1984) 'The political and organisational context of curriculum evaluation', in *Evaluating the Curriculum in the Eighties*, M Skilbeck (ed.), London: Hodder & Stoughton.

Birchenough, M (1986) 'School self-evaluation: A progress report from the GRIDS project', *The Journal of Evaluation in Education*, **9**, 30–6.

Blake, R R and Mouton, J S (1985) *The Managerial Grid*, Houston, TX: Gulf Publishing Co.

Blanchard, K and Johnson, S (1983) *The One-Minute Manager*, New York: Berkley Books.

Blase, J and Anderson, G (1995) *The Micropolitics of Educational Leadership*, London: Cassell.

Bourne, J (ed) (1994) *Thinking Through Primary Practice*, London: Routledge.

Boyd, W (1994) 'National school reform and restructuring: parallels between Britain and the United States', Paper presented at the British Educational Management and Administration Society (BEMAS) conference, Manchester, 16–18 September, 1994.

Bray, D W and Campbell, R J (1974) *Formative Years in Business: A Long-term AT&T Study of Managerial Lives*, New York: John Wiley.

Brown, M and Rutherford, D (1996) 'Servant, architect, moralist professional', *Management in Education*, **10**, 1, 3–4.

Brown, S and McIntyre, D (1993) *Making Sense of Teaching*, Milton Keynes: Open University Press.

Bruner, J (1960) *The Process of Education*, Cambridge, MA: Harvard University Press.

Bruner, J (1986) *Actual Minds, Possible Worlds*, Cambridge, MA: Harvard University Press.

Bullogh, R (1989) 'Teacher education and teacher reflectivity', *Journal of Teacher Education*, **40**, 15–21.

Burns, T and Stalker, G M (1966) *The Management of Innovation*, London: Tavistock.

Bush, T (1995) *Theories of Educational Management*, 2nd edn, London: Paul Chapman Publishing.

Bush, T (1992) *Theories of Management*, London: Paul Chapman Publishing.

Calderhead, J (1988) *Teachers' Professional Learning*, Lewes: The Falmer Press.

Capel, S, Leask, M and Turner, T (1995) *Learning to Teach in the Secondary School*, London: Routledge.

Capel, S, Leask, M and Turner, T (1996) *Starting to Teach in the Secondary School*, London: Routledge.

Chen, D (1995) *Education Toward the Twenty-First Century*, Singapore: Ministry of Education.

Claxton, G (1984) *Teaching to Learn*, London: Cassell.

Clinton B, Morrall, M and Terrell, I (1994) *Planning Student Involvement in School Development*, Lancaster: Framework Press.

Cockman, P, Evans, B and Reynolds, P (1992) *Client-Centred Consulting*, London: McGraw-Hill.

Cooper, P and McIntyre, D (1996) *Effective Teaching and Learning*, Milton Keynes: Open University Press.

Creemers, B P M (1994) *The Effective Classroom*, London: Cassell.

Cullingford, C (1995) *The Effective Teacher*, London: Cassell.

Davies, L (1994) 'The management and mismanagement of school effectiveness', *Compare*, **24**, 3, 205–17.

Day, C, Hall, C, Gammage, P and Coles, M (1993) *Leadership and Curriculum in the Primary School*, London: Paul Chapman Publishing.

Dean, J (1991) *Professional Development in School*, Milton Keynes: Open University Press.

Department for Education (1994) *Code of Practice for the Identification and Assessment of Special Educational Needs*, London: HMSO.

Department of Education and Science (1991) *Development Planning: A Practical Guide. Advice to Governors, Headteachers and Teachers*, London: DES/HMSO.

Department of Education and Science (1988) *School Indicators: A Discussion Paper*, circulated Spring, London: DES.

Department of Education and Science (1985) *Quality in Schools, Evaluation and Appraisal: An HMI Study*, London: HMSO.

Department of Employment (1993) 'The personal effectiveness model', *Competence and Assessment*, 22.

Dewey, J (1933) *How We Think*, Chicago: Regnery.

Donnelly, J (1990) *Middle Managers in Schools and Colleges*, London: Kogan Page.

Dryden, G and Vos, J (1994) *The Learning Revolution*, Aylesbury: Accelerated Learning Systems.

Duke, D L (1988) 'Why principals consider quitting', *Phi Delta Kappan*, **70**, 4, 308–14.

Edu-con (1984) *The role of the public school principal in the Toronto Board of Education*, Toronto, Edu-con of Canada.

Ekholm, M (1987) 'School reforms and local response: an evaluation of school reviews in 35 school management areas in Sweden 1980–1985', *Compare*, **17**, 2, 107–18.

Elliott, J (1982) 'Nominal group technique' *CARN Bulletin*, 5, 68.

Employment Department (1991) 'The personal effectiveness model', *Competence and Assessment*, 22.

ERA (1988) *Education Reform Act, 29 July 1988*, London: HMSO.

Etzioni, A (1975) *A Comparative Analysis of Complex Organisations*, New York: Free Press.

Fleishman, E A and Harris, E F (1972) 'Patterns of leadership behaviour related to employee behaviour', in *Personnel Psychology*, Vol. 15, pp.43–56.

French, J and Raven, B (1958) 'The bases of social power', in *Studies in Social Power*, D Cartwright (ed.), Ann Arbor, MI: Institute for Social Research.

Friebel, A J J M (1994) *Planning van Onderwijs en her Gebruik van Curriculumdocumenten (The Planning of Education and the Use of Curricular Documents)*, Enschede: Universiteit Twente.

Fritchie, R and Thorne, M (1988) 'Interpersonal skills for women managers', MSC, Bristol Polytechnic.

Fullan, M (1992) *Successful School Improvement: The Implementation Perspective and Beyond*, Milton Keynes: Open University Press.

Fullan, M (1991) *The New Meaning of Educational Change*, London: Cassell.

Furlong, J and Maynard, T (1995) *Mentoring Student Teachers*, London: Routledge.

Ghiselli, E E (1971) *Exploration in Managerial Talent*, Santa Monica, CA: Goodyear.

Gilchrist, B and Hall, V (1993) *Using Management Development Materials: A Guide for Schools, LEAs and Other Support Agencies*, London: HMSO/DfE.

Glasser, W (1992) *The Quality School: Managing Students without Coercion*, 2nd edn, New York: HarperCollins.

Goddard, D and Leask, M (1992) *The Search for Quality: Planning for Improvement and Managing Change*, London: Paul Chapman Publishing.

Goldring, E and Rallis, S F (1993) *Principals of Dynamic Schools: Taking Charge of Change*, Thousand Oaks, CA: Corwin Press.

Granström, K and Lander, R (1995a) *Professionalism i skolans ulvardering och uppfoljning Praxis, No 2 (Professionalism in the evaluation and assessment of schools)*, Goteborg: Goteborg Universitet.

Greenvald, J (1996) 'Vice-Principal – Function or Fiction', *FORUM – School Management Magazine*, September 1996.

Hägglund, S and Lander, R (1991) 'Professional development and change: Teachers in five upper secondary schools', Paper presented at the 19th Conference of the Nordic Society for Educational Researchers, Copenhagen, 7–9 March, 1991.

Hallinger, P and Hausman, C (1994) 'From Attila the Hun to Mary had a Little Lamb: Principal role ambiguity in restructured schools', in *Reshaping the Principalship Insights from Transformational Reform Efforts*, J Murphy and K S Louis (eds), Thousand Oaks, CA: Corwin Press, pp.123–53.

Hamilton, D (1976) *Curriculum Evaluation*, London: Open Books.

Hammersley, M and Atkinson, P (1995) *Ethnography, Principles in Practice*, 2nd edn, London: Routledge.

Handy, C (1976) *Understanding Organisations*, London: Penguin.

Hargreaves, A (1994a) *Changing Teachers, Changing Times: Teachers' Work and Culture in the Postmodern Age*, New York: Teachers College Press.

Hargreaves, A (1994b) 'Restructuring restructuring: Postmodernity and the prospects for educational change', in *Teacher Development and the Struggle for Authenticity*, P P Grimmett and J Neufeld (eds), New York: Teachers College Press, pp.52–8.

Hargreaves, A (1989) *Curriculum and Assessment Reform*, Milton Keynes: Open University Press.

Hargreaves, D H (1995) 'School culture', *School Effectiveness and School Improvement*, **6**, 1, 23–46.

Hargreaves, D H, Hopkins, D, Leask, M, Connolly, J and Robinson, P (1989) *Planning for School Development: Advice to Governors, Headteachers and Teachers*, London: DES/HMSO.

Harris, A, Jamieson, I and Russ, J (1996) 'What makes an effective department?' *Management in Education*, **10**, Feb/March, 7–9.

Hauge, T E (1995) 'Systemic competence building and quality development', Paper presented at the International Congress for School Effectiveness and Improvement, The Netherlands, January 3–6.

Hauge, T E (1991) *Competence Development in School Based Evaluation (Kompetanseulvikling i skolevurdering)*, Oslo: Department for Teacher Education and School Development, UiO.

Hauge, T E (1990) *Middle Management in the Oppegard Schools (Forsok med mellomleder i Oppegardskolene)*, Den pedagogiske veiledningstjenesten, Oppegard kommune.

Hauge, T E (1982) 'Openness and collaboration in the school community' (Apenhet og samarbeid i skolemiljoet), PhD, University of Trondheim.

Hauge, T E and Engeland, O (1994) *Quality Assurance and Quality development in the School* (Kvalitetssikring og kvalitetsutvikling i skolen, KIS (1991–93)), Statens utdanningskontori Oslo og Akershus.

Hauge, T E, Engeland, O, Moller, J and Aaserud, T (1995) *The Professional Development of Leaders in School and Kindergarden (Lederutvikling i skole og barnehage Evaleruing av et lederutviklingsprogram i Nittedal 1992–95)*, Department for Teacher Education, Oslo.

Henry, D A and Kelly, S (1996) *Accelerated Schools Design in Evaluation of 1995–1996 Restructuring Designs in Memphis City Schools*, Snapshot Reports, Memphis, TN: Center for Research in Educational Policy.

Hersey, P and Blanchard, K (1982) *Management of Organisational Behaviour*, New Jersey: Prentice Hall.

Herzberg, F (1966) 'Work and the nature of man', cited in *Business Psychology and Organisational Behaviour* (1994) E McKenna (ed.), Hove: Lawrence Erlbaum Associates.

Holly, P and Hopkins, D (1988) 'Evaluation and school improvement', *Cambridge Journal of Education*, **18**, 2, 221–45.

Hopkins, D (1985) *Evaluating TVEI: Some Methodological Issues*, Cambridge: Cambridge Institute of Education.

Hopkins, D (1993) *A Teacher's Guide to Classroom Research*, Milton Keynes: Open University Press.

Hopkins, D, Ainscow, M and West, M (1994) *School Improvement in an Era of Change*, London: Cassell.

Hoyle, E and John, P (1995) *Professional Knowledge and Professional Practice*, London: Cassell.

Hylkema, W F S (1990) *Docenten en hun Vaksecties (Teachers and their Departments)* Nijmegen: Katholieke Universiteit Nijmegen.

Inner London Education Authority (ILEA) (July 1988) *Secondary School Development Plans*, London: ILEA.

Jenks, J and Kelly, J (1985) *Don't Do, Delegate!* London: Kogan Page.

Joyce, B and Showers, B (1988) *Student Achievement Through Staff Development*, London: Longman.

Kallòs, D (1985) *Arbetsenheter och arbetslag i grundskolan Pedagogiska rapporter nr 40, Pedagogiska institutionen (Working-units and working-teams in the comprehensive school)*, Lunds Universitet.

Kemp, R and Nathan, M (1989) *Middle Management in Schools: A Survival Guide*, Oxford: Blackwell.

Kolb, D A (1984) *Experiential Learning: Experiences as the Source of Learning and Development*, Englewood Cliffs, NJ: Prentice Hall.

Kolb, D A (1993) 'Experiential learning', in *Culture and Process of Adult Learning*, A Thorpe, R Edwards and A Hanson (eds), Milton Keynes: Open University Press.

KUF (1996) *School Leadership Towards Year 2000 (Skuleleiing mot ar 2000)* Kompetanse- mal for pedagogisk leiing i skulen innafor Luis-programmet, Kirke-, forsknings- og utdanningsdepartementet.

Lander, R (1996) *Halsan tiger inle still Lagesbeskrivning och utvarderingsdesign for projek- tet Halsoskolor Rapport fran institutionen for pedagogik*, Goteborgs universitet 1996:3 (Report on health promoting schools in Sweden.)

Lander, R and Odhagen, T (1992) *Forlbildningskurser under luppen Om kotnp let terings- fortbildningen i vastra Sverige varen 1991 Rapport fran institutionen for pedagogik, (Look- ing at in-service-training courses)* Goteborgs universitet 1992, 8.

Langford, G (1978) *Teaching as a Profession: An Essay in the Philosophy of Education*, Manchester: Manchester University Press.

Leithwood, K A (1990) 'The principal's role in teacher development', in *Changing School Culture through Staff Development: Yearbook of the Association for Supervision and Curriculum Development*, B M Joyce (ed.), Virginia: ASCD.

Lieberman A (1994) 'Teacher development: Commitment and challenge', in *Teacher Development and the Struggle for Authenticity*, P P Grimmett and J Neufeld (eds), New York: Teachers College Press, pp.15–30.

Likert, R (1967) *The Human Organisation*, New York: McGraw Hill.

Lippet, R and White, R (1968) 'Leaders behaviour in three social climates', in *Group Dynamics Research and Theory*, D Cartwright and A Zander (eds), Tavistock: London.

Louis, K S and Miles, M B (eds)(1990) *Improving the Urban High School: What Works and Why*, New York: Teachers College Press.

Lunzer, E and Gardner, K (1984) *Learning from the Written Word*, Edinburgh: Oliver and Boyd.

Martin, W and Willower, D (1981) 'The managerial behaviour of high school princi- pals', *Education Aministration Quarterly*, **17**, 1, 69–90.

Marx, E C H (1975) *De organisatie van scholengemeenschappen in onderwijskundige optiek (The organisation of schools from an educational perspective)*, Groningen: Wolters- Noordhoff.

McGregor, D (1960) *The Human Side of Enterprise*, New York: McGraw-Hill.

McKenna E F (1991) 'Managerial leadership emergent trends', unpublished Professo- rial Inaugural Lecture, University of East London, cited in E F McKenna (1994) *Busi- ness Psychology and Organisational Behaviour*, Hove: Lawrence Erlbaum Associates.

McKenna, E F (1994) *Business Psychology and Organisational Behaviour*, Hove: Lawrence Erlbaum Associates.

McNiff, J (1988) *Action Research: Principles and Practice*, London: Routledge.

McNiff, J (1993) *Teaching as Learning: An Action Research Approach*, London: Routledge.

Manchester Open Learning (1993) *Handling Conflict and Negotiation*, London: Kogan Page.

Mezirow, J (1981) 'A critical theory of adult learning and education', *Adult Education*, **32**, 1, 324.

Miles, M B (1987) 'Practical guidelines for school administrators', Paper presented at AERA Annual Meeting.

Møller, J (1995) *The Principal as an Instructional Leader in the Basic School (Rektor som ped- agogisk leder i grunnskolen – spenningsfeltet mellom forvallning, tradisjon og profesjon)*, Drpolit graden: University of Oslo.

Mønsterplanen for grunnskolen (1987) *(The National Curriculum Plan for the Basic School)*,

Kirke-, forsknings-og utdanningsdepartementet.

Moon, B and Shelton Mayes, A (1994) *Teaching and Learning in the Secondary School*, London: Routledge.

Mortimore, P (1993) 'School effectiveness and the management of effective learning and teaching' *School Effectiveness and School Improvement*, **4**, 4, 290–310.

Murphy, J (1992) *The Landscape of Leadership Preparation*, Thousand Oaks, CA: Corwin Press.

Murphy, J and Louis, K S (1994) *Reshaping the Principalship Insights from Transformational Reform Efforts*, Thousand Oaks, CA: Corwin Press.

National Curriculum Council (1989) *Curriculum Guidance 1–5*, York: NCC.

National Commission on Excellence in Education (1983) *A Nation at Risk*, Washington DC: Washington Government Printing Office.

Nestor, B (1991) *Studieledare i grudskolan En skolledningsfunktion medforhinder?* (Study of leaders of the comprehensive school) (Diss) Acta Universitatis Upsaliensis Uppsala Studies in Education 39 Stockholm, Almqvist and Wiksell International.

NOU (1995) *The Proposal for the New Act of Education in Basic and Secondary Schools*, Ny lovgivning om opplering, Norway.

Nisbet, J (1984) 'Curriculum evaluation in context', in *Evaluating the Curriculum in the Eighties*, M Skilbeck (ed.), London: Hodder & Stoughton.

Nixon, J (1981) 'Towards a supportive framework for teachers in research', *Curriculum*, **2**, 1, 31–4.

Organisation for Economic Cooperation and Development (OECD) (1988) 'The search for educational indicators', *Innovation in Education*, **48**, February, 1–3.

OFSTED (1995) *Framework for the Inspection of Schools*, London: HMSO.

O'Hear, A (1988) *Who Teaches the Teachers*, London: Social Affairs Unit.

Osborne, M and Broadfoot, P (1992) *Perceptions of Teaching: Primary School Teachers in England and France*, London: Cassell.

Parsloe, E (1992) *Coaching, Mentoring and Assessing*, London: Kogan Page.

Peters, T and Waterman, R (1982) *In Search of Excellence*, New York: Harper & Row.

Peterson (1981) 'Making sense of the principal's work', Paper presented at the American Educational Research Association Annual Meeting.

Piaget, J and Inhelder, B (1969) *The Psychology of the Child*, New York: Basic Books.

Powell, J H (1989) 'The reflective practitioner in nursing', *Journal of Advanced Nursing*, **4**, 824–32.

Reynolds D, Creemers, B P M, Nesselrodt, P S, Schaffer, E C, Stringfield, S and Teddlie, C (1994) *Advances in School Effectiveness Research and Practice*, London: Pergamon.

Reynolds, D and Cuttance, P (1992) *School Effectiveness*, London: Cassell.

Ross, S M, Henry, D A, Phillipsen, L, Evans, K, Smith, L and Buggey, T (1996a) 'Matching restructuring programs: Selection, negotiation and preparation', Paper presented at the American Educational Research Association, New York.

Ross, S M, Smith, L J, Stringfield, S and Associates (1996b) 'Multi-dimensional support for bottom-up school reform: Implementing the Memphis restructuring initiative', Paper presented at the American Educational Research Association, New York.

Sarason, S (1982) *The Culture of the School and the Problem of Change* (revised edn), Boston, MA: Allyn & Bacon.

Sarason, S (1990) *The Predictable Failure of Educational Reform*, San Francisco: Jossey-Bass.

Schön, D A (ed.) (1990) *The Reflective Turn: Case Studies in and on Educational Practice*, New York: Teachers College Press.

School Management Task Force (SMTF) (1990) *Developing School Management: The Way Forward*, London: DES/HMSO.

Schratz, M and Walker, R (1995) *Research as Social Change: New Opportunities for Qual-*

itative Research, London: Routledge.

Sergiovanni, T J, Burlingame, M, Coombs, F and Thurston, P W (1992) *Educational Governance and Administration*, Englewood Cliffs, NJ: Prentice Hall.

Simons, H (1984) 'Issues in curriculum evaluation at the local level', in *Evaluating the Curriculum in the Eighties*, M Skilbeck (ed.), London: Hodder & Stoughton.

Siskin, L S (1991) 'Departments as different worlds: Subject subcultures in secondary schools', *Educational Administration Quarterly*, **27**, 2, 134–60.

Skilbeck, M (1984) *Evaluating the Curriculum in the Eighties*, London: Hodder & Stoughton.

Smets, P (1986) *Middenmanagement in her onderwijs in AML van Wieringen (ed) Management van onderwijsinstellingen (Management of educational institutions)*, Groningen: Wolters Noordhoff, pp.176–90.

Smyth, J (1989) *Critical Perspectives on Educational Leadership*, Lewes: Falmer Press.

Sparkes, A (1991) 'The culture of teaching, critical reflection and change: Possibilities and problems', *Educational Management and Administration*, **19**, 1, 4–19.

Speller (1994) 'Investors in people in a college of further education', in *Quality Improvement in Education*, C Parson (ed.), London: David Fulton.

Stenhouse, L (1975) *An Introduction to Curriculum Research and Development*, London: Croom Helm.

St. meld 29 (1994–95) 'White paper on principles and guidelines for the 10-year basic school and the national curriculum plan' (Om prinsipper of retningslinjer for 10-arig grunnskole -ny laereplan), Kirke-, forsknings-og utdanningsdepartementet.

St. meld 37 (1990–91) 'White paper on governing in the school system' (Om organisering og styring i utdanningssektoren), Kirke-, forsknings-og utdanningsdepartementet.

Stoll, L and Fink, D (1996) *Changing Our Schools*, Buckingham: Open University Press.

Stones, E (1992) *Quality Teaching*, London: Routledge.

Stringfield, S, Ross, S M and Smith L J (1996) *Bold new plans for school restructuring: The New American Schools Development Corporation designs*, Mahwah, NJ: Lawrence Erlbaum Associates.

Tannenbaum, R and Schmidt, W (1973) 'How to choose a leadership pattern', *Harvard Business Review*, May/June, 162–80.

Teacher Training Agency (TTA) (1995) 'Securing excellence in teaching', Teacher Training Agency – First Annual Lecture given by Anthea Millett at the Institute of Education, University of London, 31 October 1995.

Teacher Training Agency (TTA) (undated, early 1990s) *The School-Centred Initial Teacher Training Scheme*, London: Teacher Training Agency.

Teddlie, C and Stringfield, S (1993) *Schools Make a Difference: Lessons Learned from a 10-year Study of School Effects*, New York: Teachers College Press.

Terrell, I (1989) 'An evaluation of the process of constructing an IDP in a secondary school', unpublished MA dissertation, Open University.

Terrell, I (1996) *Distant and Deep: A report on the collaborative research and development of a distant and deep learning project*, Middlesex: Middlesex University Press.

Terrell, I, Terrell, K and Rowe, S (1996) *Raising Achievement at GCSE*, Lancaster: Framework Press.

The Education Council for England and Wales (1993) *Assert Your Professional Quality*, Billericay: The Education Council.

Thomas, K W (1976) 'Conflict and conflict management', in *Handbook of Industrial Management Psychology*, M Dunnette (ed.), Skokie, IL: Rand McNally.

Torrington, D and Weightman, J (1993) 'The culture and ethos in the school', in *Managing the Effective School*, M Preedy (ed.), Milton Keynes: Open University Press.

Torrington, D and Weightman, J (1989) *The Reality of School Management*, Oxford: Blackwell.

UK Inter-Professional Group (UKIPG) (1995) Annual Report, London: UKIPG.

van der Knaap, P (1995) 'Policy evaluation and learning: Feedback, enlightenment or augmentation?' *Evaluation*, **1**, 2.

West, M and Bollington, R (1988) *Teacher Appraisal*, London: David Fulton.

Whitaker, P (1993) *Managing Change in Schools*, Milton Keynes: Open University Press.

White, J (ed.) (1943) *Child Behaviour and Development*, New York: McGraw-Hill.

Wilcox, B (1992) *Time-Constrained Evaluation: A Practical Approach for LEAs and Schools*, London: Routledge.

Whitehead, M (1996) 'The drip-drip-drip despair', *Times Educational Supplement*, May 10, pp.6–7.

Witziers, B (1996) 'Coordinatie van het vakonderwijs binnen scholen voor voortgezet onderwijs: vaksectis en schoolleiding' (Coordination in secondary schools: Departments and educational leadership), *Pedagogishe studien*, **73**, 3, 198–214.

Witziers, B (1993) 'Vaksecties binnen scholen voor voortgezet onderwijz' (Departments in schools for secondary education), in *Handboek Schoolorganisatie en Onderwijsmanagement (Handbook for School Organisation and Education)*, B P M Creemers *et al.* (eds), Netherlands: Gronings Instituut voor onderzoek van onderwijs, opuoeding en ont wikkeling.

Witziers, B (1992) De coordinatie binnen scholen voor vooortgezet onderwijs (Coordination in schools for secondary education), Enschede, Universiteit Twente: Netherlands.

Witziers, B and Vilsteren, C van (1990) 'Vaksecties en de coordinatie van hun vakonderwijs' in *Curriculum en Schoolorganisatie (Curriculum and School Organisation)*, Imants, J and Eijzen, W (eds), pp 61–71, Amsterdam/Lisse: Swets en Zeitlinger.

Wragg, T and Wood, E K (1994) 'Teachers' first encounters with their classes', in *Teaching and Learning in the Secondary School*, B Moon and A Shelton Mayes (eds), London: Routledge.

Yukl, G A (1981) 'Leadership in Organisations', in *Business Psychology and Organisational Behaviour*, E McKenna (ed.), Hove: Lawrence Erlbaum Associates.

Index